Seeing the Messiah

Seeing the Messiah

An Analysis of the Postmortem Appearances of Jesus Christ and the Lubavitcher Rebbe Against the Backdrop of Apparitional Phenomena

JONATHAN KENDALL, MD

Foreword by Michael Licona

RESOURCE *Publications* • Eugene, Oregon

SEEING THE MESSIAH
An Analysis of the Postmortem Appearances of Jesus Christ and the Lubavitcher Rebbe Against the Backdrop of Apparitional Phenomena

Copyright © 2025 Jonathan Kendall. All rights reserved. Except for brief quotations in critical publications or reviews, no part of this book may be reproduced in any manner without prior written permission from the publisher. Write: Permissions, Wipf and Stock Publishers, 199 W. 8th Ave., Suite 3, Eugene, OR 97401.

Resource Publications
An Imprint of Wipf and Stock Publishers
199 W. 8th Ave., Suite 3
Eugene, OR 97401

www.wipfandstock.com

PAPERBACK ISBN: 979-8-3852-4899-5
HARDCOVER ISBN: 979-8-3852-4900-8
EBOOK ISBN: 979-8-3852-4901-5

01/07/26

The author acknowledges with gratitude permission to reprint from the following works. Material excerpted from *Induced After Death Communication: A Miraculous Therapy for Grief and Loss* © 2005, 2014 Allan L. Botkin & Craig Hogan with permission from Red Wheel/Weiser LLC. Newburyport, MA www.redwheelweiser.com. Excerpts from *Those Who Saw Her: Apparitions of Mary*, Revised and Expanded, Fourth Edition © 2023, Catherine Odell, published by OSV. Used by permission. No other use of this material is authorized. Material excerpted from *Meet the Witnesses of the Miracle of the Sun*, 2006, John Haffert, The American Society for the Defense of Tradition Family and Property. Used by permission. Excerpts from *At the Hour of Death*, Kindle edition, © 2012, Karlis Osis and Erlendur Haraldsson, published by White Crow. Used by permission. Excerpts from *The Departed Among the Living: An Investigative Study of Afterlife Encounters*, Kindle edition, © 2012, Erlendur Hardaldsson, published by White Crow Books. Used by permission.

For dad, we miss you

Contents

Foreword by Michael Licona | ix
Acknowledgments | xiii
Introduction | xv

1. The World of Apparitions | 1
2. Crisis Apparitions | 5
3. Apparitions of the Living | 16
4. Haunting Apparitions | 29
5. Rescue Apparitions | 40
6. Transitional Apparitions | 46
7. Reunion Apparitions | 53
8. Inducible Apparitions | 65
9. Apparitions of Jesus Christ | 83
10. The Marian Apparition of Knock, Ireland | 88
11. The Marian Apparition of Betania, Venezuela | 96
12. The Miracle of the Sun in Fátima, Portugal | 102
13. Assessing Apparitions as Subjective Phenomena | 111
14. Apparitions and the Fantasy Prone Personality | 121
15. Assessing Apparitions as Objective Phenomena | 128
16. Apparitions, Super-Psi and the Question of Survival | 142
17. Apparitions as Expressions of the Collective Unconscious | 148
18. Menachem Mendel Schneerson: The Lubavitcher Rebbe | 154
19. Apparitions of the Rebbe | 161

20　The Resurrection of Jesus Christ | 170

21　Jesus' Appearances: Resurrection or a Compilation of Apparitions' "Greatest Hits"? | 183

22　Apparitions as an Alternative Explanation to Jesus' Resurrection | 192

23　Comparing the Postmortem Appearances of the Lubavitcher Rebbe and Jesus Christ | 225

Concluding Reflections | 227

Appendix A: Statistics on Apparitional Phenomena | 231

Appendix B: Apparitions and Quantum Entanglement | 238

Bibliography | 243

Foreword

THE QUESTION OF JESUS' resurrection stands at the heart of Christian faith and remains one of the most deeply examined claims in religious history. But what if there exists a natural, or at least non-supernatural, explanation that accounts for the earliest experiences of the disciples? In *Seeing the Messiah: An Analysis of the Postmortem Appearances of Jesus Christ and the Lubavitcher Rebbe Against the Backdrop of Apparitional Phenomena*, Dr. Jonathan Kendall offers a provocative and thoughtful exploration of this possibility, advancing what may be the strongest alternative hypothesis: that the resurrection appearances of Jesus fall within the broader and well-documented phenomenon of apparitions.

This is not a debunking book, nor is it a theological defense. It is, rather, a methodical investigation into whether the known data about apparitional experiences—both historical and contemporary—can explain the New Testament claims without invoking divine intervention. Dr. Kendall draws deeply from the fields of parapsychology, religious studies, psychology, and historical analysis to build a framework in which the paranormal—not the miraculous—serves as a possible lens through which to interpret the postmortem appearances of Jesus.

In the early chapters, Dr. Kendall lays out eight categories of apparitions: crisis apparitions, apparitions of the living, hauntings, rescue and transitional apparitions, reunion experiences, those induced through ritualized settings such as séances and psychomanteums, and religious apparitions. Each type is accompanied by well-sourced case studies and analysis. What emerges is a clear pattern: apparitions are common, sometimes recurring, and frequently experienced by multiple percipients. They are not always mere hallucinations. In some cases, they convey accurate information the percipient could not have known. In others, they are witnessed simultaneously by groups. And in still others, they provoke physical reactions or enduring life changes.

Yet Dr. Kendall is careful not to stretch the data too far. He subjects naturalistic explanations—such as hallucination, suggestion, fraud, and fantasy-prone personality—to rigorous scrutiny and finds them lacking in explanatory power for many of the most compelling cases. The result is a cautiously persuasive case that some apparitions are objectively real, though their cause remains obscure. For most, he argues, the likely explanation is a form of telepathic projection—what parapsychologists call "super-psi"—generated unconsciously by the living mind.

The book reaches a critical turning point when it examines the postmortem appearances of Menachem Mendel Schneerson, the Lubavitcher Rebbe. After his death in 1994, followers reported a wide range of vivid encounters—some spontaneous, others induced, often bearing great emotional or spiritual significance. These accounts, too, are treated with seriousness, not credulity. Dr. Kendall concludes that the Rebbe's apparitions are best explained as paranormal but non-supernatural, fitting within the broader framework established in the book's earlier chapters.

But when it comes to Jesus of Nazareth, something different emerges. In the final third of the book, Dr. Kendall shifts from building the strongest case for the apparitional hypothesis (AH) to testing its limits against the biblical data. His assessment begins with Paul's creedal summary in 1 Cor 15—our earliest written record of the resurrection appearances—and moves through the empty tomb tradition, the conversion of Saul, and the postmortem narratives found in the Gospels. Each piece of evidence is weighed for its compatibility with known apparitional phenomena.

Here, AH shows its weakness in explaining the data. Unlike typical apparitions, Jesus' appearances are unusually physical. He walks, speaks, teaches, eats, and invites his followers to touch him. He appears not just to individuals but to groups, including skeptics and enemies. Some of the experiences do not arise from psychological need or grief in the conventional sense. Indeed, the disciples are not expecting resurrection at all. This is critical. Apparitions are often tied to deep emotional longing or traumatic loss—but the New Testament witnesses were confused, frightened, some even resistant to the idea that Jesus had returned.

Dr. Kendall acknowledges that AH may be stretched to accommodate certain aspects of these accounts. In chapter 22, he plays devil's advocate, offering the most generous reading possible for AH under three hypothetical assumptions. Even so, he finds the theory lacking. The cumulative weight of the evidence—especially the empty tomb, the physicality of the encounters, and the transformation of the early witnesses—defies categorization within any known apparitional model.

What makes this conclusion all the more striking is the honesty with which the theory is tested. Dr. Kendall does not begin with an agenda to prove or disprove the resurrection. He begins with data—real case studies, real experiences, real human testimonies—and proceeds cautiously, critically, and respectfully. His analysis is interdisciplinary in the best sense, weaving together historical theology, paranormal studies, psychology, and eyewitness reports into a coherent and deeply engaging whole.

This is a rare book. It is rare because it honors both the mysterious nature of apparitions and the unique nature of the resurrection. It does not dismiss religious claims, nor does it blindly affirm them. It seeks understanding. And in doing so, it offers something valuable to both believers and skeptics: a model of inquiry that is neither defensive nor dismissive, but open, thoughtful, and intellectually rigorous.

In the end, Dr. Kendall concludes that while apparitions are real and may explain many postmortem encounters, they do not account for the totality of the resurrection claims concerning Jesus. That event remains, in his words, "a dramatic strain" on any naturalistic or paranormal model. It is either a category of its own—or it is something more.

For the open-minded reader—whether religious, skeptical, or somewhere in between—this book will be a bracing, enlightening journey. It does not offer easy answers. But it does offer better questions. And in that, it fulfills the highest aim of any serious intellectual work.

MICHAEL LICONA
Professor of New Testament Studies
Houston Christian University

Acknowledgments

FIRST AND FOREMOST, I express immense gratitude to those who have boldly traversed the precarious realms of psychical research ahead of me. From the philosophers and scientists out of Cambridge that founded the Society for Psychical Research (SPR), including the legendary Frederic W. H. Myers, Edmund Gurney, Frank Podmore, Henry and Eleanor Sidgwick, Sir Ernest Bennett, Herbert Thurston, G. N. M. Tyrrell, and so many of their contemporaries too numerous to mention, to their modern counterparts, these thinkers have relentlessly sought to understand that force commonly referred to in the literature now as "the phenomenon."

Said modern counterparts have no less boldly served as beacons of illumination for those few in the scientific and religious communities who are willing to see. Accordingly, I find myself indebted to these revolutionary thinkers and practitioners, a lengthy list that includes Dale Allison, Dianne Arcangel, Yoram Bilu, Allan Botkin, Stephen Braude, Adam Crabtree, Simon Dein, James Dunn, Hilary Evans, Sue Fishkoff, Michael Grosso, Gary Habermas, Erlendur Haraldsson, Leslie Kean, Craig Keener, Ed and Emily Williams Kelly, Raymond Moody, Catherine Odell, Jake O'Connell, Karlis Osis, Michael Persinger, Guy Lyon Playfair, William Roll, Joseph Telushkin, Jacques Vallée, and so many others. Without their scholarly endeavors and the works that they have produced along the way, as well as those that have preserved the more-dated-yet-still-relevant seminal volumes published in the late nineteenth and early twentieth centuries, the writing of this book would not have been possible.

Certain others that also belong on the aforementioned list are worthy of special mention as it relates to my efforts on this project. Among the ranks of distinguished scholars of religion and psychical research is Jeffrey Kripal. I express great appreciation to Jeff for taking the time out of his *impossibly* busy schedule to correspond with me numerous times via email regarding topics relevant to this work, and who, like numerous others referenced, has published a plethora of groundbreaking volumes relevant to subjects discussed in this one.

I extend thanks to Debbie Licona, Michael Licona, and Bill Pratt for taking substantial time to read multiple drafts of this work and for providing me with much needed critical feedback. Whatever the merits of this volume, its content was greatly strengthened by their helpful suggestions. Any and all errors remain mine to bear. The publication of this book was made a reality by Joe George, Savanah Landerholm, Karlie Tedrick, Matthew Wimer, and others at Wipf and Stock. I will be forever grateful for their faith in this project and their painstaking efforts in getting this to print.

Two colleagues and friends in particular have been of foundational importance to my authorial efforts. James Patrick Holding talked me off the ledge many times as I first engaged the world of biblical background and scholarship. He would unfailingly answer scores of questions I would send him at a time when my faith was at its most vulnerable. He remains to this day a good friend and colleague, and a bottomless source of knowledge. Similarly, I have had the privilege of serving and working with Michael Licona for nearly a decade. In addition to his unparalleled scholarship on Jesus' resurrection, Mike has provided me with crucial feedback on my work, wrote this book's foreword, and has been a good friend. Mike has also engaged me in many hours of conversation on the material herein, both live and by telephone. Without these two individuals' inspiration and their direct and indirect engagement with me over the years, I truly do not know where I would be in my Christian faith.

I am forever and always indebted to the sacrifices made by my parents, Rhonda and Jim, who in addition to getting me to this point in my life, encouraged me in this project and served as helpful sounding boards as I progressed through my research. Most importantly of all, my wife Heather has provided enduring and unshakable support over the course of this five year project. She has stood at ground zero where a seemingly endless litany of books that may as well have originated from the Twilight Zone found their way into our house and onto my bookshelf, and has helped me find my way through the metaphysical crises that my forays into the world of psychical research inevitably produced.

Introduction

"Lord, are you at this time going to restore the kingdom to Israel?" the disciples asked Jesus.[1] While astonished and overjoyed to find him alive and well just days after his tortuous death by crucifixion, they found it fitting to simply ask in effect, "So now what?"

As far as we can tell from our ancient sources, messianic expectation in the first century chiefly involved the delivery of Israel from the yoke of Roman oppression. While the coming Messiah's vocation may have varied in the minds of the hopeful, one aspect was constant. The Messiah would overthrow Rome. Nobody expected the Messiah would be crucified, a death that was widely considered to be as shameful as it was brutal. If anything, death by crucifixion proved that one was *not* the Messiah regardless of how promising the prospects may have looked beforehand.

However, on Easter Sunday some of Jesus' women followers discovered his tomb to be empty. Not long afterwards, Jesus appeared to them and subsequently to his eleven remaining disciples. God had reversed the capital verdict of the earthly courts and raised Jesus from the dead.

As welcome as the news of resurrection was to his disciples, the Romans retained political dominance over Israel. Evil still pervaded the world. And creation had not been restored to a state of sinless incorruption, Jesus' new body notwithstanding.

The risen Jesus responded to the disciples' question, "It is not for you to know the times or dates the Father has set by his own authority. But you will receive power when the Holy Spirit comes on you; and you will be my witnesses in Jerusalem, and in all Judea and Samaria, and to the ends of the earth."[2]

1. Acts 1:6, NRSV.
2. Acts 1:7–8, NRSV.

Most religions are based on private revelations or visions experienced by a gifted or charismatic leader. Not so with Christianity. The disciples adamantly declared that Jesus was Messiah after all despite his having turned contemporary Messianic expectations on their head, and even despite his shameful death by crucifixion.[3] Despite their initially shattered hopes of national restoration, the disciples remained steadfast in their Messianic declarations because they were convinced that Jesus had been raised. Furthermore, he proved it by appearing to them in a rejuvenated body.

Jesus is unique in that he is the only religious founder who has been raised from the dead. This mantra has been repeated for centuries by Christian theologians and apologists alike. There's just one problem. Since about 1994, this Christian claim is no longer unique. Shortly after his death from complications of a stroke, some followers of Rabbi Menachem Mendel Schneerson, the Lubavitcher Rebbe,[4] declared not only that he is the Messiah, but also that he remains alive. Moreover, as with early followers of Jesus, many Meshichists[5] today claim that he has appeared to them since his death, validating their ongoing hopes that he is the Messiah.

Jesus and the Rebbe cannot *both* be the Jewish Messiah, right? There are some very old Jewish traditions that speak of the possibility of two Messiahs, but this usually involved a suffering or priestly messiah and a royal, or conquering messiah whose roles were complementary. Additionally, for reasons we won't get into here, Christianity and Hasidic Judaism are not entirely theologically compatible. What then are we to make of the postmortem appearances of these two religious leaders?

The most accessible explanation is borne in psychopathology. The followers who saw Jesus and the Rebbe were hallucinating. As we will see, this explanation falters on the fact that there are well-attested *collective* sightings of both. Collective hallucinations occur but there are caveats which often make this explanation lack conviction when considering some specific cases.[6]

3. This is certainly not to say that Jesus was not both gifted and charismatic.

4. Or "Rebbe" for short. In this book, I will mostly use "Rebbe" when referring to Rabbi Schneerson.

5. Meshichists are those within Lubavitch Hasidism that still believe the Rebbe to be Messiah. I will use this term interchangeably with "Messianists" in this book.

6. When I use the term "collective hallucination," I am referring to subjective hallucinations that occur simultaneously to two or more people in a group. In other words, the percipients' minds are generating individual, subjective hallucinations. Depending

A more plausible tenet in some cases is that the seers experienced objective apparitions. That is, they saw something representing the deceased that resulted from an *objectively real* impulse. This tenet is consistent with the disciples' initial interpretation, according to Luke, that Jesus' spirit was appearing to them. Yet they changed their mind when he invited them to touch him and demonstrated his corporeality by consuming a piece of broiled fish.[7]

In popular culture, apparitions are commonly thought to be transparent entities. They are not physical in nature and certainly cannot be touched. Neither of these purported characteristics of apparitions is universally true, however. Apparitions often appear to be just as solid as the members of our household. As such they are not uncommonly mistaken for living people when they are initially seen. Moreover, according to two recent studies, about one in eight apparitional phenomena produce tactile (physical) sensations in their percipients. Also, as will be considered in due course, there are reasonably well-evidenced apparitions that successfully consumed food; one even smoked half a cigarette for good measure.

Encounters with apparitions are also not rare. They are more common than typically believed and may manifest in a variety of different contexts. Apparitions frequently appear to multiple people at the same time and usually when *not* expected. Sometimes these encounters result in a transfer of veridical information, that is information which could not have been known outside the context of the apparitional experience. Grieving widows and widowers will not infrequently be confronted with sensory experiences of their deceased spouses. Many experience apparitions of known persons at or around the time of their death. Apparitions may presage events to soon unfold, warn percipients of impending peril, and sometimes even guide them to safety from life-threatening situations.

But these are just stories, right? Clearly such tales are the fanciful products of imagination, exaggeration, illusion, hallucination, or outright fraud? After all, the rationalist will assert, this is the scientific age and we have left such superstitions to the dustbin of history, and we are all better off for it. To be sure, I suspect many case reports in the literature

---

upon the context, such hallucinations may even be somewhat similar in content when expectation is present. In contrast, visions that are shared by two or more people that are very similar, or exactly the same, in content, I believe are objectively real in some sense, or occur because of an objectively real stimulus. I would not label these latter kinds of experiences to be hallucinatory. This will make more sense as we proceed.

7. Luke 24:36–43.

are plausibly explainable in such ways. However, I am equally convinced that not all such reports are so easily disposed of by these explanations.

The cumulative data compels me to the belief in the objective nature of at least some of the reported apparitional phenomena. Most of these encounters occur well outside the confines of people diagnosed with neurodegenerative or psychiatric disorders, or those that are suffering from substance abuse. They occur across the entire spectrum of educational levels, mostly to people who are physically and psychologically healthy and to individuals who are highly functioning members of society. Crucially, case reports of apparitions over the past 140 years or so have been collected by serious researchers and are often accompanied by corroborative reports from eyewitnesses, replete in some cases with signed affidavits.

In what follows, we will encounter well-authenticated accounts of apparitions that serve a variety of functions: the deliverance of sailors from life-threatening storms at sea; a timely vision manifested inside the mind of a young girl who uses the information to promptly save her mother's life; apparitions that come to collect the spirits of dying loved ones, sometimes with stunned bystanders present to witness the spectacle; and even an apparition that accompanied Charles Lindbergh on his record-breaking Trans-Atlantic flight. We will also encounter bone-chilling cases of haunted houses and enigmatic, yet glorious visions of Jesus Christ and the Blessed Virgin Mary.

Fascinating as all this may be, what do these phenomena have to do with claims that Jesus Christ or the Lubavitcher Rebbe have been raised from the dead?

The most important evidence for Jesus' resurrection is the evidence of his postmortem appearances to his earliest followers. That some of Jesus' early followers had experiences that led them to conclude that he had been raised from the dead is a fact accepted by even highly skeptical New Testament scholars. Similarly, many of those who have experienced postmortem appearances of the Rebbe (many of which are still alive at the time of this writing) have been interviewed and their testimonies submitted to writing.

One of the emerging theories to account for the postmortem appearances of Jesus is that his early followers saw apparitions shortly after the crucifixion.[8] As we will explicate in due course, I find this a much

---

8. Dale Allison effectively revivified debate around this theory in his 2005 book *Resurrecting Jesus: The Earliest Christian Tradition and its Interpreters* (198–375) and

superior alternative theory than that of subjective visions or hallucinations. We will discover that apparitions may be invoked in attempts of accounting for the postmortem appearances of the Rebbe as well. Resultingly most of the space in this volume will be concerned with the subject of apparitions.

What is presented here will surprise most readers who are disinclined to believe in the objective nature of apparitions or the wider world of paranormal cognition in which they find their home. It certainly had a profound impact on me. As a medical doctor, I make treatment decisions based upon the updated scientific data from clinical trials when available. When diagnosing an illness, I will try to find the best fit for the data with which we have to work, including important aspects of respective patients' histories of present illness, symptom profiles, physical exam findings, laboratory test results, and imaging test results. Before ascertaining a diagnosis, numerous other possibilities must often be considered and ruled out to feel confident that the correct treatment is being administered.

Similar processes of thought are employed by me in other aspects of life. When it comes to the matter of apparitional encounters, since I have not had such an experience, I tend to view the phenomenon through a skeptical lens. As I read through hundreds of case reports in the literature, I considered potential explanations of a more subjective nature that could adequately explain the content of the reports without resorting to a paranormal explanation. In many cases, I found non-paranormal explanations to be as plausible (if not more so) than its paranormal alternative. In the end, however, I found some of the narratives to be very resistant to "normal" explanations.[9] In this volume I restrict myself mostly to presenting such cases that I found to be compelling as likely-authentic paranormal events.

Furthermore, the literature on apparitions lends credible evidence to the veracity of certain "psi phenomena" including telepathy, psychokinesis, precognition, retrocognition, and clairvoyance.[10] This was a very

---

even more emphatically in his more recent work, *The Resurrection of Jesus: Apologetics, Polemics, History.* Jake O'Connell also delivered an important volume in this debate in his *Jesus' Resurrection and Apparitions: A Bayesian Analysis.* It is primarily the yeoman work of both Allison and O'Connell that inspired my current efforts on the topic.

9. For reasons that will become clear, I prefer the term "normal" or "prosaic" or "mundane" as opposed to "natural" to refer to non-paranormal explanations for allegedly paranormal events. These usually include fraud, hallucination, illusion, cryptomnesia, etc. I will also use the term "supernormal" as a synonym for "paranormal."

10. The term "psi" is commonly employed in the literature as shorthand denoting

unexpected and frankly shocking result of this research. However, after going down this proverbial rabbit hole, I found it difficult to reach an alternative conclusion without uncritically dismissing many well-evidenced accounts. As such, in this author's mind, apparitions serve as the best *potential* way of understanding the postmortem traditions of our two Messianic icons without endorsing resurrection claims.

I will close this introduction on a personal note. Having been educated in the West, I thought that scientific materialism posed the greatest challenge to traditional forms of theism. In ways, this held true for decades when I reflected upon the implications of certain scientific foundations such as biological evolution and Newtonian mechanics. However, having become immersed in a new world of literature that I had been unaware existed as recently as early 2020, in my mind the edifice of scientific materialism was rapidly incinerated by the fires of psychical research. The victory was short-lived however, as a dark phoenix arose from the ashes. And this foe is much more formidable than the one it replaced. This foe is commonly called Super-Psi in the literature,[11] and we will be discussing this in due course.

I was once, and remain, quite comfortable in dismissing the typical alternative interpretations to Jesus' resurrection that have been touted by skeptics, in some cases for centuries:

1. Jesus' disciples fabricated claims of resurrection.
2. Jesus' disciples went to the "wrong tomb" and found it empty.
3. Jesus somehow survived the crucifixion and later presented himself alive to the disciples (i.e., Swoon Theory).
4. The disciples hallucinated the risen Jesus.
5. Claims of resurrection by Jesus' early followers were the result of cognitive dissonance.

---

the paranormal categories listed. Briefly, telepathy is mind-to-mind communication. Psychokinesis, or PK, refers to affecting matter with the mind. Clairvoyance denotes having or obtaining knowledge of events or places without use of the five ordinary senses. Precognition refers to obtaining information about the future in a supernormal manner. Retrocognition refers to obtaining information about the past in a supernormal way. I will use "psi" often in this volume as an umbrella term for these categories when appropriate.

11. What typically falls under the umbrella of super-psi are dramatic exhibitions of psi—e.g., a trance medium at a séance materializes an apparition of the deceased spouse of one of the sitters, and the apparition produces reams of intimate knowledge that the medium could not possibly have known by normal means.

All of these theories work within the realm of scientific materialism, and all of them are severely flawed when subjected to analysis. Super-Psi, on the other hand, offers a litany of natural anomalies that may be employed to account for the historical data more plausibly without necessarily concluding that Jesus was raised from the dead. The phenomenon of objectively-produced apparitions is at the forefront here. Once science has moved on from its current stance of dogmatic materialism, these will be the arguments of tomorrow, those more commonly employed by future critics in refuting the resurrection.

Moreover, apparitional and other psi phenomena that will be discussed in this volume lend credence to the interpretation that consciousness survives bodily death. In other words, those of us more inclined towards theism will find this data to ostensibly confirm the existence of the afterlife. As will be demonstrated and what was hinted at above, this conclusion is not the only one that may be drawn from the evidence. However, in my mind it remains the most probable interpretation of the data.

Finally, there is another side to this existential coin. Not all that I have discovered fits easily within a strictly Judeo-Christian worldview, at least as traditionally conceived. Whether you are a theist or an atheist, spiritually minded or not, there will be something in what follows that will be disturbing to your worldview. On the other hand, I think you will also find this to be a fascinating read that may just change the way you see reality.

1

The World of Apparitions

As a product of this research, the single greatest epiphany for me was the discovery that ghost sightings and apparent visits of the deceased have been studied and carefully documented by very serious researchers. The Society for Psychical Research (SPR) serves as the apogee of such painstaking analyses on this phenomenon as well as other forms of psi. In an important late nineteenth-century work, Henry Sidgwick et al. published "Report on the Census of Hallucinations." The researchers asked the following question in the surveys:

> Have you ever, when believing yourself to be completely awake, had a vivid impression of seeing or being touched by a living being or inanimate object, or of hearing a voice; which impression, so far as you could discover, was not due to any external physical cause?[1]

A total of seventeen thousand individuals was asked this question by 410 different collectors. Roughly 10 percent of the respondents answered in the affirmative.[2] More recently, a survey from about 1980 indicated that 25 percent of Western Europeans and 31 percent of Americans thought that they have experienced some form of contact with a deceased person.[3]

---

1. Sidgwick et al., "Census," 353.
2. For discussion on how this number was derived, see Sidgwick et al., "Census," 36–39.
3. Haraldsson, *Departed*, 1.

Moreover, the sources from which most of the cases presented here are dependent indicate that the collections went through a rigorous vetting process. Psychotherapist Adam Crabtree writes of Frederic W. H. Myers and the SPR in general:

> Between the formation of the SPR in 1882 and his death in 1901, Myers and his colleagues published in their *Proceedings* and *Journal* something over 10,000 pages of reports on supernormal phenomena, including not only extended field observations with mediums and heavily documented studies of spontaneous cases, but early attempts to study telepathy and kindred phenomena experimentally and quantitatively. The industry, thoroughness, and care manifest in these publications is unsurpassed in any scientific literature known to me.[4]

This echoes the sentiments of the highly respected, early twentieth-century psychical researcher William James:

> In fact, were I asked to point to a scientific journal where hard-headedness and never-sleeping suspicion of sources of error might be seen in their full bloom, I think I should have to fall back on the Proceedings of the Society for Psychical Research.[5]

For whatever it may be worth from somebody that has plunged into these sources in considerable detail, I agree wholeheartedly with the comments of Crabtree and James as pertaining to the SPR.[6] After obtaining a mere passing familiarity with the work of the SPR, it becomes clear that the researchers were exceptionally cautious in their procedures. Such caution included consideration of, and ruling out, mundane causes prior to accepting cases' authenticity.[7]

More recently, Dianne Arcangel conducted a five-year, international "Afterlife Encounter Survey" in which she received 827 complete submissions. Of the respondents, 596 reported experiencing afterlife encounters. She gives narrative details on a selection of dozens of these encounters in her 2005 book *Afterlife Encounters*. Regarding her concern for authenticity, she validated the narratives she received by directly interviewing the

---

4. Crabtree, "Automatism," 353.

5. James, "Psychical Research," 304–5. See also Tyrrell's summary of the researchers' methodology. Tyrrell, *Apparitions*, 25.

6. See Gauld, *Founders*, for an excellent overview of the society's origin, motivations, and fascinating biographical information of its premiere members.

7. Sidgwick et al., "Census," 54–69.

percipients, obtaining eyewitness support when available, and in some cases procuring written documentation. In certain instances, she used external sources to provide supporting evidence.[8]

Erlendur Haraldsson, who collected stories of apparitional encounters in Iceland, also checked reported sightings with corroborating witnesses when available.[9] This is particularly the case with sightings that were collectively perceived by multiple witnesses. We will consider numerous cases from his collection.

Whatever one makes of apparitional occurrences, they cannot all be summarily dismissed as the result of fraud, subjective hallucination, or exaggeration. The evidential basis for the objective reality of at least some apparitional experiences may be argued on two grounds: 1) Some of the apparitions are witnessed by more than one person at the same time, and 2) in some cases, these experiences result in percipients' obtaining information that could not have otherwise been known to them at the time. In the examples presented subsequently, we will focus largely on cases of apparitional encounters that fit within one or both categories.

Apparitions are typically categorized by researchers based on certain characteristics and stereotypes. For instance, Tyrrell divided the cases into four categories.[10] By the time my research was completed, I could narrow the case material to no fewer than eight categories: 1) Crisis apparitions; 2) Apparitions of the living; 3) Haunting apparitions; 4) Rescue apparitions; 5) Transitional apparitions; 6) Reunion apparitions; 7) Inducible apparitions; and 8) Religious apparitions.

In what follows we will consider examples from each of these categories. Please note that the categories themselves are helpful only for organizational purposes. There exists some overlap from multiple categories in some of the cases.

Before moving on, a few things to note on definitions and methodology:

1. We will encounter the term "hallucination" multiple times in some of the cases. Some of the early researchers, especially those of the SPR, apply the term "hallucination" as a blanket for all such phenomena, not necessarily intending to judge all such experiences as subjective. For the purposes of this book, I use the term

---

8. Arcangel, *Afterlife*, xii.
9. Haraldsson, *Departed*, 1–4. See also appendix A in the same volume.
10. Tyrrell, *Apparitions*, 33.

"hallucination" to denote only subjective experiences; that is, those based on no actual, external signal, prompt, or impulse.

2. For authors who provided a title to the case reports that I reproduce in subsequent chapters, I retain the title that those respective authors used. For those that did not, I supply my own title.

2

Crisis Apparitions

MY NAME IS MARGRET

> My wife and I had living with us a little girl about two and a half years old whom we fostered. One night I woke up and felt as though a woman were standing beside the bed. She said to me, "My name is Margret." Then she vanished out the door. I looked at the clock and saw it was exactly three thirty. The day after, or the same day, I learnt that the girl's grandmother had died at that same moment from a heart attack at a town in another part of the country. Her name was Margret. I knew nothing about her health. I am not even sure I knew her name. I had never seen her when she was living.[1]

CRISIS APPARITIONS APPEAR TO percipients at about the time, or within a short period of time, of a crisis event. This most often involves the death of the agents producing them.[2] A question worth pondering: why would Margret appear to a percipient who she did not know in life? There are numerous examples in the literature where apparitions appear to unexpected percipients.

---

1. Haraldsson, *Departed*, 41
2. By use of the word "agent," I am referring to the person who apparently produces the apparition. The percipient is on the other end of the exchange, the one seeing the apparition or that has some other sensory experience that ostensibly emanated from the agent.

AT HJORSEY

> When I was in my twenties, I stayed at Hjorsey. One time in the middle of the night, I woke up and saw an elderly man from the district, a farmer, standing on the middle of the floor. I watched him for quite a while. He did not move and then he disintegrated and disappeared as soon as I was about to speak to him. In the morning I told the household members of my experience and thought that this farmer was most likely dead now. In the evening we received a message by post informing us of the death of this farmer. About two months later I met this farmer's widow and she told me she had dozed off after his death and dreamt her husband said to her: "I have already been to Hjorsey, but no one was aware of me there except Gisli (the informant)."[3]

STEAMER IN A PANTRY

Edmund Dunn was a fireman on the tug *Wolf*, a steamer that towed vessels in Chicago Harbor. On October 24th, 1889, his sister, Agnes Paquet experienced a chilling vision of his death.

> I arose about the usual hour on the morning of the accident, probably about six o'clock. . . . I awoke feeling gloomy and depressed, which feeling I could not shake off. . . . I went into the pantry, took down the tea cannister, and as I turned around my brother Edmund—or his exact image—stood before me and only a few feet away. The apparition stood with back toward me, or, rather, partially so, and was in the act of falling forward—away from me—seemingly impelled by two loops or a loop of rope drawing against his legs. The vision lasted but a moment, disappearing over a low railing or bulwark, but was very distinct. I dropped the tea, clasped my hands to my face, and explained, "My God! Ed is drowned!"
>
> At about half-past ten a.m. my husband received a telegram from Chicago, announcing the drowning of my brother. . . . I then gave him a minute description of what I had seen. I stated that my brother, as I saw him, was bareheaded, had on a heavy, blue sailor's shirt, no coat, and that he went over the rail or bulwark. I noticed that his pants' legs were rolled up enough to

---

3. Haraldsson, *Departed*, 43–44.

show the white lining inside. I also described the appearance of
the boat at the point where my brother went overboard.[4]

After the telegram had arrived, Mr. Paquet set off for Chicago. Although Agnes Paquet had never seen the vessel (outside of the vision), she accurately described the boat's description as well as Edmund's attire. Interestingly, the crew informed Mr. Paquet that Edmund had purchased a pair of pants that were too long, and he had to roll them up to compensate. The only discrepancy is that the crew thought that Edmund was wearing his hat at the time of the accident.[5]

This unusual, but not unique, feature of Agnes Paquet's disturbing vision of her brother's death was that it also featured part of Edmund's environment. Standing in her pantry at home, she sees her brother falling away from her, but also finds herself on the deck of the steamer. She is, as Tyrrell puts it, "perceptually conscious of being in two spaces *which bear no special relation to one another.*"[6]

Given the short window of time available for an appearance to be categorized as a crisis apparition (the day of the agent's death), they do occur disproportionately to that of other categories of apparitions. In Haraldsson's sample of 349 cases in Iceland, thirty-eight of the apparitions (11 percent) occurred on the same day that the person died, and in 84 percent of those cases the percipient was unaware of the agent's death prior to the apparitional experience.[7] If crisis apparitions were merely coincidences,[8] we would expect their incidence in relation to other kinds of apparitions to be a fraction of 1 percent, not 11 percent.

GO STRAIGHT TO THE DOCTOR!

Jeanie Gwynne-Bettany's story is similar to our last case in that the apparition is seen within the context of its immediate environment. Fortunately, this case has a happier ending than our first three cases:

> On one occasion (I am unable to fix the date, but I must have been about 10 years old) I was walking in a country lane at A.,

---

4. Sidgwick, "Clairvoyance," 33.
5. Sidgwick, "Clairvoyance," 33–34.
6. Tyrrell, *Apparitions*, 52, emphasis original.
7. Haraldsson, *Departed*, 50.
8. By coincidences, I mean that a percipient hallucinates a person that happened to die at about that same time, or on that same day.

> the place where my parents then resided. I was reading geometry as I walked along, a subject little likely to produce fancies or morbid phenomena of any kind, when, in a moment, I saw a bedroom known as the White Room in my home, and upon the floor lay my mother, to all appearance dead. The vision must have remained some minutes, during which time my real surroundings appeared to pale and die out; but as the vision faded, actual surroundings came back, at first dimly, and then clearly.
>
> I could not doubt that what I had seen was real so, instead of going home, I went at once to the house of our medical man and found him at home. He at once set out with me for my home, on the way putting questions I could not answer, as my mother was to all appearance well when I left home.
>
> I led the doctor straight to the White Room, where we found my mother actually lying as in my vision. This was true even to minute details. She had been seized suddenly by an attack at the heart and would soon have breathed her last but for the doctor's timely advent. I shall get my father and mother to read this and sign it.[9]

Jeanie's story was confirmed upon inquiry by both of her parents. In fact, her father, S. G. Gwynne, added the following:

> I distinctly remember being surprised by seeing my daughter, in company with the family doctor, outside the door of my residence; and I asked, "Who is ill?" She replied, "Mamma." She led the way at once to the "White Room," where we found my wife lying in a swoon on the floor. It was when I asked when she had been taken ill, that I found it must have been after my daughter had left the house. None of the servants in the house knew anything of the sudden illness, which our doctor assured me would have been *fatal* had he not arrived when he did.
>
> My wife was quite well when I left her in the morning.[10]

The following crisis apparition occurred during the Transvaal War.[11]

---

9. Gurney et al., *Phantasms I*, 194.

10. Gurney et al., *Phantasms I*, 194, emphasis original. In addition to this remarkable case, Ms. Bettany was also involved in another collectively-experienced crisis case that coincided with the death of one of her neighbors. See Gurney et al., *Phantasms II*, 173–74.

11. Also called the First Boer War, the Transvaal War took place in 1880–81 between the British and the South African Republic, in the context of the latter eventually gaining independence from the former.

CONVERSATION WITH AN APPARITION

> One night, after reading for some time in the library of the club, I had gone to my rooms late. It must have been nearly one o'clock before I turned into bed. I had slept, perhaps some three hours or so when I awoke with a start.... Standing by my bed, between me and the chest of drawers, I saw a figure, which, in spite of the unwonted dress—unwonted, at least to me—and of a full black beard, I at once recognized as that of my older brother-officer. He had on the usual kharki coat, worn by officers on active service in eastern climates. A brown leather strap, which might have been the strap of his field service glass, crossed his breast. A brown leather girdle, with sword attached on the left side, and revolver case on the right, passed round his waist. On his head he wore the ordinary white pith helmet of service.... His face was pale, but his bright black eyes shone as keenly as when, a year and a-half before, they had looked upon me as he stood with one foot on the hansom, bidding me adieu.
>
> Fully impressed for the brief moment that we were stationed together at C—in Ireland or somewhere, and thinking I was in my barrack-room, I said, "Hallo! P., am I late for parade?" P. looked at me steadily, and replied, "I'm shot."
>
> "Shot!" I exclaimed. "Good God! how and where?"
>
> "Through the lungs," replied P., and as he spoke his right hand moved slowly up the breast, until the fingers rested over the right lung.
>
> "What were you doing?" I asked.
>
> "The General sent me forward," he answered, and the right hand left the breast to move slowly to the front, pointing over my head to the window, and at the same moment the figure melted away. I rubbed my eyes, to make sure I was not dreaming, and sprang out of bed. It was 4:10 a.m. by the clock on my mantelpiece.[12]

The percipient was in London at the time, the agent of the apparition had died in the Battle of Lang's Neck in South Africa. Upon investigation, it was determined that there was likely a discrepancy in the time reported (4:10 a.m) and the actual time that the apparition appeared (likely closer to about 7:00 a.m.), as the percipient claimed that the light of dawn was filtering into his room through the window, which was impossible that early and at that time of year. However, the case's authenticity is bolstered

---

12. Gurney and Myers, "Soon After Death," 413–14.

by facts that were later confirmed by the percipient through two witnesses who had been present at the Battle of Lang's Neck. Major Poole (i.e., "P.") had been wearing the same uniform as his apparition, had grown the beard (which the percipient had never seen him with beforehand), and the mode of death was confirmed, a bullet through the right lung.[13]

Such conversations during apparitional encounters are rare per Green and McCreery. While 14 percent of the visual apparitions from their collection spoke, they comment that, among those, "few speak at length, and the speaking is not always realistic."[14] Regarding the case just presented they note,

> Cases of this kind are exceptional. Apparitions seem to have a certain reluctance to speak freely and realistically. It should not be supposed that all of the 14 per cent of cases in which visual apparitions speak correspond to cases in which the subject actually sees the apparition's lips move and hears the sound issuing from its mouth, as if it were a real person. In some cases the subject first hears someone speaking and then later sees what seems to be the author of the sound. In others he may see an apparition and at the same time hear a voice speaking, but the apparition's lips may not move, and it may seem as if the voice is coming from elsewhere and not from the apparition.[15]

Subsequent cases considered by the authors demonstrate that even when the occasion would "seem appropriate" for an apparition to speak to the percipient, often at the percipient's repeated attempts to elicit a response, a verbal reply is frequently not given. Even the famous Morton Ghost fails to provide a verbal response after multiple attempts by a percipient to elicit one.[16] Also, when they do "speak," it is not uncommon for apparitions to communicate via telepathy rather than by (apparent) voice phonation.[17] Among the reasonably well-evidenced collections, especially those assembled by the SPR, it is rare for apparitions seen in the awake state to have complex exchanges with percipients.

---

13. Gurney and Myers, "Soon After Death," 414–15.
14. Green and McCreery, *Apparitions*, 95.
15. Green and McCreery, *Apparitions*, 96.
16. We will encounter the Morton Ghost in chapter 4.
17. Green and McCreery, *Apparitions*, 96–101.

ROBERT BOWES—THE APPARITION ON THE LAKE

This fascinating narrative originally appeared in Sir Ernest Bennett's *Apparitions and Haunted Houses*, published in 1939. The apparitional encounter occurred in February 1926. A farm laborer named Robert Bowes was ill, and was visited by Miss Godley, Miss Goldsmith, and Mr. Robert Gallagher. The three conversed with Bowes through an open window. Robert seemed to be doing okay, all things considering, but did ask for them to send the doctor because he had not seen him for a long time. Continuing with Miss Godley's account:

> I then came straight back. The road runs along the shores of a big lake and, while the steward stopped to open a gate there, he asked me, "if I saw the man on the lake." I looked and saw an old man with a long white beard which floated in the wind, crossing to the other side of the lake. He appeared to be moving his arms, as though working a punt, he was standing up and gliding across but I saw no boat. I said, "Where is the boat?" The steward replied "There is no boat." I said, "What nonsense! There must be a boat, and he is standing up in it." But there was no boat and he was just gliding along on the dark water; the masseuse also saw him. The steward asked me who I thought he was like, I said, "he is exactly like Robert Bowes, the old man." The figure crossed the lake and disappeared in among the reeds and trees at the far side, and we came home.[18]

Miss Godley proceeded with the intent of writing a note for the doctor, but before finishing the task the same doctor paid her a visit. He had been to Bowes's place just after they had left, having gone by a different route. The doctor told Miss Godley that Robert had just died.[19]

The testimony of the steward, Mr. Gallagher, confirms Miss Godley's account, that while on their way home they saw the apparition walking atop the surface of the water, with its whiskers moving in the breeze, before disappearing as it neared the shore. Curiously, the third percipient, Miss Goldsmith, witnessed an identical apparitional drama, except she actually did see Bowes standing in a boat.[20]

It is extremely improbable that these accounts were hallucinatory. That this vision of Robert Bowes took place at roughly the time of his

---

18. Bennett, *Haunted Houses*, 37–38.
19. Bennett, *Haunted Houses*, 38.
20. Bennett, *Haunted Houses*, 39.

death, at the time unbeknownst to the percipients, makes any claim that they experienced subjective hallucinations a highly improbable coincidence. More pointedly, that the visions occurred simultaneously to the three who were not expecting to see anything (and indeed were surprised by what they saw), and that the content described was similar effectively rules out subjective hallucination. At the same time, the one major discrepancy of Miss Goldsmith seeing a boat while the other two did not makes collusion or fraud an untenable solution.[21]

APPARITIONS AS THE EXPRESSION OF IDEAS

According to George Tyrrell, apparitional dramas are subconscious creations of the "midlevel" regions of *both* agent(s) and percipient(s). Tyrrell calls these midlevel regions of personality the *producers*. According to this theory, in typical cases, the construction of an apparition is the result of a mental impulse sent subconsciously by the agent's *producer*. This impulse is subsequently received, and possibly modified to a certain extent, by the percipient's *producer*. The apparitional drama has now been formed by a collusion of the subconscious minds of agent(s) and percipient(s). Dramas need an appropriate stage and props, however. While the "storyline" has been written, the stage still needs to be set. Tyrrell's *stage carpenter*, another functionary of the subconscious personality of the percipient, is responsible for expressing in sensory form the finished drama.[22]

Often to a striking degree, apparitions adapt to the environment in which they are presented and mimic the physical characteristics and

---

21. Notably I ran across several such collective apparitions that appeared slightly different to the percipients. A husband and wife, Mr. and Mrs. Barber, upon returning home, saw a lady enter their gate, move up the flagged walk to their entry door, and disappear. The one apparent discrepancy was in the apparition's attire. Mr. Barber perceived the lady wearing a plaid shawl and a gray-black bonnet with "a bit of color." Mrs. Barber perceived her only to be a "gray figure." See Bennett, *Haunted Houses*, 275–78.

In another case, apparitions were seen by a Mr. Tom Horner and a Mr. Arthur Wright in March 1934. While motoring from Filey to Harrogate, England, their headlights met the light emanating from the headlights of a bus approaching from the opposite direction. Apparitions of men in uniform were seen in the road. They wore "large soft hats, dark plum-coloured cloaks and leggings." Mr. Horner saw three such apparitions while Mr. Wright claimed to see two. See Bennett, *Haunted Houses*, 284–87.

22. Just to be clear, Tyrrell's *producer* and *stage carpenter* were not theorized to exist in a literal sense. If my understanding of Tyrrell is correct, these were conceptual personifications of the subconscious mind used to explain the construction of apparitional dramas.

actions of an actual person. Apparitions may cast shadows. Their reflections may be seen in windowpanes or mirrors. If they wander into a dark area of the room, their visibility will diminish accordingly. They are "aware" of their surroundings. Unlike Dick Van Dyke's classic TV character Rob Petrie, they do not trip over ottomans. Sometimes they will even open doors upon entering the room and exit the same way, though after the drama has played out the percipient will usually discover the room to be left the way it was prior to the encounter.[23] Moreover, apparitions are virtually always fully clothed. This makes sense if apparitions are subconscious creations, akin to the content of dreams, but is problematic on the assumption that they are conscious spirits or out-of-body experiences (OBEs). Also worth noting, in cases where there are multiple percipients, the apparition is seen by the percipients appropriately from their respective positions in space. These important aspects of the drama are the domain of the percipient's *stage carpenter*.

The Robert Bowes case provides I think instructive grounds for such speculation. The three percipients received an impulse, or "message," that was likely generated by Bowes upon his death. They likely were "chosen" recipients of this impulse, albeit subconsciously, because they had just visited him prior to his passing. Miss Godley's subconscious mind, or the producer-level of her personality, received and processed the "message" and the stage carpenter-level presented it to her by projecting the apparition of Bowes floating across the surface of the lake. Even she and her steward commented that it did not make sense that there would not be a boat. However, Miss Goldsmith, who also received the "message," subconsciously produced a more appropriate and complete apparitional drama by supplying the boat.

Why though was the vision so similar among the three percipients? I suggest it is because the basic content was conjured at the producer-level of Robert Bowes's subconscious, midlevel personality. Through mechanisms that we currently do not understand, he generated an *idea* of being on the lake. Perhaps he was thinking or dreaming about being on the lake just prior to his passing. This idea was likely vague and undeveloped, as are all ideas in their initial stages. As Bowes slipped into unconsciousness,

---

23. Of course, exceptions to this "realistic" aspect of apparitions are plentiful, as we touch upon frequently in this volume. Apparitions will sometimes move through walls or rise through ceilings. They will sometimes project their own luminosity (supply their own light, to be seen clearly even in a darkened room). And, of course, sometimes apparitions will appear transparent rather than solid.

presumably for the last time, this idea was further developed by the *producer*, thereby giving life to the basic content of the vision to follow. This content was delivered in the form of a telepathic "message" to the three percipients of our case. To make sense of the differences, the "message" could be modified by each percipient's *producer* before it was presented to each consciously, in sensory form, by the percipients' respective *stage carpenters*. The construction of an apparitional drama is a combined effort on the subconscious levels of both agent and percipient.[24]

In this way, ideas are developed and conveyed telepathically, and somewhat dramatically, from agent(s) to percipient(s). Tyrrell refers to *idea patterns* being created and conveyed by such apparitional dramas. This is admittedly complex, but after my own analysis of the subjects considered in this book, I think Tyrrell's proposed mechanism is somewhere on the right track. We will be returning to the *idea pattern* concept later when we consider especially apparitions of religious figures and other folkloric entities.

ASSESSMENT OF CRISIS APPARITIONS

The general authenticity of crisis apparitions is bolstered by their frequency in contrast to those apparitions that occur well after the agent has died. A disproportionate number of apparitions that do occur seem to appear at about the time of the agent's death. A remarkable 14 percent of the apparitions in Erlendur Haraldsson's Icelandic study of 349 cases occur within twenty-four hours of the agent's death. Just over one-fifth of the appearances (22.4 percent) occur within one week, while about one-third (31.2 percent) occur within one month. Just over half (51.8 percent) of apparitions are seen within one year of the agent's death, 72.8 percent occur within five years, and 82 percent within ten years.[25] Moreover, crisis apparitions sometimes appear to multiple percipients, as in the Robert Bowes case. Just as interestingly, crisis apparitions will on rare occasion appear at about the same time to multiple percipients separated in space, sometimes by distances of hundreds of miles.[26] Finally, as was detailed in several cases in this chapter, sometimes crisis apparitions will supply the percipient with veridical information regarding the mode of

---

24. Tyrrell, *Apparitions*, 101–2.
25. Haraldsson, *Departed*, 53–55.
26. See cases 314 and 315 of Gurney et al., *Phantasms II*, 181–83.

injury or death and/or details of the surrounding environment in which the crisis occurred.

Mysterious as they are, crisis apparitions represent a genuine phenomenon of nature. That is not to say that these apparitions are necessarily conscious spirits. The balance of the evidence, in my opinion, strongly suggests that crisis apparitions are mostly unconscious, telepathic projections of agents undergoing some form of extreme distress. We will be returning to this possibility often as we proceed.

3

Apparitions of the Living

PARAMAHANSA YOGANANDA WAS ON a journey to find Kedar Nath Babu in Banaras, India on behalf of his father to deliver a letter regarding a business proposal.[1] There was one major problem. His father had lost the address! Yogananda was sent to Swami Pranabananda instead, who his father believed could be helpful as he had attained "an exalted spiritual stature." Having reached Banaras, Yogananda proceeded to the swami's address and walked inside, finding a "rather stout man, wearing only a loin-cloth, was seated in the lotus posture on a slightly raised platform."[2]

> "Are you Swami Pranabananda?"
> He nodded. "Are you Bhagabati's son?" His words were out before I had time to get Father's letter from my pocket. In astonishment, I handed him the note of introduction, which now seemed superfluous.
> "Of course I will locate Kedar Nath Babu for you." The saint again surprised me by his clairvoyance. . . .
> Abruptly terminating our conversation, the saint became gravely motionless. A sphinxlike air enveloped him. At first his eyes sparkled, as if observing something of interest, then grew dull. . . .
> "Little sir, don't get worried. The man you wish to see will be with you in half an hour." The yogi was reading my mind—a feat not too difficult at the moment!

---

1. Banaras is also known as Varanasi in the state of Uttar Pradesh.
2. Yogananda, *Autobiography*, 25.

Again he fell into inscrutable silence. When my watch informed me that thirty minutes had elapsed, the swami aroused himself.

"I think Kedar Nath Babu is nearing the door," he said.[3]

Yogananda subsequently left the room, met the visitor and confirmed that it was Kedar Nath Babu, who in turn asked if Yogananda was Bhagabati's son who had come to the swami's house to meet him. Kedar Nath Babu confirmed that the swami had approached him as he was bathing earlier in the Ganges, and informed him that Yogananda was waiting for him at his apartment. He then agreed to go with him. They initially walked hand-in-hand, but eventually the swami asked him how long it would take him to reach his place. After Kedar Nath Babu told him it would require a half hour, the swami enigmatically replied, "I have something else to do at present" and "I must leave you behind. . . . Bhagabati's son and I will be awaiting you." The swami then "dashed swiftly past me and disappeared in the crowd."[4]

Understandably puzzled, Yogananda retorted that the swami had been at his residence and within sight for the past one hour. Then he went on to recount the conversation that he had had with the swami. Kedar Nath Babu responded as most would, with similar astonishment.[5]

Swami Pranabananda gave his two visitors a quizzical smile before explaining,

> "Why are you stupefied at all this? The subtle unity of the phenomenal world is not hidden from true yogis. I instantly see and converse with my disciples in distant Calcutta. They can similarly transcend at will every obstacle of gross matter."[6]

Yogananda drew upon his own eyewitness recollection to relate this and other miraculous tales in his *Autobiography of a Yogi*. Of course, the story strikes even some of the most open-minded of us as fantastic. And perhaps it is. Maybe there is a non-paranormal explanation to be had for Swami Pranabananda's apparent "self-projection" to a distant location to summon Kedar Nath Babu?

On the other hand, there are many well-attested apparitions of living persons in the literature. For reasons that will become clear as we

---

3. Yogananda, *Autobiography*, 25–26.
4. Yogananda, *Autobiography*, 26–27.
5. Yogananda, *Autobiography*, 27–28.
6. Yogananda, *Autobiography*, 28.

proceed, this may be the most enlightening category of apparitions, especially when speculating upon their phenomenological nature. In our first case the agent and percipient of the apparition are one and the same.

BUILDING INSTRUCTIONS

The following is a case of problem-solving by self-projection:

> In the year 1944 I was asked by a milk condensation manufacturing company named *CCF* in Leeuwarden to repair a very complicated book-keeping machine (Burroughs) which I hardly knew how to work with. I started with the repair and got the machine ready except that she was not correct adding in the hundred figures. It was not so easy to find out the defect, but . . . during a night in the week I was at work with the machine, I was awakened in my sleep and saw (in colour) on the table of our bedroom that book-keeping machine, while a brilliant electric lamp was lighting, and saw myself, fully dressed, take out with the fingers of my left hand a little triangle formed from the machine and give it with a pincher or pinner at one end a pinch making it somewhat longer and placed that part back in the machine.
>
> At the day following on that nightly experiment I did the same manipulation done in the preceding night and see, the machine was working in the hundreds all correct. Mark please, the machine was *not* in my workshop but I repaired her at the *CCF*.[7]

I submit for consideration that the information required to correct the machine was in the subliminal mind of the percipient all along, or at least a working theory of how to fix the problem. The projected apparition of himself was the subliminal mind bringing this information to the surface. As we will see later, however, it may have been that this information was obtained in a supernormal (veridical) way, as much of the information in certain apparition cases seems to be.

"STANDING AT MY LEFT ELBOW"

It was February 10th, 1894. Awaiting the return of his friends who were performing at a concert, the narrator of the following case was sitting at his fireplace, immersing himself in a book when he received a visit from a familiar friend:

7. Green and McCreery, *Apparitions*, 77, emphasis original.

Suddenly, without a moment's warning, my whole being seemed aroused to the highest state of tension or aliveness, and I was aware, with an intenseness not easily imagined by those who have never experienced it, that another being or presence was not only in the room but close to me. . . . Without changing my position, and looking straight into the fire, I knew somehow that my friend A. H. was standing at my left elbow, but so far behind me as to be hidden by the arm-chair in which I was leaning back. Moving my eyes round slightly without otherwise changing my position, the lower portion of one leg became visible, and I instantly recognized the grey-blue material of trousers he often wore, but the stuff appeared semi-transparent, reminding me of tobacco smoke in consistency. . . . With that curious instinctive wish not to see more of such a "figure," I did no more than glance once or twice at the apparition and then directed my gaze steadily at the fire in front of me. An appreciable space of time passed—probably several seconds in all, but seemingly in reality much longer—when the most curious thing happened. Standing up-right between me and the window on my left, at a distance of about four feet from me and almost immediately behind my chair, I saw perfectly distinctly the figure of my friend—the face very pale, the head slightly thrown back, the eyes shut, and on one side of the throat, just under the jaw, a wound with blood on it. The figure remained motionless with the arms close to the sides, and for some time, how long I can't say, I looked steadily at it; then all at once I roused myself, turned deliberately round, the figure vanished, and I realized instantly that I had seen the figure behind me without moving from my first position—an impossible feat physically. I am perfectly certain I never moved my position from the first appearance of the figure as seen physically, until it disappeared on my turning round.[8]

The agent was the narrator's friend who had fainted, fell in the street, and sustained the throat wound represented by the apparition. Fortunately, his friend did recover from the wound. The narrator writes in his letter to Frederic Myers that he had witnessed "psychic phenomena of almost every kind" for the prior fifteen years leading up to this incident. Furthermore, he expressed the belief that he had a telepathic connection with A. H., evidenced by the two often saying the same things simultaneously, one being able to read the other's thoughts on rare occasion, and

---

8. "Apparition," 26–27.

the narrator often, somehow, becoming aware when A. H. is approaching.[9] Regarding this unique presentation, the apparition apparently "lost patience when the percipient steadily refused to cooperate by turning round and revealed that an apparition can be seen as well 'through the back of the head' as in any other direction."[10]

This case demonstrates that apparitions need not be perceived through use of ordinary sight—that is, via the reflection of light waves being processed as an inverted image upon the retina of the eyes. Rather the message was presumably received telepathically. In turn the recipient's brain/subconscious mind produced an image to deliver the information in a "supra-sensical" way to the recipient. In addition to being an apparition of a still living agent (who remained alive and well afterwards), this case could be classified as a crisis apparition as well.

FOLLOWER

> I was awake in bed and suddenly I saw a man in my room. He was walking around me and bending over me and a child of mine. I knew it was not a real man because I only saw his face as if in a fog, not clearly, there was always some mist over it. Later that morning, when I was up, a man who I had not expected came to visit me. I was later told that somebody always came ahead of him if he did not call before he visited or let you know. After this he did not come without me knowing it so it would not happen again. He had heard of it from other people, another woman who was always aware of the man. According to the description it was the same man that had been seen by both of them.[11]

Haraldsson states that the informant's sister, Steinunn, recalled being told of this occurrence by her sister.

> She said she herself had been aware of the man but never saw him. "He always sat in a special chair in the living room and soon afterwards I would be visited by a certain man. This always happened if he had not contacted me before visiting."[12]

9. "Apparition," 27–28.
10. Tyrrell, *Apparitions*, 66.
11. Haraldsson, *Departed*, 155.
12. Haraldsson, *Departed*, 155.

"GOD BLESS YOU"

> I was cleaning a large room in a business where I had recently started to work and was alone as far as I knew. Suddenly the door is opened and I hear "God bless you." I turn around and see a large woman walking into the room. I was sort of hypnotized and could not move because of fright. She stopped at a machine that was out of order and disappeared. She was in a long dress with a shawl over her shoulders and had grey hair. As she disappears, the director enters and walks the same way as the woman. I heard it much later that she had been the mother of the director.[13]

Here we have more examples of living agents remotely producing apparitions of other figures. Haraldsson observes that these cases reflect the phenomena of *fylgjur*, "fetchers/followers/doppelgangers," from Icelandic folklore. Fylgjur are "mostly connected with people coming and going and the arrival of guests," and per a 1975 survey, Haraldsson states that one-sixth of respondents had been aware of a fylgja.[14] Similarly, Norway has its *vardøgler*, that is "precognitive experiences such as footsteps and apparitions that herald the arrival of the person in question."[15]

MRS. WILMOT'S TRANSATLANTIC JOURNEY

On October 3rd, 1863, Mr. S. R. Wilmot was sailing from Liverpool to New York aboard the steamer *City of Limerick* when the crew collided with a severe storm that was of nine days' duration.

> Upon the night following the eighth day of the storm, the tempest moderated a little, and for the first time since leaving port I enjoyed refreshing sleep. Toward morning I dreamed that I saw my wife, whom I had left in the United States, come to the door of my state-room, clad in her night-dress. At the door she seemed to discover that I was not the only occupant of the room, hesitated a little, then advanced to my side, stooped down and kissed me, and after gently caressing me for a few moments, quietly withdrew.

---

13. Haraldsson, *Departed*, 155.
14. Haraldsson, *Departed*, 155.
15. Roll, "Survival Research," 403.

> Upon waking, I was surprised to see my fellow passenger [William J. Tait], whose berth was above mine, but not directly over it—owing to the fact that our room was at the stern of the vessel—leaning upon his elbow, and looking fixedly at me. "You're a pretty fellow," said he at length, "to have a lady come and visit you in this way." I pressed him for an explanation, which he at first declined to give, but at length related what he had seen while wide awake, lying in his berth. It exactly corresponded with my dream.[16]

Upon returning home to Watertown, Connecticut, Mr. Wilmot was asked by his wife, "Did you receive a visit from me a week ago Tuesday?"

> My wife then told me that on account of the severity of the weather and the reported loss of the *Africa*, which sailed from Boston the same day that we left Liverpool for New York, . . . she had been extremely anxious about me. On the night previous, the same night when . . . the storm had just begun to abate, she had lain awake for a long time thinking of me, and about four o'clock in the morning it seemed to her that she went out to seek me. Crossing the wide and stormy sea, she came at length to a low, black steamship, whose side she went up and then descended into the cabin, passed through it to the stern until she came to my state-room. "Tell me," she said, "do they ever have state-rooms like the one I saw, where the upper berth extends further back than the under one? A man was in the upper berth looking right at me, and for a moment I was afraid to go in, but soon I went up to the side of your berth, bent down and kissed you and embraced you and then went away."[17]

Mr. Wilmot's wife and his sister, Miss Wilmot, who was aboard the *City of Limerick* and had spoken to Mr. Tait about the incident, corroborated the account to the investigators.[18] Of the cases considered thus far, this one most closely approximates the tale we considered at the beginning of the chapter. However, contrary to the deliberate nature of Swami Pranabananda's astral projection, Mrs. Wilmot's transatlantic journey occurred spontaneously.[19] There are well-evidenced analogies, however, to such deliberately produced apparitions.

---

16. Sidgwick, "Clairvoyance," 42.
17. Sidgwick, "Clairvoyance," 42–43.
18. Sidgwick, "Clairvoyance," 44.
19. See Charman, *Telepathy, Clairvoyance and Precognition*, ch. 5 for a good summary of this case along with discussion of the various interpretations offered, including

LUCIAN AND EILEEN LANDAU'S EXPERIMENT IN PSYCHOKINESIS

Andrew MacKenzie once paid a visit to two fellow members of the Society for Psychical Research, Lucian and Eileen Landau, husband and wife, both of whom had "strong psychic gifts." MacKenzie relates the account of an experiment performed by the couple (prior to when they were married) that took place in London, UK. Eileen slept in a spare bedroom opposite that of Lucian's bedroom at the time. Lucian had not been feeling well. One night in September 1955, Eileen apparently had a spontaneous out-of-body experience where she came into Lucian's room to "check his pulse and respiration." Having subsequently reported this to Lucian, he asked her to repeat this the following night, and also gave her a light diary (38 grams in weight) to bring with her. MacKenzie writes:

> He woke up suddenly. It was dawn, and there was just about enough light coming in through the partly drawn curtains to enable one to read. At a point near the door stood the figure of Mrs Landau, looking straight ahead towards the window. The figure was wearing a nightdress; its face was extremely pale, almost white. It moved slowly backwards towards the door with a gliding motion. When the figure reached the middle of the landing Landau left his bed and followed it. He could then clearly see the moving figure, which was quite opaque and looked like that of a living person, but for the extreme pallor of the face, and at the same time the head of Mrs Landau, asleep in her bed, the bedclothes rising and falling as she breathed.[20]

Upon reaching a spot near the bed, the apparition vanished. All the while, Eileen Landau stayed in bed, without movement except for her typical rate of breathing. Lucian went back to his room and found a rubber toy dog that weighed 107.5 grams that belonged to his wife. The toy was originally standing on a chest of drawers near her bed in the other room. After breakfast the next morning, Lucian asked his wife why she did not move the diary as originally planned. Eileen replied that she initially attempted to get the diary but "somehow could not pick it up" and added that she had been taught as a child never to handle diaries or letters of

---

non-paranormal ones. I side with the apparent majority of interpreters that deem this an authentic psi event that is most likely to be classified as a reciprocal out-of-body experience ("reciprocal" meaning that the apparition was seen at the location to which she seems to have projected her consciousness).

20. MacKenzie, *Hauntings*, 19.

other people. She recalled taking the toy dog to the other room, seeing her husband asleep, and then feeling exhausted and wanting to go back to her bed, but was unable to remember doing so. Her consciousness was apparently normal to that point, as was her ability to see her surroundings, which appeared normal.[21]

MacKenzie adds,

> Landau told me that this case was the most unusual one in his experience, "but its nature makes it difficult to provide the necessary supporting evidence." I agree with this assessment. The case is remarkable in that it involves what purports to be the movement of a solid object, a rubber toy dog, by the astral (or etheric) body of Mrs Landau. Some writers would classify this case as an out-of-the-body experience, as Landau did, and others as an apparition of the living, but if we accept the evidence of both witnesses, the most important point is that it took place in an experimental setting.[22]

AN APPARITION THAT CONSUMES BISCUITS AND TEA

> While lying on a bed, she [Roma] heard a noise and, on looking up, discovered Dadaji in the study, which was visible to her through an open door. At first, she could see objects in the room through him, and then he became solid. She screamed and was heard by her brother, a medical doctor, and her mother. Dadaji did not speak, but through sign language told her to be silent and to bring him a cup of tea.... When she returned to the study with the tea, Roma was followed by her mother and physician brother. She reached in through the partly open door and gave Dadaji the tea and a biscuit. The mother, through a crack in the door, saw Dadaji; the brother, standing in a different position, only saw Roma's hand reach in through the opening and come back without the tea. There was no place she could have set the cup without entering the room. Then the father, a bank director, came home from doing the morning shopping at the bazaar. He didn't believe what they told him, and, brushing away their objections, peeked in through the crack in the door and saw a man's figure sitting on a chair. The family remained in the living room keeping the study door in full sight. When they

---

21. MacKenzie, *Hauntings*, 19–20.
22. MacKenzie, *Hauntings*, 20.

heard a noise and thought Dadaji had left, the family entered the study. The four of them saw that the door leading from the study to the stairwell was locked from the inside by an iron bar across it and was also bolted from above. Dadaji was no longer there; half of the cup of tea and part of the biscuit were gone, and on the table was a cigarette, still burning—Dadaji's favorite brand![23]

This account took place in 1970 when Dadaji was in Allahabad, India. Dadaji deliberately produced this apparition from a prayer room and subsequently asked one of the ladies there to confirm that her sister-in-law (in Calcutta) had seen his apparition. Osis and Haraldsson interviewed this lady, the Mukherjee family, and Dadaji's hosts in Allahabad. Roma was a devotee of Dadaji while her brother and father, both skeptical of the phenomena, visited him only on occasion and her mother did not visit him at all.[24]

23. Osis and Haraldsson, "Swamis," 148–49.

24. Osis and Haraldsson, "Swamis," 148–49. The authors also examined an apparent case of bilocation produced by Sathya Sai Baba, in which he had been present at a location for at least one hour, handled objects, and administered gifts that the hosts still had up to the time of being interviewed by the authors. At the same time, however, they were able to establish that the same Sai Baba was present on the opposite side of the Indian peninsula at the Palace of Vankatagiri, confirmed with an official register. Osis and Haraldsson interviewed eight witnesses ten years after the event took place. The memories of those interviewed produced inconsistencies. However, in broad contour the accounts were similar. See Haraldsson, *Modern Miracles*, 271–88 for a detailed account. Sai Baba's apparition was also said to consume "simple foods."

There are other rare accounts of food consumption in the literature. In another apparent case of bilocation, psychical researcher Alex Tanous was said to have "dropped in" on a friend in Canada while simultaneously "resting in a hotel room" in New York City. Tanous was invited inside his friend's house for refreshments. He "stayed for a while, drinking tea and conversing with his friend." After Tanous left, his friend did not hear a car start outside. Concerned that Alex may have been having car trouble, he "opened the door but saw no sign of a car, or even footsteps in the snow. It was later that he learned Alex had been in New York City during the time he was 'visiting.'" See Auerbach, *ESP*, 46.

At 11:00 a.m. on April 18th, 1961, in Eagle River, Wisconsin, sixty-year-old chicken farmer, Joe Simonton, encountered occupants of a silver-colored flying saucer. Upon request, Simonton filled up a jug with water for one of the occupants and was given three cookies, which were perforated with small holes and roughly three inches in diameter that "tasted like cardboard." The Food and Drug Laboratory of the US Department of Health, Education and Welfare analyzed one of the "pancakes" with chemical, infrared and other tests. In terms of its ingredients, bacteria, and radiation readings the conclusion was "that the material was an ordinary pancake of terrestrial origin." The US Air Force concluded that Simonton had had a "sudden dream" while awake and "inserted his dream into the continuum of events around him of which he was conscious." J. Allen Hynek and Major Robert Friend, who investigated the case on behalf of the US Air Force stated, "There is no question that Mr. Simonton felt that his contact had been

The authors write that such OBE reports as those of Dadaji and Sai Baba distinguish them from Western OBE reports, having discovered numerous cases where a swami's apparition was seen handling animate objects, engaging in acts of healing, and lifting the bodies of the percipients. Upon investigation, some of the witnesses were unreliable and there were fraudulent accounts. However, at other times the reports by witnesses were reasonably consistent. Also, the observers were often trustworthy and well-trained, some of them being scientists.[25]

FIFTH EXPERIMENT AT A DISTANCE OF NINE MILES

The following case illustrates that an apparition representing a particular person need not be the actual agent producing it.

> The intention was that Lieutenant N. should see in a dream, at 11 o'clock p.m., a lady who had been five years dead, who was to incite him to a good action. Herr N., however, contrary to expectation, had not gone to sleep by 11 o'clock, but was conversing with his friend S. on the French campaign. Suddenly the door of the chamber opens; the lady, dressed in white, with black kerchief turns to N., nods to him, and then returns through the door. Both follow quickly, and call the sentinel at the entrance; but all had vanished, and nothing was to be found. Some months afterward, Herr S. informed me by letter that the chamber door used to creak when opened, but did not do so when the lady opened it—whence it is to be inferred that the opening of the door was only a dream-picture, like all the rest of the apparition.[26]

---

a real experience." See Vallee, *Dimensions*, 64–66.

While praying inside her Presbyterian church in Oakland, California, Joy Kinsey lost consciousness for three hours. During this time, she had a vision of being inside of a temple that was "beautiful beyond description" with Jesus sitting on the throne. In the context of the vision, she saw a goblet of wine that Jesus told her to drink as a "new anointing" for her sins. She did so. Upon awakening and being reoriented to the surroundings of her church, "she found the people around her were distressed because they smelled a strong aroma of sweet wine coming from her mouth." This aroma filled the church and she felt drunk to the point where two people had to support her when she stood and walked. Interestingly, she had never had an alcoholic beverage and her church taught complete abstinence. See Wiebe, *Visions*, Ch. 4, "In the Temple of the Lord."

25. Osis and Haraldsson, "Swamis," 150.
26. Gurney, *Phantasms I*, 102.

This apparition was seen in the awake state and was viewed collectively by two percipients. Most interestingly, Wesermann was unaware that the second percipient was present and intended for the apparition of the deceased woman to appear to Lieutenant N. in a dream rather than in the awake state. This case has I think far-reaching implications as it illustrates that appearances of deceased individuals need not lead us to conclude that the agent is that deceased individual. Rather, the phenomenon could be the result of a telepathic message produced either purposely or, as we have seen in a couple of the other cases, involuntarily by a living agent.[27] We will have more to say about this important case later.

Wesermann's achievement calls to mind Dr. Morton Schatzman's patient pseudonymously named "Ruth." Ruth was haunted, literally in this case, by recurrent apparitions of her still-living father, who had been both physically and sexually abusive to her as she was growing up. With therapy, Ruth gained insight into these apparitional encounters and was eventually able to *control* them. She could conjure them up and make them go away, though they seemed to operate outside of her control in between being created and made to leave. Ruth was able to conjure apparitions of seemingly anybody on command, including one of herself. The apparitions could touch her and vice versa. However, with a couple of rare exceptions, only she was able to see, hear, or feel her apparitional creations. One time, her father did see the apparition of her husband Paul that she had created. Another time, Paul was able to see an apparition of Ruth herself, seeing her in the same position on the couch and in the same clothing that Ruth saw.[28] In the spirit of trance mediums, Ruth was also able to become entranced and take on other personalities, specifically

---

27. Tyrrell, *Apparitions*, 131–33. The agent who produced the apparition of the deceased woman was a man named Wesermann, who was the government assessor and Chief Inspector of Roads at *Düsseldorf* at the time. The authors of *Phantasms of the Living* detail five examples where Wesermann successfully impressed upon percipients particular images. Save for the cited case above, these impressions were seen in the percipients' dreams. While successful generally, the impressions were not necessarily completely accurate. In one instance (*Third Experiment at a Distance of One Mile*), Wesermann attempted to impress upon a particular percipient a funeral procession of a friend of his who had died. Upon inquiry the next day, the percipient had indeed seen a funeral procession in her sleep. However, in her dream it was Wesermann that was the corpse, not Wesermann's friend.

28. Schatzman, *Ruth*, 239–40, 259–61. Notably, Ruth was unsuccessful in creating apparitions that could be seen by other subjects in an experimental setting.

that of her father, on command. As with mediums, she was unable to remember what transpired upon awakening.[29]

The SPR researchers recorded fifteen cases of apparitions deliberately produced by agents to unwitting percipients. In all cases, the records were first hand and the evidence from both the agent/experimenter and the percipient were retrieved. Thirteen of these experiments were recorded less than two years after the fact. In six of these thirteen cases, a record had been made by the experimenter prior to obtaining the results or by the percipient before becoming aware that the apparition was the result of an experiment. Seven of the ten experimenters were successful on their first trial. Finally, in most of these cases, the percipient saw the apparition after the experimenter had fallen asleep or had been hypnotized.[30]

ASSESSMENT OF APPARITIONS OF THE LIVING

The cases in this chapter demonstrate that 1) a living agent can produce an apparition, both advertently and inadvertently; and 2) a living agent can produce an apparition of a different person (or figure), advertently and inadvertently. That living agents can produce apparitions of people who are deceased has implications for when we consider reunion apparitions, as well as those that have experienced apparitions of religious figures.

Unless the material we have surveyed in this chapter somehow has an alternative explanation, apparitions of the living provide further evidence that the images are unconscious, telepathic projections of a particular agent. The experimental cases we have considered seem to particularly demand such a conclusion.

---

29. Schatzman, *Ruth*, 187–234.

30. Sidgwick et al., "Census," 29; ten of the cases mentioned are detailed, both narrative and evidence, in Gurney et al., *Phantasms I*, lxxxi–lxxxiv, 101–10 and Gurney et al., *Phantasms II*, 671–76.

4

Haunting Apparitions

Sometimes classified as "recurrent apparitions," hauntings are the substance of popular ghost stories, urban legends, and Hollywood horror movies. It seems that most people know somebody that claims to have seen a ghost or visited a location, usually a house, and that has experienced haunting phenomena.

My grandmother used to tell stories of her childhood home that she believed to be haunted. Her experiences varied from hearing loud noises that went unexplained to seeing shadowy figures running up a nearby hillside through her window. If there was nobody home when she returned from school, she would sit on the porch until somebody arrived. She recounted to me that while sitting on the porch, she would sometimes hear footsteps coming down the stairs on the other side of the door despite nobody being home.

Are ghosts and haunted houses based on legitimate reports of paranormal activity or do they have more mundane explanations? I would surmise that for every authentic case there are probably ten that can be explained by hoaxing, illusions, hallucinations, aberrant geomagnetic and/or electromagnetic activity, or simply rooted in folklore.[1] However, well-evidenced hauntings like the ones we consider here resist being reduced to these latter categories. Notably, they also tend not to reflect the blood-curdling tales of popular fiction and imagination.

---

1. The great majority of "Phantom Hitchhiker" tales the world over likely are based in folklore and cannot be reliably traced to living eyewitnesses. See Goss, *Phantom Hitch-Hikers*, where this is forcefully demonstrated.

THE MORTON GHOST

Also known as the Cheltenham Ghost, this is probably the most famous and best-authenticated haunting in the literature. Rosina Despard, otherwise identified with the pseudonym "Miss R. C. Morton" in the original accounts, was a medical student in the late nineteenth century and one of the first observers of the ghostly figure.

> All the observers agreed as to the description of the figure, which was tall, wearing a dark dress with widow's weeds. With one hand usually half hidden in the folds and a handkerchief held to the face . . . the face was never well seen, but the general description tallied with the appearance and habits of Mrs. S., the second wife of a former tenant.[2]

The Morton Ghost appeared over a period of at least seven years (1882–1889), peaking in 1885 and thereafter fading. At least seven people saw the ghost and twenty people heard it over this period. The house had been built around 1860 and was occupied by only two families, whose history was known (i.e., the Despards), before becoming occupied by the Mortons.

> The phenomena consisted of the visual apparition, which followed, more or less, a routine, going down the stairs from the bedroom landing to the drawing-room, standing at a particular spot in the bow-window, then leaving the drawing-room by the door, going along the passage and disappearing by the garden door. Also, footsteps were heard by many percipients always of the same description. . . . The swish of woollen drapery was also heard. These footsteps were unlike any of those of the Morton family. All the servants were changed during the period of the hauntings; but the footsteps went on unaltered. There were other sounds, especially the peak period, of bumps, turning of door-handles, heavy and irregular footsteps, heavy thuds and bumpings, noises like heavy articles, such as boots, being thrown across the passage, and the sound of something heavy being dragged.[3]

The sounds were heard collectively by as many as five people at once. While the apparition was not apparently seen by more than one person simultaneously, it was once observed by four people individually and in

---

2. Tyrrell, *Apparitions*, 140.
3. Tyrrell, *Apparitions*, 141.

rapid succession as it made its typical trek from the drawing-room to the orchard.

While the apparition appeared to be solid and was mistaken on at least a couple of occasions for a real person, it seemed to be non-physical in nature. It would appear inside of rooms where the doors were closed and vanish while being observed. On a couple of occasions, it passed right through threads that Despard had tied across the stairway. One person may see the figure when it was present while another person would fail to see it. On one occasion, Captain Morton (Rosina Despard's father), who was never able to see the figure, walked over to where it was standing (the location of which was pointed out to him by Rosina) only to have the apparition subsequently move around him. Also, despite numerous attempts, Rosina was unable to touch the apparition. Somehow it always managed to evade her, placing "its visible surface beyond her reach."[4]

The Morton Ghost had "no luminosity of its own, behaved with reference to the lighting of the scene," and was frequently accompanied by the occurrence of cold feelings or a cold breeze. The house dogs were able to see her or at least sense her, as "a retriever was several times found in the kitchen in a state of terror. A skye terrier twice ran to the foot of the stairs, wagging its tail at an invisible something, and jumping up and fawning. Then it suddenly slunk away with its tail between its legs and ran under a sofa."[5]

The appearances were also spontaneous, never occurring at times of obvious expectation. Several times, Despard stayed up at night with other family members and/or friends hoping to see the ghost, but to no avail. She also claims that the figure did not appear after it was a topic of discussion amongst the family or even if they had merely been thinking about it.[6]

Whatever we make of this fascinating specter, the appearances to at least seven different people, once to four different individuals in succession, along with multiple cases of collectively experienced auditory phenomena, betrays the objective nature of the Morton Ghost.[7] Notably, like

4. Tyrrell, *Apparitions*, 141–42.
5. Tyrrell, *Apparitions*, 142.
6. Tyrrell, *Apparitions*, 142.
7. For more on the Morton Ghost, see the original article, "A Record of a Haunted House," by R. C. Morton in volume 8 of *Proceedings of the Society for Psychical Research*. See also Bennett, *Haunted Houses*, 185–209, which contains details of the SPR investigation, including the contents of signed statements made by several percipients. See also MacKenzie, *Hauntings*, 40–64. MacKenzie, writing in 1982, details the subsequent

many apparitions, the Morton Ghost seemed resistant to being touched. The same holds true of our next case.

THE CLERGYMAN ON THE HAUNTED ROAD

The location of this haunting was in the former county of Roxburghshire in Scotland. Miss Louisa Scott saw the figure on May 7th, 1892:

> I saw advancing towards me at an ordinary pace a tall man, dressed in black, whom I believed to be a clergyman. I removed my gaze but for a second, when great was my surprise on looking up again to find that he had gone from my sight.[8]

Miss Scott's sister, not present initially, would also see the apparition, though curiously not at the same time. Her sister saw the man at a time when he was still within proximity to Miss Scott.

> Upon coming up to me she said, "Where on earth is that man who was standing only about ten feet from you?" And here, what makes it still more striking, is that I was facing the tall spectre, *yet could not see him when my sister did*. She was more fortunate than I, for she saw the entire dress of the man, while I only noticed his long black coat, the lower part of his body to me being invisible; while she had the satisfaction of seeing him entirely and also seeing him vanish, as she did not remove her eyes, as I did, from the first time of seeing him.[9]

About one month later, Miss Scott saw the specter in the same place:

> On Sunday last, June 12th, at a few minutes before ten in the morning, . . . I perceived far in front a dark figure. . . . hoping to get a nearer inspection, I boldly followed, running in close pursuit; but here the strangest part of it all is that, though he was apparently walking slowly, I never could get any closer than

---

history and developments of the house well into the twentieth century, including further apparitional sightings that were alleged to have occurred. For instance, an apparition very similar to the Morton Ghost was seen in 1958 and 1961 in Cotswold Lodge, located on the *opposite* side of the road from the Despard house (which was at that time St. Anne's Nursery College, used for training nannies). The apparition was of a solid-appearing woman with a black dress who extended to the ground and whose features were obscured to some degree because of a handkerchief she held to her face with her right hand. MacKenzie, *Hauntings*, 54–56.

8. "Collective Apparition," 148–49.

9. "Collective Apparition," 149, emphasis original.

within a few yards, for in but a moment he seemed to *float or skim away*. Presently he came to a standstill, and I began to feel very much afraid and stopped also. There he was!—the tall spectre dressed as I have described before. He turned round and gazed at me with a vacant expression, and the same ghastly, pallid features. I can liken him to no one I have ever seen. While I stood, he still looked intently at me for a few seconds, then resumed his former position. Moving on a few steps, he again stood and looked back for the second time, finally *fading from view* at his usual spot by the hedge to the right.[10]

Left in a state of terror over the incident, Miss Scott rushed home. On the way, she ran into a woman, informing her of the ghostly encounter. This woman was also aware of the road's bad reputation and was also frightened, afraid at that point to proceed alone. Miss Scott accompanied her home, both reaching their destinations safely without running into the clergyman.[11] The clergyman continued to haunt the road, having been seen by numerous percipients at various points along it, over the course of at least the next seven to eight years.[12]

The disturbing nature of the specter's features is not uncommon with hauntings. This is clear after a cursory reading of several of Sir Ernest Bennett's catalogue of haunting cases:

> I looked at her in horror, and dared not cry out lest I might move the awful thing to speech or action.[13]

> "I stood, too frightened to move, especially as I had to pass her to reach the lower staircase. If I saw her face now, after all these years, I should know it. The hair was very dark and smooth; the one eye not covered by the shawl was turned up, and the face like death."[14]

> She seemed to stare straight at me with a horrible look on her face.... We both saw the apparition and my friend fainted, and altogether it was a mercy that we were not all killed![15]

10. "Collective Apparition," 149–50, emphasis original.
11. "Collective Apparition," 150.
12. See MacKenzie, *Hauntings*, 114–23.
13. Bennett, *Haunted Houses*, 220. The narrator's brother would also experience this apparition in the same room two weeks later, describing her as a "villainous looking hag."
14. Bennett, *Haunted Houses*, 280.
15. Bennett, *Haunted Houses*, 297.

And of all the fiendish faces, it was the most horrible you can imagine.[16]

The visage of haunting apparitions, to be sure, is not always so horrific as these examples suggest. Bennett discusses another apparition which one percipient described as "a very gentle, mild-faced old man, and not one bit like a story-book ghost," though the same apparition was also described as looking "very ill."[17]

THE CASE OF SAMUEL BULL

The Samuel Bull haunting, investigated by Lord Balfour, Admiral Hyde Parker, and Mr. Piddington, took place in the village of Ramsbury in Wiltshire County, England in the early 1930s. Samuel Bull was a chimneysweep who died of cancer in his home on Oxford Street in June 1931. His widow, who unfortunately became bed ridden shortly after her husband's death, continued to live in the same cottage with a grandson, James Bull. The widow had a married daughter, Mrs. Edwards, come to live with her, along with her husband and their five children, in August of the same year. It was about six months after, in February 1932, that the apparitions began.

The first paranormal encounter was a sense of presence detected by some of the children outside of their bedroom door. Upon examination, there was nobody there. This experience caused Mrs. Edwards to be anxious and the children were in a restless state. Later, the apparition of Samuel Bull was seen to ascend the cottage stairs and pass through a shut door into the room in which he had died. This was also where his widow was staying until the room had been condemned as unsafe for habitation. This first visual encounter was experienced by Mrs. Edwards and her grandson, who was twenty-one years of age. Similar experiences were often repeated. Initially they horrified the percipients, causing the children to scream, but as the encounters multiplied the seers tended to be calmer.

The investigators interviewed Mrs. Edwards regarding the details of these experiences. Everybody that happened to be present when the apparition materialized would see it, and in at least one case the apparition was perceived simultaneously by all family members that lived in

---

16. Bennett, *Haunted Houses*, 299.
17. Bennett, *Haunted Houses*, 81–83.

the house. The apparition did not materialize when strangers happened to be present. It was solid, appearing in the same way that Samuel Bull would have in life, "dressed as he usually was in the evenings when he had finished work." When the apparition appeared, it would make its way to the bed and touch his widow's forehead with a cold, firm hand. Curiously, the hands of the apparition were in bad shape, the knuckles seemingly protruding through the skin. Equally curiously, Mrs. Edwards said that the appearances "take a great deal out of the members of the family," especially the widow, Mrs. Bull.

The apparition's countenance was always one of sadness, the family understanding this to represent the deceased man's displeasure of their circumstances of living in a dilapidated cottage. Interestingly, its countenance was reportedly happier in two of its last appearances. The family suggested this may have been due to changing life circumstances because they were soon to move into a council house. It would appear day and night though the house was always dark, illuminated only with the aid of candles. He would also apparently "appear" even when there was no candlelight because the family could sense his presence.

When the apparition would appear, it would "come and go" frequently for a period of several hours. It would not speak except on one occasion when his widow heard the figure say her name, "Jane." The apparition appeared over a period of roughly two months, the last appearance being on April 9th of the same year. Mr. Piddington wrote an account of the investigatory interview of Mrs. Edwards and Mrs. Bull that had occurred on April 15th. By the time of the interview, the cottage had been dismantled except for the bed in which Mrs. Bull was still lying and a single chair. The investigators and the vicar of Ramsbury, Geo. Hackett, attested to the witnesses' integrity and believed them to be truthful in this account.[18]

Writing seven years later, Sir Ernest Bennett commented that he knew of no other case of an apparition appearing to as many as nine people at one time.[19] Fast-forward some eighty-six years to the present, I am unaware of any reasonably well-evidenced apparition appearing to this many percipients, except some that have been reported at séances or within a religious context.

---

18. "Ramsbury, Wilts," 297–304.
19. Bennett, *Haunted Houses*, 72.

Bennett does, however, lament that by the time the matter was investigated by representatives of the SPR, and interviews with the family were conducted, the cottage had been dismantled and mostly emptied of its furniture, occurring after the family had moved into a district council house.[20] This protestation aside, I am inclined to grant the case authenticity. While the investigatory interview for this remarkable case transpired after the dilapidated house had been largely dismantled, it did occur within one week of the time that the last apparition had been seen.

One additional point to note before moving on: One could make the argument that this case could have been categorized a reunion apparition rather than a haunting.[21] Unlike most haunting cases where the apparition's identity is not initially recognized by the percipients, that is clearly not the case here.[22] Nevertheless, I placed this case in this chapter because of the mechanical and highly repetitive nature of the apparition.

THE GERMAN KNIGHT

> Two ladies were staying with a German family at Cassel, and were sleeping in a room supposed to be haunted by a knight. They both saw an apparition, and, the narrator says, "As soon as it came close to my bed, I seized it, and seemed to take hold of something soft, like flimsy drapery, but whatever it was seemed dragged from me by some invisible power."[23]

Tactile phenomena, sensations of touch, in apparitional encounters are not as uncommon as one may think. However, as we have seen and will see elsewhere, the touch is usually initiated by the apparition on the percipient, not the other way around. Indeed, as we've seen, many apparitions prove to be quite resistant to being touched by percipients.

Green and McCreery state,

> It is usually the apparition which touches the percipient, and not the percipient who touches the apparition. This is true both of our collection of cases, and of cases previously published. When

---

20. Bennett, *Haunted Houses*, 72–73.
21. See chapter 7.
22. Though in some cases the apparition may be identified later by an old photograph.
23. Tyrrell, *Apparitions*, 59.

a percipient does try to touch or catch hold of an apparition, it often eludes him in some way.[24]

Tyrrell espouses the same findings, indicating that he had read 56 cases where the apparition touched the percipient.[25] However, as he wrote in 1953, stated that the German Knight case was the only one he was aware of where an apparition was successfully touched by a percipient(s), or more specifically, "was successful in taking hold of a ghost."[26] Even here, we note that the apparition still exhibited a similar aversion to being touched. Tyrrell apparently overlooked a few cases that were narrated in the "Census of Hallucinations." Per the authors of the "Census", "In the great majority of tactile hallucinations, the idea produced is that something is touching the percipient."[27] However, of the tactile cases in the "Census", six cases give the percipient the impression of actively touching the apparitional object. In only four of these six cases does the percipient see the apparition and successfully touch it.[28] In one apparition of the living, there was a lady who was able to reach out and briefly feel the coat of an apparition of her husband.[29] Also in the "Census", there were a couple of cases narrated where the percipient shakes hands with the apparition, though in both cases the apparition offered its "hand" to the percipient.[30] In more recent times, Dianne Arcangel narrates the case of a lady who was able to successfully initiate an embrace with her deceased father. These rare occurrences are the exceptions that prove the general rule.[31]

24. Green and McCreery, *Apparitions*, 104.
25. Tyrrell, *Apparitions*, 58–59.
26. Tyrrell, *Apparitions*, 59–60.
27. Sidgwick et al., "Census," 132.
28. Sidgwick et al., "Census," 132.
29. Sidgwick et al., "Census," 295–97.

30. Sidgwick et al., "Census," 378–79, 385–87. Both handshaking cases took place in Russia and represent apparitions of individuals who had died. In the former case, the apparition was of a deceased father appearing to his son four years after death. In the latter case, a deceased man appears to his son-in-law a mere nine days following death. Note that the first case as it appears in the "Census of Hallucinations" is narrated in French. For an English translation of this case and a discussion of both cases, see Green and McCreery, *Apparitions*, 108–10.

31. An executive assistant for a venture capital firm reported a visitation from her deceased father. During the experience, she "grabbed him again around his waist and held on for dear life. I could feel him hugging me. Neither of us would let go." Arcangel, *Afterlife*, 44–47.

ANNE AND JACK

This auditory account is consistent with "place theory" as described by Massullo. This case occurred in Akron, Ohio, in the 1940s. Anne and Jack were renting the house that had been built in the 1860s. On May 24th, the couple heard loud footsteps starting on the upper floor, then come down the steps. Hearing the words "Ma! Oh, Ma!" by the voice of a young boy, they rushed into the living room. By that time the trailing voice emanated from beyond the front door.

> Before Jack could open the door, there came a horrific crash and a series of blood-chilling screams ending in a gurgling choke. Then dead stillness as Jack and Anne swung the door open and looked out into the spring twilight.[32]

The episode was repeated daily, prompting Anne to inquire about the source. A local grocer confirmed that nobody had stayed in the house past May 24th. The grocer further told Anne that in 1871, the household's youngest son had left for Chicago to become a bricklayer. While at work, he fell from a high scaffolding and supposedly screamed something as he plummeted to his death.

> Just about that time of day, his mother, resting in her chair (in Akron), heard her son rushing down the stairs calling her name. The mother reported that she then heard her son go out the front door and she heard his body falling. It was reported that she started crying and knew her son had died (she received a telepathic message).[33]

This case is instructive in that it provides a potential link between some examples of haunting apparitions and crisis apparitions. What originally could be categorized as a crisis apparition was repeated when other sensitive percipients were nearby. The implication being that, if some apparitions are the result of telepathy, the person represented by the apparition does not necessarily have to be linked to the location where the event that produced it occurs. Rather in some cases, the haunting location may be the place where the telepathic message was delivered (which was originally delivered to a specific recipient who occupied that location in the past, in this case decades earlier).[34]

---

32. Massullo, *Ghost*, ch. 9, paras. 19–20.
33. Massullo, *Ghost*, ch. 9, paras. 21.
34. Massullo, *Ghost*, ch. 9, paras. 22–23.

ASSESSMENT OF HAUNTING APPARITIONS

Most of the cases we have considered in this chapter are dated, but there are evidential haunting cases in modern times.[35] Haunting apparitions are generally confined to a single location; usually a house, but it could be a stretch of road or even an entire village. These apparitions are usually spotted at times when they are *not* expected. However, they tend to "act" as if a three-dimensional pre-recorded image is somehow being projected onto space. It's rare when there is meaningful interaction between the apparitions and the percipient(s), though they do commonly surprise and frighten seers. This fright is not only the result of the surprise of the apparitions' appearance, but often because of the disturbing nature of their features. Finally, locales that are haunted, particularly in the case of haunted houses, are frequently accompanied by loud and mysterious, usually unpleasant noises such as doorknobs rattling, disembodied footsteps, and doors that open and close on their own.

Believers in the objective reality of haunted houses commonly attribute apparitional manifestations to actual visitations from spirits of the deceased. In other words, ghosts are exactly what they appear to be. Some who view the matter through a theistic lens may believe that ghosts are demons that are impersonating spirits of the deceased. Skeptics are more likely to assert that hauntings can all be explained under the umbrella of fraud, hallucinations, illusions, etc.[36] As a general rule, I do not believe that ghosts in haunted houses are actual spirits of the departed nor demonic imposters. I do believe that some are objective in nature, however. As will be discussed later, I believe apparitions are the result of telepathic impressions in most cases.[37]

---

35. See "Ghost of Fame Cleaners." Arcangel, *Afterlife*, 18–20.
36. See chapters 13 and 14.
37. See especially chapter 15.

5

Rescue Apparitions

IN ESSENCE, RESCUE APPARITIONS are the opposite of crisis apparitions, and the associated case reports are predictably more uplifting. Crisis apparitions present sensory information to a percipient (frequently a family member or friend) of an agent that is undergoing a traumatic event (one that often leads to death). Contrarily, the agent of a rescue apparition appears to save a person that is undergoing a life-threatening event. Consider the following examples from Erlendur Haraldsson.

GOOD GUIDANCE REPORTED BY A SEAMAN IN HIS FORTIES FROM ISAFJORD

> I was with another man on a small boat and we were going to cross Faxabay to Arnarstapi. When we were out on the bay we suddenly had stormy weather and it became hopeless for us to find our way because we had no equipment of any sort and the boat was filled time and again with water. My partner was exhausted and lay down and I was of course dreadfully tired and sleepy. Then a man appeared at the stern of the boat. I remember to this day how he was dressed. He wore jeans and a green checkered shirt and had grey hair. I did not recognize him, I did not know him. I was tired and drowsy and thought it was quite normal for him to be there. I did not think it unusual until we came ashore, but I did find it strange how courageous he was to be standing there in the wild storm as the waves broke on the

boat. He spoke to me, but I could not hear a word. He became very angry when he saw I was about to give up. Each time I was about to fall asleep he took out a key and held it to my face and pointed in the direction I should steer. I did as the man told me, and of course did not realize what was really happening. The remarkable thing was that I landed in Arnarstapi, passed the reefs and landed at the dock. And it was all the doing of this man.... The voyage across Faxabay lasted for about 24 hours.

I told my mother about how odd this had been. She told me that this man had been an engineer, a friend of my father and that he was dead.... Oh, of course I had seen him before, I just did not remember him at the time.[1]

Haraldsson adds,

G. Sigurjonsson, the friend who was with the informant on the voyage, said he remembered him telling him about the incident when they reached the shore. He added that when they came ashore, they met a man who asked them where they had come from. When they said they had sailed from Reykjavik, the man walked away from them because he did not believe them.[2]

SEVENTY-YEAR-OLD FISHMONGER AND FORMER SEAMAN

I was on a fishing boat from Stykkisholm. We were out in the bay in storm and rain and had just laid our nets and should be awakened at six in the following morning. I slept in a narrow cabin with others and one man was on duty in the deckhouse. About five in the morning I and some others woke up as someone called, "Rise." I went up to the cabin door and called to the man in the deckhouse and asked if he had been calling. No, he said, it was not time for that. I went back to my bunk and was not yet asleep when again there was a shout, "Rise, are you not going to get out of bed?" It was as if someone was calling loudly from the cabin door some two meters away. Everyone woke up and jumped out of bed. That surprised me; generally the crew was not that quick. I told the engine-operator to run aft and start the donkey engine to haul in the nets. As the engine-operator went down to the engine room he saw that the generator was on

1. Haraldsson, *Departed*, 158.
2. Haraldsson, *Departed*, 158.

fire. He barely managed to disconnect the electricity so that it came to a halt. I am convinced that if he had been later we would have caught fire and there would have been a fatal explosion in the engine room. I did not recognize the voice. It called in a typical seaman fashion. I had reasons to suspect that it was my deceased grandfather.[3]

SEAMAN IN HIS FIFTIES FROM THE FISHING VILLAGE OF FLATEYRI

I often saw my deceased father stand behind the wheelhouse of my boat. I got so used to this that I no more paid particular attention to it, nor did it startle me. . . . We were fishing with a Scottish seine and we were drifting in the fjord. A man should have been on watch in the wheelhouse. Then I heard that I was called twice in my bunk below deck. I was sleepy and was not quick to react, but when I was called the third time, I was thrown out of my bunk and onto the floor. I went up to the deck but thought this was my imaginary nonsense. Then I saw that the boat was almost standing on the shore. I could not have turned the boat from the shore any later. The man supposed to be on watch and lookout was asleep on the floor of the wheelhouse. I recognized that the voice calling me was my father's voice. I am convinced he saved us.[4]

JOSHUA SLOCUM'S SEA VOYAGE

Joshua Slocum was attempting to become the first person to circumnavigate the entire globe by sea. Following a stop at the Azores on his way to Gibralter, he had apparently become afflicted with food poisoning while his ship *Spray* was being rocked by a violent storm. Slocum believed that a "strange guest" helped steer the ship for a forty-eight-hour period during the squall. Having given to delirium, he awakened to seeing a tall man holding the wheel spokes, gripping them as a vise.

Prior to succumbing to illness, the former merchant navy captain had been "overtaken by a pervasive loneliness, 'a sense of solitude, which

---

3. Haraldsson, *Departed*, 159.
4. Haraldsson, *Departed*, 159–60.

I could not shake off.'" Yet, amidst the storm, Slocum was compelled to the belief that a sailor, one he described as having "an ancient cast of visage," was in the boat with him. The tall man told Slocum, "I have come to do you no harm" and that he had "come to aid you." He further told Slocum, "Lie quiet . . . and I will guide your ship tonight."

Most amazingly, upon recovery, Slocum found that the *Spray* was "still heading as I had left her, and . . . going like a racehorse." The ship had voyaged ninety miles in the night through the storm and was still on course to Gibraltar. Slocum detailed his account of this encounter for the *Boston Globe* in a piece entitled "Spook on Spray," published October 14th, 1985. He experienced this visitor several times over the course of the voyage; one time via an auditory experience: a shouted warning had awakened him, "allowing him to narrowly avert disaster during a storm off Cape Horn."[5]

CHARLES LINDBERGH'S CO-PILOTS

Charles Lindbergh is famous for having made the first solo transatlantic flight from New York to Paris. Twenty-five years of age at the time, Lindbergh took off in the *Spirit of St. Louis* from Roosevelt Field in New York City on May 20th, 1927.[6] Ice caked the wings of the plane and a magnetic storm disrupted his bearings. He was flying blind through fog banks. After seventeen hours, the desire for sleep became overwhelming.

> He gradually became aware that, while his body demanded sleep, and his mind made decisions his body failed to heed, he had ceded control to a "separate mind," a force that he recognized as being something of himself, and yet not.[7]

It was in the twenty-second hour of his flight that Lindbergh discovered that he was not alone. Quoting from "The Spirit of St. Louis" published in 1953, Geiger writes the following:

> The fuselage behind me becomes filled with ghostly presences— vaguely outlined forms, transparent, moving, riding weightless with me in the plane. I feel no surprise at their coming. There's

---

5. Geiger, *Third Man*, 50–51.
6. Geiger, *Third Man*, 83.
7. Geiger, *Third Man*, 84.

no suddenness to their appearance. Without turning my head,
I see them as clearly as though in my normal field of vision.[8]

He thought that these ghostly presences were speaking to him, were friendly, even familiar in some sense, not at all frightening or even startling, and there to help him, "conversing and advising on my flight, discussing problems of my navigation, reassuring me, giving me messages of importance unattainable in ordinary life."[9]

Lindbergh eventually spotted fishing boats on the sea. Shortly afterwards he found himself flying over the southwestern coast of Ireland. At this point his body's demand for sleep as well as the ghostly presences left him. Expecting to be fifty miles off course, Lindbergh calculated that he was but a mere three miles from his intended path. Upon reaching Paris, having already broken the world record for longest distance for a nonstop airplane flight, Lindbergh circled the Eiffel Tower before landing on the airfield Le Bourdet Aerodome in front of 150,000 witnesses.[10]

Lindbergh did not publicly discuss his ephemeral "co-pilots" until the 1950s. Geiger quotes Lindberg from the June 6th, 1953, publication of the *Saturday Evening Post*:

> I've never believed in apparitions, but how can I explain the forms I carried with me through so many hours of this day? Transparent forms in human outline—voices that spoke with authority and clearness—that told me—that told me—but what did they tell me? I can't remember a single word they said.[11]

Such stories can be easily multiplied. John Geiger catalogs dozens of similar stories in *The Third Man Factor*. People facing extreme, life-threatening situations, will often encounter this "third man" that delivers them from certain death.[12]

---

8. Geiger, *Third Man*, 85.
9. Geiger, *Third Man*, 85.
10. Geiger, *Third Man*, 85–86.
11. Geiger, *Third Man*, 87.

12. Geiger writes, for instance, of Ron DiFrancesco, the last person to escape the South Tower just after the 9/11 terrorist bombings, being guided to safety by a disembodied voice with mere seconds to spare. See Geiger, *Third Man*, 1–6. In his book, Geiger details "third man" encounters with people finding themselves in a variety of extreme, life-threatening, conditions. These include explorers to dangerous, unchartered lands, polar regions such as Antarctica, mountain climbers, and undersea explorers. "But the amazing thing is this: over the years, the experience has occurred again and again, not only to 9/11 survivors, mountaineers, and divers, but also to polar explorers, prisoners of war, solo sailors, shipwreck survivors, aviators, and astronauts. All have

ASSESSMENT OF RESCUE APPARITIONS

Who are these "third man" entities? Guardian angels? Loved ones that have passed on watching over us? Or perhaps the "third man" is an apparition projected from the subliminal minds of those in danger, one that provides vital information obtained or abilities applied in supernormal ways. We have seen that apparitions can be generated both deliberately and non-deliberately by the living. Later it will be demonstrated that the subliminal mind can also produce remarkable effects on both living and inanimate matter. Can such subliminal influences guide a lost, desperate sailor amidst a storm-tossed sea to safety? If so, the third man, inasmuch as it is understood to be a guardian entity, need be nothing more than the subliminal mind of the beleaguered person undergoing a life-threatening crisis. It's a relevant possibility to ponder.

---

escaped traumatic events only to tell strikingly similar stories of having experienced the close presence of a companion and helper, and even 'of a sort of mighty person.' This presence offered a sense of protection, relief, guidance, and hope, and left the person convinced he or she was not alone but that there was some other being at his or her side, when by any normal calculation there was none." Geiger, *Third Man*, 14.

6

Transitional Apparitions

"MY WORLDVIEW UNDERWENT A RADICAL TRANSFORMATION"

The moment he died, when his EEG flattened, I "saw" that his mother came to collect him. You must bear in mind that she'd died five days earlier. There was this incredibly beautiful reunion. And at one point they reached out for me and included me in their embrace. This was an indescribable, ecstatic reunion. Part of me left my body and accompanied them to the light. I know this must sound very strange indeed, but I was fully conscious and with Anne and her son as they went to the light, just as I was fully conscious and in the room where all the relatives were incredibly sad because their nephew and grandson had just died. And I joined them, we were heading toward the light, but at a certain point it was clear that I had to return, so I fell back. I simply fell back into my body. It was such an overwhelming experience, I glowed with happiness, but then I suddenly realized that I had a big smile on my face amid all these people who'd just lost a child dear to them. I quickly covered my face with my hands because I didn't want to be disrespectful toward all these mourning and crying people in the room. And I never said a word about the experience. Talking about it seemed completely inappropriate at the time, and bedsides I didn't have the words to describe what had happened to me. I used to think that

I knew what was what. But my worldview underwent a radical transformation.¹

ALSO CALLED "TAKE AWAY apparitions" or "bystander apparitions," transitional apparitions are those seen by a percipient in his or her final days and moments of life. While usually only the dying person claims to see the apparition, there are documented cases of apparitions seen by another person, or persons, present at the time of the visitation.

Speaking from her experience as a former Hospice chaplain, Dianne Arcangel makes the astonishing claim that "I have never sat with a dying patient who was not in the accompaniment of an apparition as their time grew near. *No one ever dies alone.*"²

OLD AUNT ANN

My aunt, Miss Harriet Pearson, who was taken very ill at Brighton in November, 1864, craved to be back in her own home in London, where she and her sister Ann (who had died some years previously) had spent practically all their lives. I accordingly made the necessary arrangements, and had her moved home. Her two nieces (Mrs. Coppinger and Mrs. John Pearson), Eliza Quinton the housekeeper, and myself did the nursing between us. . . . On the night of Dec. 23rd, Mrs. John Pearson was sitting up with her, while Mrs. Coppinger and I lay down in the adjoining room, leaving the door ajar to hear any sound from the next room. We were neither of us asleep, and suddenly we both started up in bed, as we saw someone pass the door, wrapped up in an old shawl, having a wig with three curls each side, and an old black cap. Mrs. Coppinger called to me, "Emma, get up, it is old Aunt Ann!" I said, "So it is; then Aunt Harriet will die today!" As we jumped up, Mrs. John Pearson came rushing out of Aunt Harriet's room, saying, "That was old Aunt Ann. Where has she gone?" I said to sooth her, "Perhaps it was Eliza come down to see how her old mistress is." Mrs. Coppinger ran upstairs and found Eliza asleep. Every room was searched, no

---

1. van Lommel, *Consciousness*, "Empathetic NDE," ch. 2, para. 2. The narrator is the boyfriend of a lady named Anne that had died five days earlier in a motor vehicle accident. Her seven-year-old son also was unfortunately mortally-injured in the accident, "His brain virtually spilled out of his skull—it looked like a smashed watermelon—it took him about five days to make the transition." The percipient was in the company of some sixty relatives that were gathered around the young man's bed when he passed.

2. Arcangel, *Afterlife*, 120, emphasis original.

> one was there; and from that day to this no explanation has ever been given of this appearance, except that it was old Aunt Ann come to call her sister. Aunt Harriet died at 6 p.m. that day.
>
> Eliza Quinton, the housekeeper, confirms the above statement, and adds: "We searched in every room but could not find anyone in the house."
>
> Miss Harriet died on the evening of that day, but before that she told us all that she had seen her sister, and that she had come to call her.[3]

Barrett adds,

> This last statement is further confirmed by Miss Emma Pearson in a later letter, in which she states that she remembers her Aunt saying that "her sister had come for her, for she had seen her."[4]

In summary, "Old Aunt Ann" was seen briefly, though unmistakably, roaming the halls of the London home by three witnesses simultaneously. Moreover, Miss Harriet Pearson also claimed to see her deceased sister. Finally, the appearance of the apparition to the three healthy witnesses was interpreted as a forecast that Miss Harriet Pearson would pass that day, which occurred later that same evening.

There exist fascinating testimonies of people that have had what Raymond Moody has coined "shared death experiences." Shared death experiences are vivid visions of bystanders that happen to be present at the time that a dying person transitions from life to death. Consider the following:

"PAT AND NANCY"

> Another case that serves to illustrate the sharing of a death experience by more than one person comes from two women in their forties who were the first to tell me about jointly sharing the life review of a dying loved one. I'll call them Pat and Nancy.
>
> The sisters were at their mother's bedside as she was dying of lung cancer. As her breathing became more labored, the room began to "light up," said one of the sisters. Both of them told how the room began to swirl, quickly at first before slowing to a

---

3. Barrett, *Visions*, 35–36.
4. Barrett, *Visions*, 36.

stop. Then the two women found themselves standing with their mother, who looked decades younger.

Together, they were immersed in their mother's life review, which was filled with many scenes they had lived and many they had not. They saw their mother's first boyfriend and experienced her heartbreak at their breakup. They saw small things that had meant a lot to their mother, like the times she had helped poor children at their school without telling anyone. They also discovered the feelings their mother had for a widower who lived down the street, and how she had longed to strike up a conversation with him.

"What we saw was so real that we thought we had died too," said one of the sisters. "For months it was beyond belief until we finally accepted it."[5]

ADAMINA LAZARO

The Review "Verdade e Luz" of San Paolo, Brazil, in its number of September, 1924, has remarks on the striking incident of which the dying Adamina Lazaro was the heroine.

A few hours before her death, the patient said to her father that she saw near the bed several members of the family, all deceased some years previously. The father attributed this declaration *in extremis* to a state of delirium, but Adamina insisted with renewed force, and among the invisible "visitors" named her own brother, Alfredo, who was employed at the time at a distance of 423 kilometres, on the lighthouse of the port of Sisal.

The father was more and more convinced of the imaginary nature of these visions, well knowing that his son Alfredo was in perfect health, for a few days previously he had sent the best possible news of himself.

Adamina died the same evening, and the next morning her father received a telegram informing him of the death of the young Alfredo. A comparison of times showed that the dying girl was still living at the time of the death of her brother.[6]

In the books cited, Dr. Moody and Sir William Barrett collectively detail many narratives of the kind presented here. Many of the "shared death

---

5. Moody and Perry, *Glimpses*, "A bright light appeared in the room," ch. 1, paras. 7–10.

6. Barrett, *Visions*, 21–22, emphasis original.

experiences" involve not only seeing apparitions, but also experiencing any of a combination of potential elements peculiar to near-death experiences (NDEs). These include dark tunnels, brilliant lights, vivid colors, hearing beautiful music, feelings of unparalleled joy and peace, changes in the geometrical structure of the room where the dying individual is laying, spontaneous changes in the spatial perspectives of the percipients, etc.[7] Many of these experiences are corroborated directly by the witnesses themselves.

TRANSITIONAL APPARITIONS OF RELIGIOUS FIGURES

Most transitional apparitions are in the form of deceased loved ones.[8] However, sometimes religious figures are seen by those making the transition from life to death. The identity of the religious figure seen is largely dependent upon cultural and religious factors. A Christian is more likely to see Jesus or an angel, or at least interpret what was seen in that way. Hindus, by contrast, are more likely to see, or interpret what was seen, as a Hindu figure or deity.

Hindus often experience visions of a Yamdoot during their transition. Yamdoots are messengers of Yamaraj, the Hindu god of death and justice, and appear at the bedside of the dying to collect them. Whether or not a Yamdoot appears in a pleasing form or a more fearful one depends upon the deeds of the dying person (Karma). "If he has accumulated good deeds, a pleasant Yamdoot appears, but if he has not acquitted himself well in his lifetime, a fearful Yamdoot might come."[9]

"YAMDOOT IS COMING TO TAKE ME AWAY"

> The patient, a Hindu policeman in his forties, was suffering from pulmonary tuberculosis. He had, at that time, a low fever and had to be lightly touched or shaken before he would respond to questions. Suddenly he said: "Yamdoot is coming to take me away. Take me down from the bed so that Yamdoot does not find me." He pointed outwards and upwards. "There he is."

---

7. See Moody and Perry, *Glimpses*, ch. 4, where this is discussed at length.

8. This is persuasively and systematically demonstrated in Osis and Haraldsson, *Hour of Death*.

9. Osis and Haraldsson, *Hour of Death*, 93.

> This hospital room was on a ground floor. Outside, at the wall of the building, there was a large tree with a great number of crows sitting on its branches. Just as the patient had his vision, all the crows suddenly flew away from the tree with much noise, as if someone had fired a gun. We were very surprised by this and ran outside through an open door in the room, but we saw nothing that might have disturbed the crows.[10]

The nurse who reported this case was surprised by the policeman's purported vision and the surrounding circumstances since it apparently differed from what he and the others present had experienced in instances prior to this.

> They were usually peaceful, so it was very memorable to all of us present when the crows flew away with a great uproar, exactly at the time the patient had his vision. It was as if they, too, had become aware of something terrible. As this happened, the patient fell into a coma and expired a few minutes later.

THE EXPLODING DRINKING GLASS

Another case reported by a Christian nurse in India revolves around a close friend of her family, also a male in his forties who was dying of pulmonary tuberculosis.

> He was unsedated, fully conscious and had a low temperature.
> He was a rather religious person and believed in life after death.
> We expected him to die and he probably did too as he was asking us to pray for him. In the room where he was lying, there was a staircase leading to the second floor. Suddenly he exclaimed, "See, the angels are coming down the stairs. The glass has fallen and broken." All of us in the room looked towards the staircase where a drinking glass had been placed on one of the steps. As we looked, we saw the glass break into a thousand pieces without any apparent cause. It did not fall; it simply exploded. The angels, of course, we did not see. A happy and peaceful expression came over the patient's face and the next moment he expired. Even after his death, the serene, peaceful expression remained on his face.[11]

---

10. Osis and Haraldsson, *Hour of Death*, 44.
11. Osis and Haraldsson, *Hour of Death*, 44.

ASSESSMENT OF TRANSITIONAL APPARITIONS

As with other categories of apparitions, I find the collective cases, at least where there is more than one healthy percipient, to be practically self-authenticating. When expectation does not seem to be present, simultaneous hallucinations that are highly similar in content are very unlikely to occur. Obtaining what would otherwise be unknown information also argues strongly for authenticity. The numerous cases of apparitions of the deceased that appear to those on their deathbed who were previously unaware that the person had died is certainly thought-provoking in this regard.[12] The door is always open for the skeptic to claim that fraud is at play in these cases, but this explanation seems problematic in accounting for the multitude of such reported cases where the eyewitnesses do not apparently have anything material to gain by fabrication.[13]

Excluding cases that are collectively perceived or that render information previously unknown to the percipient, one may reasonably posit that transitional apparitions are hallucinations caused by the patients' illness. Depending on the clinical situation, as a physician I can account from firsthand experience that critically ill patients frequently have several reasons to hallucinate, and very frequently do hallucinate. Hallucinations of hospitalized patients may be caused by hospital delirium ("sun-downing"), side effects of medications (especially analgesic opioid medications and anxiety-reducing medications), and symptoms from their underlying illness(es) such as hypoxia (low blood oxygen), hypercarbia (abnormally high blood levels of carbon dioxide), hypoglycemia (low blood sugar), fever, etc. In my experience, the content of such hallucinations does not tend to be in the form of transitional apparitions.

---

12. See Barrett, *Visions*, where numerous such case reports are discussed along with corroborating lines of evidence. More recently, Allison, *Mystery*, 99–124, provides an excellent overview incorporating more recent sources.

13. See chapter 13.

7

Reunion Apparitions

DOUBTS

A young lady had lost her mother at a very early age and then two elder brothers when she was eighteen. Her father suffered "many doubts regarding various points of Christian faith" in the aftermath of having lost his wife. At forty-eight years of age, he became "sadly depressed and worn-looking." Not long afterwards, her father was found dead.[1]

> I was lying in deepest anguish, beset not only with the grief of the sudden loss sustained, but with wretched fear that my beloved father had died too suddenly to find peace with God, regarding those miserable doubts that had so troubled him. As the night wore on, the pain of heart and thought grew worse and worse, and at length I knelt in prayer, earnestly pleading that my distressful thoughts might be taken away, and an assurance of my father's peace be given me by God's most Holy Spirit. No immediate relief came, however, and it was early dawn when I rose from my knees and felt that I must be patient and wait for the answer to my prayer.[2]

Shortly afterwards, in an attempt to relieve some of her loneliness, she climbed into the bed of a "motherly-looking personage" she assumed to

---

1. "G.—476—Collective," 274–75.
2. "G.—476—Collective," 275.

be her cousin's nurse, who was sleeping in the same room. The room was still mostly dark with the light of dawn just appearing.

> I was just about to slip quietly down into bed, when on the opposite side of it (that on which the nurse was sleeping) the room became suddenly full of beautiful light, in the midst of which stood my father, absolutely transfigured, clothed with brightness. He slowly moved towards the bed, raising his hands, as I thought, to clasp me in his arms.[3]

Startled by the vision, she exclaimed, "Father!" He replied, "Blessed for ever, my child! For ever blessed!"

> I moved to climb over the nurse and kiss him, reaching out my arms to him; but with a look of mingled sadness and love he appeared to float back with the light towards the wall and was gone. The vision occupied so short a time that, glancing involuntarily at the window again, I saw the morning dawn and the little bird just as they had looked a few minutes before. I felt that God had vouchsafed to me a wonderful vision, and was not in the least afraid, but, on the contrary, full of joy that brought floods of grateful tears, and completely removed all anguish except that of having lost my father from earth. I offer no explanation, and can only say most simply and truthfully that it all happened just as I have related.[4]

This category most approximates what Tyrrell categorized as "postmortem apparitions," a designation I did not employ since at least five of the eight categories we discuss in this volume could be considered postmortem in nature. In contrast to crisis apparitions which occur on the same day that an agent is in peril, usually resulting in death, this category of apparition is typically reserved for those occurring after the day of death. The time demarcation for when a crisis apparition crosses into "reunion" territory is frankly arbitrary and may vary depending upon the researcher.[5]

I struggled to come up with a name for this category since it encompasses a broad spectrum of experiences, from individuals undergoing bereavement to apparent encounters with the dead that occur months to years after the agent's death.[6] Unlike with hauntings, apparitions in this

3. "G.—476—Collective," 276.
4. "G.—476—Collective," 276.
5. See the discussion in Tyrrell, *Apparitions*, 133–36.
6. I am indebted to Dr. Raymond Moody for the label upon which I eventually settled.

category tend to be recognized figures, are more purposeful, and sometimes, as with rescue apparitions, exhibit intelligence. Haunting apparitions are often frightening in appearance and are accompanied by other disturbing phenomena such as cold spots, disembodied footsteps, doors apparently opening and closing on their own, and unpleasant noises that cannot be traced to sources, such as tortured groans and sounds that resemble heavy objects being dragged across floors. Reunion apparitions, however, are typically devoid of these disturbing elements, are far more often received positively by their percipients, even to the point that they can be a source of great psychological healing. Accordingly, those represented by reunion apparitions are commonly described in similar terms as those employed in our last case: "beautiful," "radiant," "fully healed," and "transfigured."

Importantly, as with the other categories, there are evidential reunion apparitions. Consider the next case where veridical information is obtained by the percipient.

A FAMILIAR SCRATCH

This case was sent by Mr. F. G. to the American SPR. The investigators Mr. Hodgson and Professor Royce vouch for the integrity and "high character" of the informants. In 1867, Mr. F. G.'s only sister died of cholera in St. Louis, Missouri, at the age of eighteen.[7] The reunion encounter occurred nine years later, when Mr. F. G. was at his lodging in St. Joseph, Missouri working on orders.

> My thoughts, of course, were about these orders, knowing how pleased my house would be at my success. I had not been thinking of my late sister, or in any manner reflecting on the past. The hour was high noon, and the sun was shining carefully into my room. While busily smoking a cigar, and writing out my orders, I suddenly became conscious that someone was sitting on my left, with one arm resting on the table. Quick as a flash, I turned and distinctly saw the form of my dead sister and for a brief second or so looked her squarely in the face; and so sure was I that it was she, that I sprang forward in delight, calling her by name, and as I did so, the apparition instantly vanished. . . . I was near enough to touch her, had it been a physical possibility, and noted her features, expression, and details of dress, etc. She

---

7. Myers, "Recognized Apparitions," 17.

> appeared as if alive. Her eyes looked kindly and perfectly natural into mine. Her skin was so life-like that I could see the glow or moisture on its surface, and on the whole, there was no change in her appearance, otherwise than when alive.[8]

Like many we have encountered, this apparition appeared to be solid and lifelike. Yet this is not what makes this case the most remarkable. Mr. F. G. relates that the appearance made such a profound impression upon him that he jumped on the next train home and told his parents about the visit from his sister.

> My father, a man of rare good sense and very practical, was inclined to ridicule me, as he saw how earnestly I believed what I stated; but he too was amazed when later on I told them of a bright red line or *scratch* on the right-hand side of my sister's face, which I distinctly had seen. When I mentioned this, my mother rose trembling to her feet and nearly fainted away, and as soon as she sufficiently recovered her self-possession, with tears streaming down her face, she exclaimed that I had indeed seen my sister, as no living mortal but herself was aware of that scratch, which she had accidentally made while doing some little act of kindness after my sister's death. She said she well remembered how pained she was to think she should have, unintentionally, marred the features of her dead daughter, and that unknown to all, how she had carefully obliterated all traces of the slight scratch with the aid of powder, . . . and that she had never mentioned it to a human being from that day to this.[9]

Mr. F. G. stated in his letter to Mr. Hodgson that neither his father nor any of the family had detected the scratch at the time of the funeral. A letter from Mr. F. G.'s father, Mr. H. G., which was also endorsed by Mr. F. G.'s brother, corroborated Mr. F. G.'s testimony.[10]

CAPTAIN TOWNS

> On the 5th April, 1873, my wife's father, Captain Towns, died at his residence, Crankbrook, Rose Bay, near Syndey, N. S. Wales. About six weeks after his death, my wife had occasion one evening about 9 o'clock, to go to one of the bedrooms in the house.

8. Myers, "Recognized Apparitions," 18.
9. Myers, "Recognized Apparitions," 18, emphasis added.
10. Myers, "Recognized Apparitions," 19–20.

> She was accompanied by a young lady, Miss Berthon, and as they entered the room—the gas was burning all the time—they were amazed to see, reflected as it were on the polished surface of the wardrobe, the image of Captain Towns. It was barely half figure, the head, shoulders, and part of the arms only showing—in fact, it was like an ordinary medallion portrait, but life-size. The face appeared wan and pale, as it did before his death; and he wore a kind of grey flannel jacket, in which he had been accustomed to sleep. Surprised and half alarmed at what they saw, their first idea was that a portrait had been hung in the room, and that what they saw was its reflection—but there was no picture of the kind.[11]

The author of this recorded statement and Towns's son-in-law, C. A. W. Lett, did not see the apparition. He was in the house at the time, but did not hear upon being summoned. Numerous others did, however, see it. Aside from Sara Lett (Lett's wife) and Miss Berthon, the percipients included Miss Towns (Sara Lett's sister), a housemaid, Graham (Captain Towns's prior body servant), the butler, Mrs. Crane (Sara Lett's nurse), and lastly, Mrs. Towns (Captain Towns's widow). It was Mrs. Towns who passed her hand over the wardrobe panel, causing the apparition to gradually fade from existence. It never recurred though the room was occupied on a regular basis thereafter. Two witnesses of the apparition, Sarah Lett and her sister, Sibbie Smyth (née Towns) signed Lett's statement.[12]

This apparition contains at least four characteristics I find particularly worthy of note. First, unlike most that are externalized projections in three-dimensional space, Captain Towns's appearance occurs on a two-dimensional surface. Second, only part of Captain Towns's body is visible, unlike most apparitions that manifest the whole body.[13] Third, like most cases in the literature, this apparition had an aversion to touch resulting in its dissolution when Mrs. Towns made the attempt. Finally, and most remarkably, Captain Towns appears collectively to eight individuals.

For the final case, I will draw from the rich and fascinating collection of cases detailed in Dianne Arcangel's *Afterlife Encounters*. Dream cases are a departure from our modus operandi of considering apparitions that seem to occur exclusively in the awake state. Nevertheless, I feel that the following case merits consideration for a couple of reasons. First,

---

11. Gurney et al., *Phantasms II*, 213.
12. Gurney et al., *Phantasms II*, 213–14.
13. See Haraldsson, *Departed*, 125. In his Icelandic study, about 78 percent manifest the whole body.

I find it a compelling example of visits of the deceased that yield information that could not have otherwise been known (veridical information). Also, it parallels a similar case we will later discuss regarding Menachem Mendel Schneerson's appearances to his followers. For purposes of space, this is an abridged version of the original. Readers are encouraged to read Arcangel's full version of this fascinating case.

"I'VE LEFT SOMETHING INSIDE THAT WALL"— CHARLES'S AND JEAN'S EXPERIENCES[14]

Charles, a successful businessman from Houston, shared in an apparitional experience that is arguably the most remarkable story I have run across in preparing this volume. The subject was a good friend named Murphy, who ran a hole-in-the-wall vacuum cleaner store before having passed.

Charles relates the following regarding exchanges he used to have with Murphy about the afterlife.

> He'd get on these discussions with me, Jean, and his wife Lorraine. He'd say, "When I die, I'll let you know if there's something over there. I believe in God, I believe in an afterlife, and I'm a really mentally strong person, so I'll contact you. If there really is a God, I'll come back and tell you." I'd say, "Yeah, yeah, yeah."[15]

Murphy eventually became "real religious," and Charles and Jean had stopped going to his house because the conversations frequently "became a preach-a-thon." While reportedly healthy overall, two days after having corrective surgery Murphy unexpectedly died.

About one year later, Charles had a remarkably vivid dream where Murphy appeared to him. Oddly, he was in the middle of another dream, and it was as if the vision of Murphy literally intruded into the dream he was having. Charles compared it to being in a theater with the film on the projector burning through the center. A brilliant light emanated from this center and eventually took shape. Eventually, the imaging came into focus. It was Murphy, standing in front of a small house with a picket fence and flowers, all decked out in stunningly vibrant colors. In the yard was a sign that read, "At Peace with Jesus." Murphy was healthy, and Charles thought him to look to be about thirty-five years of age, simply appearing as the best version of himself.

14. Arcangel, *Afterlife*, 75–82.
15. Arcangel, *Afterlife*, 77.

Then he said, "I've made it. I'm here. Tell Lorraine to look in the hall, at the dead end, just south of the bedroom to the right of the light socket. I've left something inside that wall. Be sure to give her that message."[16]

It had been more than a year since Charles and Jean had seen Lorraine. That, along with an understandable reluctance to pass along a purported message from her deceased husband that he had received in a dream, kept Charles from making the call. The dream repeated another three or four times. At that point, Jean (whom Charles had told about the dream), called Lorraine to inform her about Charles's dream. This was, of course, despite Charles's protestations to the contrary. In reaction, Lorraine was reportedly upset that Murphy had not contacted her himself.[17] Soon after Jean had given Lorraine the message that her deceased husband gave to Charles, Lorraine called her back:

> But soon, she called back and said, "Oh my God! You'll never believe this, but I just dug into the wall where Murphy told Charles to look and I found a whole lot of cash—*thousands and thousands* of dollars."[18]

Lorraine was going to have the house remodeled the very next week without knowledge of that money, and hence being unable to secure it. Interestingly, Lorraine's daughter, who lived in Florida, had been having the same dream as Charles, replete with the yard sign that read, "At Peace with Jesus."

Arcangel interviewed Charles and Jean. She asked Charles, "Had you ever seen the message 'At Peace with Jesus' around Murphy in any way?" He replied, "Oh no! Never!" and, "to this day, I've never seen anything like it. . . . Lorraine described the sign that her daughter saw, and it was the same one, in the same place, just as I'd told Jean. And we both saw Murphy standing on the walkway with the sign to his left. I've never seen anything like that, and I don't know the daughter. She was from Lorraine's first marriage."[19]

This vision is astonishing in several surprising ways. The information content that proved to be accurate, the finding of a cache of thousands

16. Arcangel, *Afterlife*, 77–78, emphasis original.

17. Arcangel, *Afterlife*, 78. The aforementioned "promise" was that Charles would give Lorraine a sign after his death. This was the sign though it was not given directly to her.

18. Arcangel, *Afterlife*, 79, emphasis original.

19. Arcangel, *Afterlife*, 79–80.

of dollars hidden in the wall that nobody knew about, came as a shock to everyone involved. In the narrative, Lorraine reportedly commented that Murphy would switch banks if it meant earning an extra half a percentage point of interest on their savings and that it seemed extremely improbable that he would have hidden a hoard of money inside a wall.[20] While we can't classify this vision to be collective per se, it seems more than coincidental that two people close to Murphy—one of his friends and his daughter-in-law—during roughly the same time period, would have the same dream, even down to matters of detail. Also, the percipient selection seems unpredictable, to put it mildly: a daughter-in-law and a friend who had lost touch with Murphy and was not overtly religious. Meanwhile Lorraine, the intended recipient of Murphy's message, received no such visitation.

ASSESSMENT OF REUNION APPARITIONS

Contrary to hauntings and most crisis apparitions, reunion apparitions tend to appear as healthy, sometimes even glorious, versions of those they represent. As well, they often seem to come with a purpose.[21] This does not, however, detract from their generally ephemeral nature.

Bill and Judy Guggenheim produced a diverse compendium of scores of such postmortem encounters.[22] As is evident from their collection, not all afterdeath communications (ADCs) are visual in nature, producing apparitions of the deceased. Many percipients feel a sense of presence, while other such encounters may be purely auditory in nature (e.g., hearing a deceased loved one's voice), tactile, olfactory, or a combination of more than one of these senses.

Apparent spirits of the deceased seem to have limitations imposed upon their ability to get through to their targeted percipient(s) and upon the extent they may accomplish such ends. In Murphy's case, he does appear against a vivid, heavenly backdrop in the percipients' dreams, though one which, nonetheless, leaves the reader with more questions than answers about life on the other side. One also wonders why Murphy did not (could not?) appear directly to his wife Lorraine, for whom the

---

20. Arcangel, *Afterlife*, 82.
21. The Captain Towns case and a few others notwithstanding.
22. Guggenheim and Guggenheim, *Hello from Heaven!*

message was intended, rather than having to convey it indirectly to an old, estranged friend and Lorraine's daughter from a prior marriage.[23]

Indeed, I find myself repeatedly struck by the simplicity of most of these accounts, as well as the dearth of details regarding afterlife activities in the case reports. This is particularly noticeable as one traverses the many testimonies in the Guggenheims' book. ADCs, regardless of which sense or combination of senses are invoked, generally prove to be brief encounters evidently intended to convey reassuring messages to their percipients. Typically, the agents' messages, in one manner or another, simply convey to percipients that they are okay or that those currently grieving need to move on with their lives. This inherent simplicity I find to be a marker of authenticity.

REUNION ENCOUNTERS PROVIDE COMFORT TO MOST

The simplicity of such accounts, however, does not detract from their often serving as life-changing events for the percipients. In Arcangel's survey of the 596 respondents who had experienced an afterlife encounter, 98 percent found that the experience ultimately brought them some degree of comfort and that this did not tend to erode with time.[24] Similarly, Rees states that nearly 70 percent of widows and widowers in his Welsh study found the encounters "helpful and pleasant," while only 6 percent found

---

23. Dianne Arcangel details another remarkable case regarding a young man named Tommy, who had been murdered but managed to alert his mother through an auditory ADC of vital information that, when checked and reported by his mother and followed-up by police investigators, led to the arrest of his murderer. Prior to the auditory ADC, chandelier lights repeatedly flickered for minutes when police investigators went to the house to report the tragedy to his mother, Beverly. In the aftermath of the investigation and eventual arrest, it was later thought that this could have been Tommy's way of symbolically identifying his murderer, a man who went by the nickname "Light." Four months later, Beverly and Tommy's dog, Baby, saw an apparition of Tommy on the street. After being identified by the two percipients as an apparition of Tommy, it smiled, turned, and floated away, suspended just above pavement. Baby and Beverly desperately tried to catch up to Tommy, but to no avail. Eventually their view of the apparition was obstructed by passersby and not seen again. Arcangel, *Afterlife*, 66–74.

Amazing though this series of paranormal events is, the case also illustrates remarkable restraint on the part of the apparent. Without restraints, one easily imagines Tommy appearing to Beverly and the police detectives in solid form and verbally giving them the information from the start. Also worth noting, the reunion apparition that occurred four months later exhibited a resistance to being touched, as we have seen with so many in this volume.

24. See Arcangel, *Afterlife*, 51–64.

them unpleasant, the latter being mostly tactile cases.[25] To a degree, how such encounters are received seems to be culturally specific. In Japan, where such encounters are desired and even nurtured, nearly 90 percent of widows had some form of experience with their deceased husbands.[26] In some cultures, such as the Hopi Indians of northern Arizona, ADCs may be predominantly distressing in nature. Consider the following excerpt cited from William Foster Matchett.

> She described how she would sit alone in her room in the evening and draw all the shades, and then, almost nightly, a vision of her deceased husband would appear before her chair. He would say little to her. At first she found this experience a very comforting one and looked forward to his presence. Later, he began quite persistently to say things like "I'm gone now, don't bring me back any more; I don't want to come back." In the last month before her hospitalization, the apparition stood in front of her chair, caressed her hair, then softly touched her check [sic]. She could distinctly feel his fingers move gently from her cheek to her neck; then suddenly he began to strangle her. She sprang to her feet in terror, "struggled free," threw on the light, and "he was gone." Gradually, the apparition began to show signs of physical decay. She reported that flesh on his hands and arms was turning to "skin and bones" and that his clothing was deteriorating.[27]

Distressing afterdeath communications seem to predominate in cultures that fear the return of the dead. The Navajo, for instance, "believe that most of the deceased return as malevolent ghosts that haunt their relatives." To prevent their return, emotions of grief are discouraged after a four-day mourning period. The Amazonian Jivaro tribe that inhabits the jungle area between Ecuador and Peru have similar beliefs. The Jivaro believe that a visual or verbal afterdeath communication is dangerous to the living, and they "strive to erase any remembrance of the dead after the loss." To do this, they will even avoid sleep for one day to prevent dreaming of the deceased. Also, the chanting of soul songs is employed to break the bonds between living and dead. Another Amazonian tribe, the Kagwahiva, encourages mitigating sorrow even during mourning and will change the name of the deceased person into that of an inanimate noun

---

25. Rees, *Eternity*, ch. 10, para. 7.
26. Aleman and Larøi, *Hallucinations*, ch. 2, para. 10.
27. Sabucedo et al., "Perceiving," 881.

in an attempt at distancing the deceased person from the living. A mortuary rite is then used to "keep the ghosts at bay: the eyes of the corpse are closed and their face is tied with a cloth." The Matsigenka of the Amazon believe that, following a sudden death, the deceased may return in the form of a beast to assault their loved ones, either in nightmares or when they are walking alone through a forest.[28]

Numerous studies have replicated the findings of W. D. Rees and have found ADCs to be a prevalent phenomenon across many cultures. Likely between 30–60 percent of the bereaved experience such encounters. In Rees's day, it was exceptionally rare for widows and widowers to share their experiences with their doctors or even their clergy for fear of psychological stigmatization. This is undoubtedly still the case with many today for similar reasons, though as Western society becomes increasingly aware of such occurrences, they are likely disclosed more often now than half a century ago.

As with hauntings, reunion apparitions/encounters may be recurrent.[29] The difference is that haunting apparitions usually recur at a specific location, whereas reunion apparitions tend to center around a specific person. Although typically centered around an individual, reunion apparitions are occasionally collectively perceived.

ARE REUNION ENCOUNTERS OBJECTIVE IN NATURE?

The various studies seem to be divided as to what kind of sensory experience predominates in reunion encounters. Several studies indicate that a sense of presence—without accompanying visual, auditory, tactile, or olfactory manifestations—is the most common experience. Other studies indicate that percipients more often experience the deceased as an apparition, with or without the invocation of other senses.[30]

Are these experiences hallucinatory? Are they subjective experiences that do not correspond to any form of externally produced reality? I think this could be true of many such occurrences, especially those that

---

28. Sabucedo et al., "Perceiving," 881–82.

29. 78 percent of survey respondents in Arcangel's study reported having had more than one such experience, though this does not always involve recurrent *visual* afterlife encounters, and respondents who had multiple encounters may have in some cases been referring to the appearances of different persons or entities. See Arcangel, *Afterlife*, 284.

30. See appendix A for further discussion of some of these statistics.

are purely auditory in nature. Aleman and Larøi demonstrate that many auditory phenomena related to hearing voices may plausibly be explained in large measure by "misattribution of inner speech." Effectively, the hallucinator is producing the voices by subtle use of his or her own vocal cords/muscles (subvocalization) without realizing it. This has been demonstrated through the utilization of electromyographic and neuroimaging studies while subjects are reporting auditory hallucinations.[31] This makes sense with what we find elsewhere. Apparitions that are visual and auditory in nature do not tend to produce lengthy conversations, as we find reported in some of the purely auditory afterdeath communications. In fact, per Rees, bereavement apparitions that are engaged verbally by their percipients tend to disappear faster.[32]

As with most ADCs that are experienced by a single individual, it is frankly difficult to rule out hallucination as a potential cause regardless of which sensory modality (or combination of sensory modalities) is in play. However, this explanation runs into difficulties in the cases where there is a supernormal information transfer and in those experienced collectively by two or more percipients.

Finally, I find it plausible that some reunion apparitions, ostensibly visits from the great beyond, may be objectively produced apparitions of the living. As we will discuss in chapter 15, we have yet to fully unlock all the secrets of human consciousness. Among other things, the subliminal consciousness of the human mind can achieve dramatic physical and psychological healing that extends beyond the capabilities of modern medical technology. As we will see further in the next chapter, apparitions of the deceased may be deliberately induced to achieve nearly miraculous psychotherapeutic benefits.

---

31. Aleman and Larøi, *Hallucinations*, ch. 5.
32. Rees, *Eternity*, ch. 10, "Talking to the deceased."

8

Inducible Apparitions

To this point, every category of apparition that we have considered occurs spontaneously. That is, there is generally no hint of expectation being present among percipients. Furthermore, the percipient(s) took no deliberate action(s) to produce such appearances, though with apparitions of the living, the agents clearly did.

As the name of this chapter suggests, however, apparent encounters with deceased loved ones can frequently be produced deliberately. Here we will delve into the phenomena of inducible apparitions by looking at some cases from two researchers in particular, Dr. Raymond Moody and Dr. Allan Botkin, as well as materializations produced in séances.

THEATER OF THE MIND

Seemingly an accident of history, Dr. Raymond Moody came across the book *Crystal Gazing* by Northcote Thomas, who Moody describes as a "compulsive and serious scholar." Initially skeptical, Moody trudged through the book with an open mind because of a conversation he once had with fellow paranormal investigator Dr. William Roll about reports of people who experienced visions by looking at mirrors.[1] Reflective surfaces have been used by multiple cultures throughout history with the goal of communing with the dead.[2]

---

1. Moody and Perry, *Reunions*, ix.
2. Moody and Perry, *Reunions*, 53–54.

Dr. Moody was so influenced by one tradition, that of the Greek Oracles of the Dead, that he decided to create an apparition chamber in his Alabama home. He called it a modernized version of the apparition chambers used in ancient Greece, where people could come to see the spirits of their deceased loved ones.[3] The "apparition chamber," or psychomanteum, was a single room that contained an easy chair with a headrest situated three feet above the floor and facing a mirror about three feet away. Draped around the chair was a black velvet curtain that hung from the ceiling. The mirror was four feet in height, three-and-a-half feet in width and was mounted on a wall such that its lower edge was about three feet from the ground. A person sitting in the easy chair would not see his or her reflection, rather a "crystal-clear pool of darkness" that was the reflection of the space behind where the person was sitting. Behind the chair was the room's only source of light, a "small stained-glass lamp with a fifteen-watt bulb."[4]

Subsequently, Moody recruited subjects that fit certain criteria: 1) mature and interested in human consciousness; 2) emotionally stable, inquisitive, and articulate; 3) no emotional or mental disorders; 4) no occult ideologies. Included in his initial recruitment list were counselors, psychologists, medical doctors, graduate students, etc.[5]

Subjects were informed that the goal of the experiment was to invoke an apparition of a departed person to whom the subject had been close. Furthermore, the subjects were instructed to bring mementos that had been owned by and were strongly associated with the departed person, as well as relevant photo albums if available. Focusing attention on one subject at a time, Moody had each arrive around 10:00 a.m. the day of testing. The day would begin with a walk through the countryside, where they would discuss the subject's motivation for experiencing an apparition of the specific departed person in mind. This was followed by a light lunch, after which they would discuss in detail the person who the subject hoped to see later in the apparition chamber. Details included key aspects of the person's life, habits, personality, character, relevant memories, etc. The mementos the subjects brought with them would also be present and sometimes touched during this conversation.[6]

---

3. Moody and Perry, *Reunions*, 65–66.
4. Moody and Perry, *Reunions*, 66.
5. Moody and Perry, *Reunions*, 67.
6. Moody and Perry, *Reunions*, 67–68.

Around dusk, the subject would be brought to the apparition chamber, the lamp would be activated, and any remaining light in the chamber would be eliminated. After resting in the easy chair, the subject was instructed to "gaze deeply into the mirror and to relax, clearing his or her mind of everything but thoughts of the deceased person." This subject could stay in the apparition chamber for as long as he or she wanted while an attendant sat in a nearby room to render any assistance that may have been needed. Afterwards, the subject discussed what occurred while in the chamber.[7]

Initially, Moody ran trials with ten different subjects, five of whom experienced apparitional phenomena. Surprised by his initial success, Moody made future refinements to his facility and technique, and this success rate eventually increased.[8]

Moody's results yielded several unpredictable surprises beyond the actual success rate. The apparitions of deceased persons that appeared inside the chamber were sometimes different from the ones that were expected to appear. In fact, this occurred at a rate of about 25 percent of the time.[9] As also reflected in this case, 10 percent of the apparitions did not stay confined within the mirror but apparently stepped into the subject's surrounding environment. Conversely, 10 percent of the time subjects would report being drawn "into the mirror" where they would encounter a deceased relative.[10] Perhaps most surprisingly, sometimes the apparition occurs *after* the subject exits the psychomanteum.

TOUR OF THE HOUSE

Dr. Moody relates the story of a woman who came to him with the goal of seeing her son, who had died from cancer two years earlier. After spending a full day in preparation, she went into the psychomanteum and, as if in a dreamlike state, relived memories from her son's childhood. She felt as if her son was in the room reliving them with her. After the experience ended, she went home.

A few days later, she phoned Moody and recounted to him that she had awakened from "a deep sleep into a state of 'hyper-awareness.'"

---

7. Moody and Perry, *Reunions*, 69
8. Moody and Perry, *Reunions*, 72–73
9. Moody and Perry, *Reunions*, 90.
10. Moody and Perry, *Reunions*, 90–91.

There, standing in the room, was her son, appearing fully healed, as he had been before the cancer had taken its ill effects. He told her that he was happy and no longer in pain. They carried on a conversation that lasted for several minutes. She even spoke to him about mundane matters, such as about the house remodel that had taken place after his death. Amazingly, he accompanied her on a tour of the rooms that had undergone remodeling, and she explained to him the changes that had been made in each.[11] Then it seems that the reality of what was happening set in.

> Suddenly she stopped. She realized that she was talking to an apparition. And even though he seemed to be flesh and bone, he had come to her as a result of a lot of time spent before a mirror. She asked what had been unthinkable just a few minutes earlier. She asked if she could touch him.
> Without a moment's hesitation, the apparition of her son stepped forward and hugged her, lifting her right off the ground.
> "What happened was as real as if he had been standing right there," the woman told me. "I now feel as though I can put my son's death behind me and get on fully with my life."[12]

As with some other cases of apparitions discussed heretofore, apparitional phenomena are not confined to audiovisual experiences. Here we have one of the more remarkable examples of a tactile apparitional experience. Furthermore, Moody states that "complex communications," such as was clearly present in this case, were reported in nearly 50 percent of psychomanteum experiences. He states that these communications "ranged from a few words of reassurance and love to lengthy and involved communications, even to conversational exchanges."[13]

Moody indicates that about 15 percent of the time, the subjects heard the words of the apparition being phonated in terms of what we would consider normal verbal communication. The rest reported that the communication was more a form of telepathy, as we have seen with other postmortem visitations.[14] Perhaps most fascinating, about 25 percent of the apparitions experienced were of the take away variety, having occurred well after the subject leaves the psychomanteum, usually within twenty four hours.[15]

   11. Moody and Perry, *Paranormal*, 207.
   12. Moody and Perry, *Paranormal*, 208–9.
   13. Moody and Perry, *Reunions*, 95.
   14. Moody and Perry, *Reunions*, 95.
   15. Moody and Perry, *Reunions*, 95–96.

Consider Dr. Moody's own psychomanteum experience.

DR. MOODY'S TAKE AWAY VISIT

Having studied the theoretical constructs of crystal gazing (or scrying), Dr. Moody decided to put the matter to the test. Before constructing the somewhat more elaborate psychomanteum described earlier, his first experiment took place in a small closet in which he hung a mirror on one wall, high enough to where it would only reflect the wall behind where he was positioned. Minimal light was provided by a 25-watt bulb.[16]

> My goal was to see Grandmother Waddleton, my maternal grandmother. . . .
>
> Sitting in the room's dim light, I gazed into the crystal clear, three-dimensional depth of the offset mirror, which was like looking into a deep mountain lake. I gazed into the mirror for an hour or more, thinking of Grandmother Waddleton and bringing scenes to life from the photos I had looked at for so long.
>
> Yet despite two hours of effort, my beloved grandmother did not appear.
>
> "*Had I done something wrong?*" I wondered as I left the booth.
>
> I went downstairs to the living room. It was twilight now, and the experience of scrying had left me surprisingly tired. I remember sitting on the couch, thinking of nothing at all.
>
> Suddenly a woman walked into the room! It took me a moment to realize that this was not my *maternal* grandmother, Grandmother Waddleton, but my *paternal* grandmother, Grandmother Moody, who had died several years earlier.
>
> "Grandma!" I exclaimed, throwing my hands up to my face.[17]

Moody relates that he had initially hoped to experience visions of Grandmother Waddleton because of a history of mostly positive experiences with her. In contrast, his prior experiences with Grandmother Moody had been generally unpleasant. Other than a luminous white line that separated her from her surroundings, she appeared solid and was much younger-appearing than how she looked when she had died. When she spoke, he was "aware of what she was saying even before she said it," describing it as a form of "mind-to-mind" communication. Her voice had

---

16. Moody and Perry, *Paranormal*, 187–88.
17. Moody and Perry, *Paranormal*, 188, emphasis original.

an "electric quality" to it that was clearer and louder than her voice had sounded before she had died.

During the conversation with his apparent grandmother, they discussed family, and she revealed information that he had previously been unaware of, but he said that the information made sense of some of the "dysfunction" that had been present during his life. The encounter had a very positive impact on him, as it "changed my impression of my paternal grandmother" for the better. He did not have a definite feeling for the length of the conversation. Curiously, he said that it seemed like two hours but it could have been a matter of mere seconds. At the end of the conversation, he tried twice to approach her for a hug, but each time she resisted being touched. Finally, he left the room to get water, and the apparition had disappeared by the time he returned.[18]

Dr. Moody's experience differed from the prior case in that, as with most apparitions, that of Grandmother Moody was resistant to being touched. As we have seen, tactile experiences within the context of an apparitional visit occur in a minority of cases, and in most (not all) of those, the touch is initiated by the apparition, not the subject. As with the prior case, however, Dr. Moody did engage in a lengthy conversation with the apparition. Induced apparitions seem to produce lengthier experiences that sometimes include complex, multi-faceted conversations than their spontaneous counterparts in which such complex communications are extremely rare.

INDUCED AFTER-DEATH COMMUNICATIONS

Another form of inducible apparitions occurred in the psychotherapist's office. Dr. Allan Botkin details his experiences with a type of therapy called "eye movement desensitization and reprocessing," or EMDR. EMDR is used to help alleviate patients' suffering from severe emotional duress resulting from a traumatic event that occurred at some time in the past.

In this form of therapy, the psychotherapist is positioned in front of and just to the side of the patient and waves his or her hand back and forth in a rhythmic manner, with the index and third finger extended. Meanwhile, the patient is instructed to focus on a particular disturbing

---

18. Moody and Perry, *Paranormal*, 189.

thought or image, usually from the patient's past.[19] Botkin relates that this is helpful in a range of psychological disorders, including multiple-personality disorder and post-traumatic stress disorder (PTSD). While not completely understood in terms of how it proves to be so efficacious, this technique serves to "access" the traumatic memory in a way that it can be further processed, thereby eliminating the harmful cycle of it being continuously relived.[20]

> No one is quite sure how it works, although it's clear that it speeds up mental processing and is similar to the rapid eye movements (REMs) people experience in dream sleep. It is well known that during dream sleep, our brains process and integrate information more efficiently than when we are awake. It has been assumed that this increased processing during sleep causes the rapid, back and forth eye movement. Having a fully awake person purposely shift the eyes in the same way, as in EMDR, seems to cause the brain to process information rapidly and efficiently. Thus EMDR draws upon the person's own natural ability to heal.[21]

According to Botkin, neuroimaging studies support that EMDR therapy allows patients to remember the traumatic event in question in a more emotionally detached and abstract way. Unlike hypnosis, which in theory can be used to access memories, including suppressed memories, EMDR "accelerates information processing in the brain so it speeds up the consciousness projector." In essence, for patients suffering from repeatedly having to reexperience a traumatic event, this technique "speeds up the projector, unsticking it to allow it to run smoothly. The traumatic event then ceases to intrude in an unwanted way into consciousness."[22]

While hypnosis enhances suggestibility and unfortunately may produce false memories, this is not the case for the EMDR technique. Dr. Botkin even indicates he has used EMDR to "undo false memories."[23] At the time of his writing, per the author, more than fifty thousand professionals have been trained to apply EMDR therapy across the world, and the therapy has been officially endorsed by the American Psychological Association Division 12: Clinical Psychology (1998), International Society

19. Botkin and Hogan, *Induced*, 3.
20. Botkin and Hogan, *Induced*, 3–4.
21. Botkin and Hogan, *Induced*, 4.
22. Botkin and Hogan, *Induced*, 5.
23. Botkin and Hogan, *Induced*, 5.

for Traumatic Stress Studies (2000), Northern Ireland Department of Health (2001), Israeli National Council for National Health (2002), and US Veterans Administration/Department of Defense (2004).[24]

Dr. Botkin utilized EMDR in the post-traumatic stress disorder (PTSD) unit at a VA hospital.

> The results were dramatic. Often we achieved in a single session changes in patients that we had not been able to approximate after years of conventional psychotherapy.[25]

He indicates that it is particularly effective in treating grief, along with other negative emotions that may result (such as anger and guilt). When processing what he calls "the core sadness" properly, "guilt and anger simply vanished without even being directly addressed."[26]

While this is undeniably remarkable, what does it have to do with apparitions? Botkin happened upon these phenomena within the context of EMDR therapy practically by accident.

SAM AND LE

This case was Dr. Botkin's first induced after-death communication (IADC) and was produced, so to speak, unintentionally as part of the therapeutic program. Sam was forty-six years of age and a Vietnam veteran. While in Vietnam, he had become close to an orphaned Vietnamese girl named Le who was only ten years of age at the time. Her parents having been killed in the war, Le stayed on the American base. In exchange for performing daily chores on the base, she was provided with food and shelter. Per Botkin, "Le reminded Sam of his two younger sisters, and helped him maintain a sense of his own humanity amid the dehumanizing brutality of war."[27]

Eventually orders came in that all orphaned Vietnamese children on Sam's base were to be delivered to a Catholic orphanage at a village some distance from Sam's base. Sam was saddened by the situation but loaded Le, along with the other orphans, onto a flatbed truck with the intent of following orders. At about that time, they were attacked by a barrage of gunfire. Most of the children were saved by Sam and the other American

---

24. Botkin and Hogan, *Induced*, 6.
25. Botkin and Hogan, *Induced*, 7.
26. Botkin and Hogan, *Induced*, 9.
27. Botkin and Hogan, *Induced*, 11.

soldiers, but Le had been shot and killed; her front torso had been "blown open from a bullet that had entered from behind."[28]

Devastated, Sam was plagued with rage and sadness, even to the point of signing up for perilous missions with the goal of killing all the enemies he could find or getting himself killed. After his tour in Vietnam, Sam came home and became a father. However, he avoided his daughter for many years "because she triggered anger, guilt, deep sadness over Le's death and gruesome images of Le's dead body."[29] According to Botkin, Sam remained mostly in seclusion from his family for nearly twenty-eight years.

Botkin performed EMDR therapy on Sam, administering a set of eye movements while instructing him to focus on his sadness. A subsequent set of eye movements was then applied to lessen the sadness after it peaked. What occurred next surprised both the doctor and patient.

> While tears ran down his face, I administered a final eye movement procedure and asked him to close his eyes. Neither of us was prepared for what happened next. The tears that had been flowing from his closed eyes suddenly stopped, and he smiled broadly.... When he opened his eyes, he was euphoric.
>
> "When I closed my eyes, I saw Le as a beautiful woman with long black hair in a white gown surrounded by a radiant light. She seemed genuinely happier and more content than anyone I have ever known." Sam's tear-reddened face glowed. "She thanked me for taking care of her before she died. I said, 'I love you, Le,' and she said, 'I love you too, Sam,' and she put her arms around me and embraced me. Then she faded away."
>
> Sam was ecstatic and absolutely convinced that he had just communicated with Le. "I could actually feel her arms around me," he proclaimed.[30]

Botkin initially assumed that Sam had experienced a grief hallucination. In any event, and most importantly for Botkin, the experience proved dramatically effective:

> If that was a hallucination, then his mind had miraculously created an experience that was completely healing. During my clinical rotations on wards with the chronic and severely mentally

---

28. Botkin and Hogan, *Induced*, 11.
29. Botkin and Hogan, *Induced*, 12.
30. Botkin and Hogan, *Induced*, 12.

ill, no patient ever reported a hallucination that was so positive and healing.[31]

The very next day, Botkin had inadvertently induced yet another after-death communication with his patient Victor, this time a Korean War veteran who had lost his best friend, Charlie, in the heat of a firefight. The image of Charlie's lifeless body had intruded upon Victor's consciousness for decades. Botkin's EMDR procedure produced a vision of Charlie in Victor's mind. Charlie "looked very happy" and "looked healthy, not bloody and dead, the way I've always remembered him since Korea" and expressed to Victor, "It's okay." Unorthodox though it may have been, the vision provided Victor with dramatic psychological healing.[32]

Within the next three weeks, Botkin was inducing these IADCs within about 15 percent of his patients.

> I had witnessed six of these remarkable occurrences, all with the same reported vividness, the certainty the vets expressed that it was real, the positive assurances they reported from the person who had died, and the unprecedented resolution of longstanding, intractable traumatic grief. . . . Astonishingly, while I had become accustomed to seeing the patients' sadness and associated feelings reduce when I used core-focused EMDR, after most of these unusual sessions, the patients left the office joyous.[33]

Puzzled initially at why his EMDR procedure was producing so many of these apparitions, Botkin eventually came to realize that he was administering another series of eye movements after the "core-focused EMDR" procedure without giving the patients specific instruction.[34] The procedural details need not concern us here. After this realization, Dr. Botkin was able to reliably produce these experiences in 98 percent of his patients.[35]

---

31. Botkin and Hogan, *Induced*, 13.
32. Botkin and Hogan, *Induced*, 16.
33. Botkin and Hogan, *Induced*, 16.
34. Botkin and Hogan, *Induced*, 17.
35. Botkin and Hogan, *Induced*, 19.

MELINDA'S CASE: "I SAID 'SIT,' AND THEY STOPPED JUMPING ON ME"

Melinda came to see Dr. Botkin for therapy three weeks after her Uncle Darren, who had "been like a father to her," died of a heart attack. Per Botkin, she would stay with Uncle Darren and her aunt when her parents worked evenings at the family restaurant. He notes that Melinda especially enjoyed playing with her uncle and aunt's dogs Paris and Rinnie. The two dogs were large breeds, reportedly a Border collie and a German shepherd that had died when Melinda was in her teens. After the usual EMDR sequence had been applied, Melinda experienced something that was initially unpleasant.

> She closed her eyes and almost immediately opened them, lurching forward in her chair. "Something jumped on me," she blurted with her eyes open wide. "I don't know what it was."
>
> "Melinda," I said, "IADCs are always positive. There's nothing to be afraid of. If you go back to it, you probably will understand what is happening, whatever that is." She looked at me out of the corner of her eye. "Okay, I'll do it, but if it happens again, that's it for this stuff."
>
> I provided another set of eye movements and Melinda, a little tense, closed her eyes. After a few seconds, she relaxed, smiled, and shook her head. She opened her eyes.
>
> "I saw my uncle very clearly," she said. "He was holding Paris and Rinnie on leashes. They were straining to come to me and wagging their tails. He said he loves me and will always be with me."
>
> Melinda was overjoyed about her experience and felt sure her uncle was still alive with Paris and Rinnie, just in a different form. She left my office happy, without the feelings of grief she had when she came to me.[36]

Melinda came back to see the doctor the next day, upset over strange, frightening sensations of "things jumping on me" that occurred the night following her EMDR. Botkin performed another IADC procedure. In her mind's eye, she saw apparitions of Paris and Rinnie being held by her Uncle Darren. He had loosed them and "they jumped up on me and were licking my face," which were the same sensations that she had experienced the night prior. She looked at her uncle who told her, "Paris and Rinnie want you to know they're all right too." About two months later,

---

36. Botkin and Hogan, *Induced*, 77.

Botkin spoke with Melinda, who reported no further episodes of sensations of something jumping on her. "She was sure it was because she had told Paris and Rinnie to sit and they were still obeying."[37]

If IADCs are properly interpreted to be actual reunions with deceased loved ones, this episode serves as an indicator that our pets take part in the afterlife. Comparable to some of the reports from Moody's psychomanteum, we find that Melinda experienced take-away phenomena later at home, notably tactile experiences, courtesy of her uncle's deceased German shepherd and Border collie misbehaving. This was one of two IADCs involving pets that Dr. Botkin details.[38]

COLLECTIVE IADCS

As with most other categories of apparitions we have surveyed, there are documented cases of inducible apparitions being experienced simultaneously by multiple percipients. Dr. Botkin first witnessed this indirectly when an observing psychologist in training sat in on a session with a patient. While Botkin performed the EMDR procedure with the patient, the psychologist closed his eyes and performed eye movements to relax.

> Images appeared to the psychologist in training: a vivid scene of a swampy area with cattails, a pond, and a willow tree. He felt as though he was lying on the grass with the pond at eye level. It made no sense to him, so he opened his eyes and continued to observe the patient and me. The patient had not yet begun speaking, so the psychologist had no knowledge of what the patient was experiencing during the IADC.[39]

When the patient opened his eyes and described what he saw, he disclosed that he was present in the same swampy area and saw the cattails, pond, and willow tree. The reason the patient saw the swamp was because it was "in the backyard of my uncle's farm. I used to play there and would lie in the grass by the pond." There was one discrepancy between the two accounts. The training psychologist saw ducks fly overhead whereas the patient did not. In a follow-up session the patient and psychologist-observer agreed to simultaneously induce IADCs. After they opened their eyes from the experience, the psychologist detailed a conversation

---

37. Botkin and Hogan, *Induced*, 78.
38. See Botkin and Hogan, *Induced*, 74–76.
39. Botkin and Hogan, *Induced*, 109–10.

between the patient and the patient's uncle. The patient subsequently confirmed the particulars of that conversation with his uncle in his own IADC experience.[40]

Botkin further notes, regarding the phenomenon of collective IADCs,

> We were intrigued by this development, so the observer psychologist and I experimented with eight other patients who agreed to participate. This time, the psychologist wrote down everything he experienced before the patients reported what happened during their IADCs. In every instance, the psychologist's accounts matched the patients' IADCs with great accuracy.[41]

That IADCs could evidently be shared led Dr. Botkin to determine that this phenomenon could not be attributable to hallucinations.

> A hallucination is idiosyncratic—two people cannot have identical hallucinations at the same time. During shared IADCs, the experiencers are observing the same reality, so it probably is independent of both of them. Further study of the phenomenon is warranted.[42]

Worthy of note is that all observers of shared IADCs had undergone their own individual IADC before participating in the shared event. This was done as a way of sensitizing them to the phenomenon. Also, the observers "had a rapport with the IADC experiencer from listening to the experiencer's story and understanding the accompanying grief." Importantly, when the observer joined the session without knowledge of the patient's issues beforehand, the collective IADC could not be produced.[43]

ASSESSING INDUCIBLE APPARITIONS

Apparitions tend to be unexpected. Not so with inducible apparitions, essentially by definition. Given the expectation present, along with the deliberate processes used to invoke them, it becomes very difficult to rule out explaining inducible apparitions merely as hallucinations elicited by suggestion. The collective IADCs, however, resist such an explanation.

40. Botkin and Hogan, *Induced*, 111.
41. Botkin and Hogan, *Induced*, 111–12.
42. Botkin and Hogan, *Induced*, 113–14.
43. Botkin and Hogan, *Induced*, 114.

While mass hallucinations may occur when expectation is present, the very similar content (even when not a 100 percent match) in collective IADCs, I think, strains an interpretation based on subjective hallucinations.

As with our other categories, inducible apparitions that yield veridical information and are experienced collectively are difficult to explain in non-paranormal ways. During the EMDR therapy sessions, somehow the bystanders were on numerous occasions able to mentally tap in to the visual construct that the patients were experiencing.

Considering the general characteristics of these experiences, there are several aspects worthy of emphasis. First, as with spontaneous reunion apparitions and other forms of ADCs, inducible apparitions tend to provide great comfort and often profound psychological healing to the percipients. Second, as with reunion apparitions, the messages to percipients tend to be simple and frustratingly terse. Their purpose, with rare exception, seems to be in delivering reassurance. We do not find elaborate accounts of the intrepid adventures the deceased are experiencing in the great beyond. Third, inducible apparitions, particularly those produced through EMDR, have similar features as NDEs. Botkin notes numerous similarities, including the vividness and indescribable beauty that often form the backdrop of apparitions' surroundings, the profound sense of peace, the apparitions' appearances as younger (or in children's cases sometimes older), vibrant, healed versions of themselves, and the experiencer traversing a dark tunnel. One common experience of an NDE is an out-of-body experience (OBE). Botkin notes that while those experiencing IADCs do not experience OBEs, they do sometimes "report going back to the scene of the death of the person for whom they are grieving and witnessing the spirit moving out of the body."[44]

Scientists and doctors are still learning of the enormous complexity of the human body and its multifaceted physiological systems. This includes its ability to physically heal, often in ways that do not conform easily to materialist assumptions. Perhaps Dr. Botkin has managed to tap into a mechanism whereby psychological healing may be achieved in ways that even modern psychotherapy cannot often produce? He notes that IADCs are essentially just far richer versions of their more spontaneous ADC counterparts.[45] Spontaneous ADCs, including reunion appari-

---

44. Botkin and Hogan, *Induced*, 175–82.
45. Botkin and Hogan, *Induced*, 184–88.

tions, may be projections of one's subconscious onto external reality for the purposes of psychological healing. According to such a theory, the sources from which ADCs are derived are somewhere deep within the recesses of the agents' subliminal consciousness.[46]

MATERIALIZATIONS PRODUCED DURING SÉANCES

Prior to closing this chapter, it is worthwhile to consider the apparitions produced by entranced mediums. Mediumship is unfortunately fraught with fraud. Despite my general openness to the supernormal world, and although mediumship was a large area of focus amongst the earliest SPR researchers, I was not initially enthusiastic about studying this area of inquiry. Like most, I was once more likely to summarily dismiss mediumship altogether than to consider the possibility that legitimate supernormal events were produced by its practitioners. It does not help that mediums such as Eusapia Palladino and Carlos Mirabelli, who likely produced authentic psi phenomena, were also discovered to have in some cases engaged in fraud.[47]

Nevertheless, unbeknownst to most, authentic mediumship may in fact serve as the apogee of strongly evidenced supernormal manifestations. Often in very controlled conditions, séances have purportedly produced numerous instances of spirit possession, automatic writing, healings, and levitations of the sitter's table, the mediums themselves, and other objects. Sometimes material objects are made to pass through other material objects ("matter through matter"). Then there are apports, the transportation/teleportation of solid objects from houses miles away into the séance room. And of course, there are sometimes materialized entities produced who claim to be spirits of the deceased. Often the apparent is known to one or more of the sitters.

Along with some famous religious apparitions, materializations at séances are sometimes seen by large groups of people. Journalist Leslie Kean narrates the remarkable materialization of an apparition identified

---

46. Evidently, other psychotherapists have successfully produced IADCs using EMDR. See Induced After Death, "IADC Therapy."

47. Charles Richet lists more than thirty scientists who investigated Palladino's mediumship, and later notes, "During twenty years, from 1888 to 1908, she submitted, at the hands of the most skilled European and American experimentalists, to tests of the most rigorous and decisive kind, and during all this time men of science, resolved not to be deceived, have verified that even very large and massive objects were displaced without contact." Richet, *Thirty Years*, 412–13, 421.

as "Dr. Barnett" that she shared with nine other sitters on August 20th, 2015, during a séance of medium Stewart Alexander she had attended.[48] Kean also writes of one of Alec Harris's séances in 1952 that was attended by Theodore Johannes Haarhoff. Haarhoff was educated at Oxford, had earned two doctorates in classical languages, and was professor at the University of Witwatersrand in Johannesburg. The professor experienced the materialization of a "Greek philosopher he had worked with who came close to him and spoke in ancient Greek, using the correct pronunciation, which is different from that of modern Greek." He had examined the room beforehand and stated, "The materializing powers of Mr. Harris are astounding, unique, and entirely above suspicion."[49]

> And a very skeptical Albert Fletcher-Desborough, professional stage illusionist who did not believe anything he had heard about these séances, did such a thorough examination of the room and cabinet, looking for structural mechanisms like floor escapes and wall slides, that he was certain no one could come in or out. As he wrote in the *Liverpool Evening Express* and for *Psychic News* in 1974, "There was no chance for deception."[50]

Kean also relates the experience of former editor of *Psychic News* journal Maurice Barbanell, who "saw thirty forms materialize in good red light with twenty-seven sitters present for almost three hours" at one of Harris's séances. Barbanell claimed that he handled the "flowing ectoplasmic draperies, which were soft and silky to the touch" and even "shook hands with two forms" that were "firm and normal."[51]

Icelandic medium Indridi Indridason's séances commonly included drop-in visits by an entity that claimed to be the spirit of Emil Jensen. In one séance in 1907, Jensen's apparition was seen by forty sitters at once, including Hallgrimur Sveinsson, then bishop of Iceland, the magistrate of Reykjavik (who was eventually one of Iceland's five Supreme Court Judges), and the British consul. The large group "saw Jensen appear eleven times that evening in bright, luminous light," and the three officials "were unable to find any indication of fraud." Subsequently, the Bishop arranged for a séance to take place at the library in his own house where Indridi again accomplished various supernormal feats. "The Bishop

48. Kean, *Surviving Death*, 336–38.
49. Kean, *Surviving Death*, 312.
50. Kean, *Surviving Death*, 313.
51. Kean, *Surviving Death*, 313.

declared later that he was completely convinced that what he had observed was genuine."[52]

Another case that produced sixty signed witnesses is worth quoting at length. The following occurred during a séance of Brazilian medium, Carlos Mirabelli:

> The fifth sitting quoted occurred in Santos in the academy, 15:30 p.m. with 60 signing witnesses. First a woman appeared, talked and disappeared. A bell then raised itself into the air and began ringing. Mirabelli announced an apparition clad in white linen. The bell continued ringing. Dr. Bezerra de Menezes, well-known to all the people present, materialized. He talked to them about himself and about his presence. Various photos were made of him. Dr. Assumpcion and Dr. Mendonça examined the apparition physically. After 15 minutes of examination they announced to have found a perfectly human body with all the human physical qualities and functions. Dr. Archimedes Mendonça, when the apparition began to float just before its dematerialization, and when slowly the limbs disappeared, grasped at the torso, and fell in a faint. He awakened later in the next room, stating that he felt a sticky mass, before he lost his senses. Mirabelli was tied throughout the performance and the seals were found in order.[53]

In other accounts, Dr. Mendonça was reported to have experienced an electric shock that caused him to faint when grabbing the apparition's torso.[54] The generally skeptical psychical researcher Eric Dingwall assessed the case.

> I must confess, that, on a lengthy examination of the documents concerning Mirabelli, I find myself totally at a loss to come to any decision whatever on the case. It would be easy to condemn the man as a monstrous fraud and the sitters as equally monstrous fools. But I do not think that such a supposition will help even him who makes it. If the phenomena of Mirabelli took place in darkness or even in semi-darkness, ... then such an hypothesis would not be, perhaps, wholly impossible. I will even grant the possibility of wholesale confederacy and assume (for the sake

---

52. Haraldsson and Gissurarson, *Indridi Indridason*, 114–17. See also Haraldsson's more recent, complementary treatment where the circumstances surrounding one of Jensen's appearances support the survival of consciousness beyond bodily death. Haraldsson, "Possible Evidence of Survival," 294–300.

53. Driesch, "Carlos Mirabelli," 305–6.

54. See Dingwall, "Mirabelli" 300.

of argument) that the materializations are confederates of the medium or of the sitters. But confederates are human beings and human beings do not usually rise into the air, dissolve into pieces and float about in clouds of vapor. Confederates do not lose half their bodies, feel like flaccid sponges and give violent shocks to people who try to seize them. Not one of these things can be explained on the hypothesis of confederacy. Can they be explained at all? We cannot assume that the whole of the Report is a hoax. The alleged facts were the talk of Santos for months. It is clear that certain events happened which were described by those who witnessed them in the terms we have read above. What were those events? The answer to that question must be left to each individual reader.[55]

Unlike spontaneous apparitions, this one, if authentic, was able to undergo some manner of examination by the two physicians present, even if it did resist being grasped. Magicians are frequently able to duplicate the accomplishments of trance mediums as well as certain other paranormal manifestations. However, some mediums who have undergone serious investigation have produced remarkable supernormal feats, often despite very rigorously controlled conditions.[56]

---

55. Dingwall, "Amazing Case," 301–2.

56. The reader may be surprised to learn that the evidence supporting authentic mediumship is immense. Dramatic pyrotechnic displays of paranormal activity have been produced in séances by mediums such as Eusapia Palladino, D. D. Home, Indridi Indridason, Alec Harris, and Stewart Alexander, to name but a few. Authentic paranormal phenomena were often produced in séances in which these mediums were bound and which were held in many different locations—some of which were unfamiliar to the medium—were scrutinized beforehand by investigators, and were sometimes in good light. Not uncommonly, skeptics who attended the demonstrations left convinced that the supernormal occurrences were genuine. For extensive discussion of mediumship, possession, and the potential implications for survival, see Gauld, *Mediumship*, especially chs. 3–4 regarding Leonora Piper and Gladys Osborne Leonard. See also Alexander, *Memoirs*; Braude, *Dangerous*; Braude, *Immortal*, chs. 3 and 6; Braude, *Limits*, 53–148; Haraldsson, *Indridi Indridason*; Kean, *Surviving Death*, chs. 12–17 and 21–26; Myers, *Human Personality*, 2:189–277 and 2:500–627; Richet, *Thirty Years*, 401–545.

9

Apparitions of Jesus Christ

THERE ARE NUMEROUS APPARITIONS of Jesus Christ and the Blessed Virgin Mary that are not easily reduced to any of the prior seven categories of a more secular flavor that we have considered. While, for instance, reunion apparitions and induced apparitions frequently result in dramatic healing of a psychological nature, religious apparitions will sometimes bring physical healing.

Since New Testament times, adherents of some form of Christianity, and some who were not adherents, have experienced visions of Jesus Christ. Numerous such encounters, including in modern times, have been documented in books devoted to the subject.[1] Many of the percipients experience visions of Jesus that resemble the more secularized apparitions we have considered from the other categories. Below, I present a few reports that differ in important ways to what we have encountered thus far.

MIRACULOUS HEALING OF SPINAL MENINGITIS

Laura was eleven years old when she was diagnosed with meningitis, reportedly developing from a case of scarlet fever. Suffering from horrendous pain and what she described as "twisted legs," hers was a particularly complicated and severe case. She was at Ohio State University.

---

1. See Wiebe, *Visions*; Rees, *Eternity*; Sparrow, *I Am With You*; Sparrow, *Sacred Encounters*.

A doctor was flown in from Chicago to consult on her case. Towards the end, the doctors informed her parents that her death "would be a terrible thing; that it would be best for them not to see or hear, to go home."[2]

> I lost my sight and hearing, but before that, I saw my parents, grandparents, and the Reverend John Lang standing in the door of my room, not permitted to come in. The smiles, the thrown kisses, the waving good-bye I remember, and then the sea of pain.
>
> Later, after losing my eyesight, I was lying on my right side. I heard a voice behind me say, "Laura, turn over." . . . Turning, I saw Jesus. I remember no other words Jesus said to me, yet I know we talked. I watched his beautifully-shaped hand reach out and touch my leg.
>
> Sometime later, I remember remarking to a nurse about what pretty red hair she had. She looked at me in shocked surprise and rushed from the room. The room soon filled up with doctors asking questions. I was a very shy person and there were too many doctors, too many questions. . . .
>
> The Reverend Lang listened, asked questions, and took many notes. I couldn't see the face of Christ, as it was like looking into a light bulb. But his clothes, the color and material I had never seen—all that I can remember. I was very blonde with very pale skin—the skin of Christ was much darker. The color of a piece of his hair I saw fall on his left shoulder as he reached out his left hand to touch me was a color I had never seen. The Reverend Lang called it auburn.
>
> My parents were told I could not live—I did. I sat in a chair and heard I never would walk—I did. They were told I would never have children—I had three.[3]

COMBINED TOUCH AND SIGHT

This vision, having taken place in 1958, involves two young men, John and Nathan, who were attending a Bible college in Texas to prepare for pastoral work. Nathan was reportedly stricken with a viral illness that was not thought to be serious. John was taking care of Nathan during this time while the latter stayed in bed to recover.

> As he was praying for Nathan one night, he opened his eyes to look at his friend lying about eight feet away. John was shocked

---

2. Sparrow, *Sacred*, 22.
3. Sparrow, *Sacred*, 22–23.

to see someone standing over Nathan's bed, but facing and looking at him. John immediately identified the person as Jesus, in part because of the sense of awe that his appearance evoked. John was about to tell his sick friend what he was seeing when Jesus reached over and placed his hand on Nathan's forehead and disappeared. At that instant, Nathan leaped out of bed and ran down the halls of the dormitory shouting, "I've been healed, I've been healed."[4]

Nathan did not see anything but did feel something touch his head. John reports that Jesus appeared in line with traditional portrayals, about six feet tall, with no radiance, and was solid with "a long white robe, shoulder-length hair, and a short beard."[5]

Numerous other case reports of physical healings accompanying appearances of Jesus exist in the literature.[6]

Another aspect of certain religious apparitions that differs from the other categories is that the number of percipients may be larger by orders of magnitude.

JESUS APPEARS TO LARGE GROUPS IN OAKLAND, CA

Kenneth Logie was preaching one Sunday night at Lakeshore Gospel Chapel in April 1954, and about 9:15 p.m., he "saw a shadow on the exterior glass doors, made by someone standing outside." The door opened and Logie saw Jesus plainly walk down the aisle, turning to people on both sides and smiling as he made his way to the pulpit. He then reportedly moved right through the pulpit, placed his hand on Logie's shoulder, and Logie collapsed to the floor. Subsequently, Jesus knelt beside Logie and

---

4. Wiebe, *Visions*, ch. 7, para. 12.
5. Wiebe, *Visions*, ch. 7, para. 13.
6. See the case of Barry Dyck, who suffered three vertebral fractures and a herniated disc after a skiing accident. Jesus appeared to Barry at night, eight days into his hospitalization. Barry grasped Jesus' outstretched hand and pleaded, "Take me with you," being drawn by what he described as "an indescribable feeling of love." Jesus instead "somehow indicated" that his request would not be granted, but that he would be fine. Awakening the next day, Barry could see perfectly and was free of swelling and pain. Despite an anticipated three month hospitalization, Barry persuaded his attending physician to discharge him that day and within three to four days was able to resume an exercise plan that included running. Several weeks later, his primary care doctor ordered X-rays and found no evidence of fracture in his neck vertebrae at that point. The author was able to speak to some of Barry's friends who verified the claims. Wiebe, *Visions*, ch. 7, paras. 1–9.

spoke to him in a foreign language which Kenneth was able to interpret and responded in English. The event was witnessed by a congregation of about fifty people.[7]

Five years later, in May 1959, Jesus reportedly appeared to an even larger group. Mrs. Lucero was giving her testimony of a vision of Jesus she had experienced during a hospitalization when she "was thought to have died."[8]

> Kenneth said when Mrs. Lucero got up to tell her story, she was wearing a black rain-coat because the weather had been rainy that day. As she spoke about the vision she had experienced about a week earlier, she disappeared from view, and in her place stood a figure taken to be Jesus. He wore sandals, a glistening white robe, and had nail prints in his hands—hands that dripped with oil. Kenneth reports that this figure was seen by virtually everyone in the congregation, which he estimated at 200 people. He also reports that the figure was filmed (in color) by the church organist with the kind of eight-millimeter movie camera popular at the time. Kenneth says the organist was so awestruck that he shook and placed the camera on top of the organ in order to keep it steady. The appearance of the man was much like Sallman's *Head of Christ*. Kenneth says the effect upon the people in the church was electrifying. After several minutes, Jesus disappeared and Mrs. Lucero was again visible.[9]

Interestingly, the author of this source, New Testament scholar Phillip Wiebe, viewed the video in 1965. Hoping to see it again when he visited Kenneth Logie in 1991, it had unfortunately been stolen by that time. He discussed this reported apparition of Jesus in detail with not only Logie but also four or five other people who had been present when the event occurred.[10]

---

7. Wiebe, *Visions*, ch. 7, paras. 16–17.
8. Wiebe, *Visions*, ch. 7, para. 18.
9. Wiebe, *Visions*, ch. 7, para. 19.
10. See Wiebe, *Visions*, ch. 7, paras. 20–29. Regarding the controversy around the event, Wiebe states that Logie had dozens of fascinating stories revolving around the church, which included exorcisms, extraordinary healings, prophesies, and stigmata events.

JESUS APPEARS IN CHINA

Another interesting account of a religious vision occurred in China in January 1994. Karen Feaver, an aide to Frank Wolf, then a Virginia congressman, writes about phenomena that occurred when a message of faith and repentance was being preached before a crowd that was, for the first time ever, hearing the gospel preached.

> A vision of Jesus walking among them and then suffering on the cross appeared to all gathered. When the teacher told of Jesus rising from the dead, the vision showed Jesus ascending "to heaven gloriously." Through that vision, many people surrendered their lives to the Lord.[11]

---

11. Feaver, "Lessons," 34.

10

The Marian Apparition of Knock, Ireland

No two Marian apparitions are exactly alike, though there are often striking similarities. These appearances frequently occur when the religious community is undergoing tumultuous times, such as when being persecuted or suppressed by the rule of governments with anti-religious sentiments. This was particularly the case in Fátima, Portugal, early in the twentieth century, which we will discuss in the next chapter. Typically, there are one to a few initial seers, usually a child or children. A beautiful, sometimes luminous, woman appears unexpectedly to a seer or seers, at a particular location, such as a rock grotto. In prophetic fashion, the apparition may communicate information that is to be conveyed to the masses. This is often a warning of impending tragedy, such as war or famine, if the people do not repent and turn to God. This woman is eventually identified to be the Blessed Virgin Mary. Frequently, she will reappear at regular preannounced times and places to the seers. As knowledge of these visits grows, crowds gather around the seers at the time of the appearances. Generally, only the seer(s) will see and react with the apparition even though there may be hundreds to thousands of others present.

During these experiences, the visionaries may enter an altered state of consciousness. For instance, Bernadette Soubirous of Lourdes became entranced during her encounters and was seemingly impervious to distraction or pain.¹ Eventually, and most often at the request of the apparition, the appearances would be memorialized, often with the construction of a chapel or a shrine.² Over the ensuing decades, countless thousands of people would make pilgrimages to these sites. In some cases, most famously Lourdes, France, these sites serve as healing shrines where thousands of people over the course of decades to centuries would claim to experience miraculous healing. Not long after gaining notoriety, these visionary encounters would be subjected to scrutiny by the Roman Catholic Church, beginning typically with the local diocesan authorities. Some Marian apparitions would eventually be granted a seal of authenticity by the Church, or deemed worthy of belief.

In this chapter and the two following, I will discuss two Marian apparitions and one phenomenon ostensibly linked to a Marian apparition, that were each witnessed by a large collection of witnesses.

KNOCK, IRELAND

On August 21st, 1879, Margaret Beirne left her home to lock up the nearby parish church. Unexpectedly, she saw a bright light emanating near a large gable on the church's south end. Amidst a downpour of rain, she did not immediately investigate. Thirty minutes earlier, about 7:00 p.m., Mary McLoughlin, the housekeeper of the parish priest Archdeacon Cavanagh, had discovered the same mysterious light. Deciding to inspect the phenomenon a bit more closely, she "thought she saw three large figures standing against the gable, silhouetted by the light." At first, McLoughlin mistook the figures as statues, assuming they were the replacement for two others that had been toppled by a storm.

Somewhat later, around 8:00 p.m., accompanied by Margaret Beirne's sister Mary Beirne, McLoughlin once again passed by the church.³ Mary Beirne described the spectacle as follows.

> And at the distance of three hundred yards or so from the church, I beheld all at once, standing out from the gable, and rather to the west of it, three figures which, on more attentive inspection,

---

1. Odell, *Apparitions of Mary*, 99–100, 109.

2. The visions of the Blessed Virgin Mary on the Rue du Bac in Paris, France in 1830 were memorialized by the mass production and distribution of medals that reproduced and commemorated the vision of Catherine Labouré. See Odell, *Apparitions of Mary*, 65–79.

3. Odell, *Apparitions of Mary*, 146–48.

> appeared to be that of the Blessed Virgin, of Saint Joseph, and Saint John. That of the Blessed Virgin was life-size, the others apparently either not so big or not so high as her figure; they stood a little distance out from the gable wall, and as well as I could judge, a foot and a half or two feet from the ground. The Virgin stood erect, with eyes raised to heaven, her hands elevated to the shoulders or bosom; she wore a large cloak of a white color, hanging in full folds and somewhat loosely around her shoulders and fastened to the neck; she wore a crown on the head—rather a large crown—and it [the cloak] appeared to me somewhat yellower than the dress or robes worn by Our Blessed Lady.[4]

Within the apparitional tableau, Saint Joseph's head was bent towards the Blessed Virgin "as if paying her respect." He was aged, with a gray beard and graying hair. The third figure was thought by Mary Beirne to be a young version of Saint John. This figure donned a bishop's miter atop his head and held a book in his left hand, while his right hand was "raised in blessing."[5]

Mary Beirne compares the figure interpreted to be Saint John with a statue at a chapel in nearby Lekanvey. Unlike the Saint John figure, the statue at Lekanvey wore no miter on its head. However, like the apparitional figure, the statue did hold a book in the left hand with the fingers of the right hand raised. As was common with other seers, Beirne submitted that it was a matter of opinion and conjecture that this third figure in the apparitional tableau represented Saint John.[6]

Eleven-year-old Patrick Hill described the vision in vivid detail.

> The figures were full and round, as if they had a body and life; they said nothing, but as we approached, they seemed to go back a little toward the gable. I distinctly beheld the Blessed Virgin Mary, life size, standing about two feet or so above the ground, clothed in white robes.... She appeared to be praying; her eyes were turned, as I saw, towards heaven; she wore a brilliant crown on her head, and over the forehead, where the crown fitted the brow, a beautiful rose; the crown appeared brilliant, and of a golden brightness, of a deeper hue, inclined to a mellow yellow, than the striking whiteness of the robes she wore; the upper parts of the crown appeared to be a series of sparkles, or glittering crosses.[7]

---

4. Odell, *Apparitions of Mary*, 148.
5. Odell, *Apparitions of Mary*, 37.
6. MacPhilpin, *Depositions*, 37–38.
7. MacPhilpin, *Depositions*, 32–33.

Like the testimony of Mary Beirne, Hill said of the Saint John figure that he was holding a "Mass Book" or a "Book of the Gospels" in his left hand. He said that when he came near the apparitions, he was even able to see the lines and the letters in the book.[8]

Another witness, seventy-four-year-old Bridget French, tried to touch the feet of the Blessed Virgin in an act of devotion but was unsuccessful. As with Patrick Hill, when approached the figures seemed to recede out of reach yet never left their sight.[9] Despite the pouring rain, the figures appeared to remain dry and continued to emit their radiant light.[10] Eventually, many of the seers went to see an ill neighbor to pray with her. By the time they passed by the church again, the apparitional figures, along with the mysterious light, had disappeared. The vision lasted for at least two hours.[11]

Even when large crowds are present when a principal seer (or seers) experience a vision of Mary, the crowds themselves usually see nothing. This Marian apparition was different, as all who came to the church that night saw it. At least fifteen people witnessed the spectacle and would later be deposed by the local diocesan authorities. As we will see below, however, there were some elements that were reported by some to be part of the apparitional tableau, such as an altar, a lamb, and a cross, that went unreported by others.

As with many sites of famous Marian apparitions, the church at Knock, Ireland had to expand to accommodate the many people that would subsequently visit the site. That is probably why Knock has its own international airport. A new church that could accommodate thousands of pilgrims was dedicated there in 1976, the Church of Our Lady Queen of Ireland. Well over one to one-half million travelers have visited Knock by recent times.[12] Similar to Lourdes, France and Betania, Venezuela (see next chapter), hundreds of miraculous cures have been reported at the Knock shrine.[13]

---

8. MacPhilpin, *Depositions*, 34.
9. MacPhilpin, *Depositions*, 33, 42–43.
10. MacPhilpin, *Depositions*, 43; Odell, *Apparitions of Mary*, 150.
11. MacPhilpin, *Depositions*, 132.
12. MacPhilpin, *Depositions*, 135–36.
13. MacPhilpin published a list of several dozen people allegedly cured (miraculously) within seven months of the night of the Knock apparition. See MacPhilpin, *Depositions*, 64–71.

SOURCE EVALUATION OF THE KNOCK APPARITION

Overall, I find the earliness of the published reports to be impressive evidence favoring the authenticity of the vision. That is not to deny that there are some problems. Academic sociologist Eugene Hynes writes,

> That an investigating commission heard testimony from witnesses in Knock church for one day only, 8 October 1879, six weeks after the reports of the apparitions is not questioned, but practically everything else about it is. Who set up the commission? Who were its members and how many were there? What was its task or who decided this question? How did it do its work? To whom, if anybody, did it report? And what did it report? What relationship do the available published versions of the seers' testimony bear to what witnesses might have told the commission? Answers to these and numerous other basic questions are unclear or unavailable.[14]

The earliest evidence indicates that the archbishop of Tuam, John MacHale, appointed the investigative commission, though some later sources from the 1920s–1930s claim that his successor, John MacEvilly, did so. Hynes concludes that because MacEvilly himself later wrote that MacHale appointed the commission, the latter is likely the case.[15]

The investigative commission was comprised of at least three parish priests: Archdeacon Bartholomew Cavanagh of Knock, Canon James Waldron of Ballyhaunis, and Canon Ulick Bourke of Claremorris.[16] The commission undertook an investigation and heard testimony from fifteen of the eyewitnesses on October 8th, 1879.[17] Unfortunately the commission's report is not available, nor is it clear how or when or to whom it was reported.[18] Early the following year, however, versions of the witnesses' testimonies were published in two books by sympathetic authors, John MacPhilpin and Thomas Sexton.[19]

14. Hynes, *Knock*, 174.

15. Hynes, *Knock*, 174–76.

16. A discrepancy exists among the earliest sources regarding the number of appointed priests. According to a writing by Jesuit priest Friar Edward Murphy, MacHale appointed four priests. See Hynes, *Knock*, 176.

17. One of the fifteen witnesses, Patrick Walsh, did not see the apparition but testified to seeing "a bright light at the church from his farm half a mile away." Hynes, *Knock*, 178.

18. Hynes, *Knock*, 176–78.

19. Regarding one of the authors, John MacPhilpin, Hynes states that his book "is not just a report of what the witnesses said but a sustained and detailed argument for

It appears that the priests who collected the witnesses' testimonies, as well as the authors who published the content of their interviews, were sympathetic to the view that Knock had received a supernatural visitation. Moreover, the clergy had discouraged earlier newspaper coverage of the event, and the first reports to be subject to media publication were only those endorsed by Friar Cavanagh and/or Canon Bourke. Hynes states that the reports also "gave no hint about how the seers interpreted (as opposed to described) the episode."[20]

MacPhilpin's book reads as a summary of the interviewees' experiences rather than as a question and answer session that we may have otherwise expected.[21] Nevertheless, on my read of MacPhilpin, it remains clear from the summaries that some of the interpretive speculations of the seers were preserved. Still, Hynes fairly asks,

> If one book claims to present the "official testimony, . . . the best reliable and authentic evidence," . . . and another book prints a "full and perfect copy of the text of the deposition," . . . how can we account for differences between the versions of the same original witness statements?[22]
>
> Even unquestioning believers such as Walsh accept that the published "depositions" in Sexton and MacPhilpin must have gone through many stages of development and elaboration. The secretary of the Second Commission of Enquiry that sat in the 1930s recorded that "it appeared to the judges that all the old depositions attributed to the witnesses must have been cast into form by someone."[23]

---

the truth of the claims of a supernatural apparition and the occurrence of miracles." MacPhilpin also was owner and editor of the first newspaper to cover the apparitional event on January 9th, 1880. *Tuam News* had also been founded by Canon Bourke, who was MacPhilpin's uncle and one of the members of the investigative commission. The author of the other very early book, Thomas Sexton, was similarly connected and was, per Hynes, "clerical" in orientation. Sexton served as "special correspondent" on reporting the events in Dublin's newspaper *Nation* (and its "cheaper sister version the *Weekly News*") in eight weekly reports between January 31st, 1880 through March 20th, 1880. Sexton was likewise "on excellent terms" with at least two of the priests who comprised the commission, Bourke and Cavanagh. Hynes, *Knock*, 179, 180-82.

20. "The burden of proof was thereby shifted from those who would claim a supernatural miracle to those who might question or deny it, while all the evidence provided was framed to support the claim." Hynes, *Knock*, 182.

21. MacPhilpin, *Depositions*, 30–47.

22. Hynes, *Knock*, 183.

23. Hynes, *Knock*, 185.

The evolution of the reports conforms to the event's interpretation. This may be seen by the following comparison of MacPhilpin's rendition of Mary McLoughlin's testimony to the same excerpt in Sexton's book.

> I saw a wonderful number of strange figures or appearances at the gable, one like the B. V. Mary, and one like St Joseph, another a bishop.[24]

> I saw a vision in which there appeared to be three figures—one that of the Blessed Virgin Mary, one of St Joseph, and the other to be, as I thought, the likeness of St John the Evangelist.[25]

Some seers reported the presence of an altar, a lamb, and/or a cross in the apparitional tableau, while others did not report these elements.
Patrick Hill said,

> On the altar stood a Lamb-the size of a lamb eight weeks old; the face of the Lamb was fronting the west, and looking in the direction of the Blessed Virgin and Saint Joseph; behind the Lamb a large cross was placed erect or perpendicular on the altar.[26]

Mary McLoughlin also specifically mentioned seeing the cross.[27] Mary Beirne and Margaret Beirne claimed to see an altar and a lamb, but specifically mention *not* seeing a cross.[28] More than half of the witnesses do not mention an altar, lamb, or a cross in their interviews, and others who did report them were found upon future interviews to be doubtful of these elements' presence.[29]

By way of summary, we have a commission of three (or four) priests who interviewed fifteen of the witnesses of the Knock apparition six weeks after the event. Two sympathetic authors published the content from these interviews early the next year. The content of the vision was framed by the investigators, who also apparently exerted some control over the media coverage it was to receive, and the content evolved in later publications. Moreover, some of the elements in traditional depictions of the Knock apparition may have been added at an early stage.

24. MacPhilpin's version as quoted in Hynes, *Knock*, 186.
25. Sexton's version as quoted in Hynes, *Knock*, 186.
26. MacPhilpin, *Depositions*, 34. Based on all the seers' interview summaries, Hill was apparently alone in seeing angels around the lamb whose wings were fluttering.
27. MacPhilpin, *Depositions*, 35.
28. MacPhilpin, *Depositions*, 38, 40.
29. Hynes, *Knock*, 198–203.

What I think may be reasonably concluded from the data is that at least fourteen people saw an apparition of three figures, two of which were identified to represent the Blessed Virgin Mary and St. Joseph from a very early stage. The third figure was thought initially to be an unknown bishop based on the attire, but subsequent speculation at a very early stage identified this third figure as St. John the Evangelist. Despite early reports of the presence of an altar, lamb, and cross, these elements may be later inauthentic adornments of the core event.[30]

ALTERNATIVE EXPLANATIONS

As the figures in the Knock apparition remained stationary, did not communicate with any of the seers, and projected their own luminosity, the question naturally arises as to whether this could have been simply a projected image upon the gable wall by a magic lantern.[31] In other words, perhaps this was the result of pious fraud.[32] Nickell argues that the apparition may have been an optical illusion created by sunrays, rainy mist, and reflective windows. Perhaps a natural, optical phenomenon projected upon the gable wall, combined with individuals' hopes of experiencing a miracle, led to the description and interpretation it was ultimately given.[33]

I think a man made projection by a magic lantern or similar device is highly unlikely, as this possibility was considered and refuted even at the time of the vision. A more complex optical illusion, requiring the right constellation of atmospheric conditions and an imaginative desire on the part of multiple witnesses to convince themselves that vague silhouettes projected on a gable wall were the Blessed Virgin Mary, St. Joseph, and an unknown bishop, I think is only slightly better speculation. Most likely, the witnesses experienced well-defined, objective apparitions of three figures that appeared in similar ways as other apparitions do in nature. Perhaps the location (at a church) and pious desire aided the apparent interpretation of who these figures specifically represented.

---

30. We have seen that collectively experienced apparitions may appear somewhat differently to percipients.

31. Magic lanterns require an image to be placed on a transparent plate. When a light source is supplied, an inverted image is projected.

32. See Hynes, *Knock*, 211–14, for a discussion of this view and a refutation.

33. Nickell, "Tableau," accessed on 6/1/25.

11

The Marian Apparition of Betania, Venezuela

FOLLOWING NOON MASS ON March 25th, 1984, children played near a man made rock grotto that was bordered by a panoply of fresh flowers, a spring-fed waterfall on the right side of the structure, and a statue of Our Lady of Lourdes at its focal point. The adults were relaxing nearby shortly after a lunch supplied by a variety of tropical fruit trees that grew on the farm.

Around 3:00 p.m., one child ran excitedly back to the picnic tables and shady spots where the adults were relaxing. Breathlessly, the child told the grown-ups that the Blessed Mother was appearing above the waterfall, near the grotto. Word spread. Soon, all of the people rushed to the rock grotto to see what they could see. There, more than one hundred people saw her.

Our Lady's glowing white figure stood out against the dark green trees near the waterfall. Many people began to pray the Rosary, cry out, and weep with joy as they pointed to the figure of the Virgin. The apparition of Mary didn't speak or move. In that sense, she initially seemed like a statue. "It's Our Lady of Lourdes," a few whispered to one another. While some people saw her facial features, which were breathtakingly beautiful, others couldn't seem to see her that clearly.

A blue sash was tied around her waist, many reported. A few also said that they saw her holding a baby, the Infant Jesus.[1]

---

1. Odell, *Apparitions of Mary*, 266.

At first blush, the vision strikes one as potentially being accounted for by false sensory experiences. The vision was of Our Lady of Lourdes, a manifestation of the Blessed Virgin that was clearly revered by those that attended mass there, as evidenced by the statue in the rock grotto. Expectation of a vision at that time and place was created by the young child who reported it to the adults. Of the many seers, some saw her features clearly, but others did not. Some apparently saw additional aspects of the vision that were not visible to most. I think hallucinatory aspects of this vision cannot be ruled out for these reasons. Also, one wonders if illusion is a possible explanation. Could the vision have been produced by the way the sunlight filtered through the dark green forest? Perhaps the light reflecting off the water and the statue somehow played a factor?

I think illusion is less likely because it was apparently considered by the seers at the time of the vision.

> Nonetheless, the visual presence of a woman's figure was so clear and unmistakable that a few people began to look around to see if something "natural" was producing the image. Could the figure be a reflection of the statue in the grotto? Was it an image thrown against the leafy backdrop by a hidden projector? Was there technological trickery involved?
>
> After about fifteen minutes, it seemed as if the image of Our Lady evaporated, or was absorbed back into the trees. Suddenly, she was gone—just as suddenly as she had arrived. Within a short time, however, she appeared again, even as people discussed their first experiences....
>
> During the last (seventh) appearance, just before sundown, the Virgin Mary stayed for about thirty minutes, the longest visit. This time, everyone agreed that she looked like a real person, although a person whose beauty had no earthly comparisons. The image was sharper, more defined. None of the visionaries was now inclined to describe the figure as a statue or as a filmy figure. It was a woman, a heavenly woman! As before, the Virgin spoke no words to those who prayed and sang in front of her.
>
> There were many young people and many poor people from the city at Betania on this March day. Also among the witnesses, however, were students, doctors, lawyers, a judge, priests, an army general, and even some atheists (who had no idea that the farm "Finca Betania" already had a reputation as a place favored by Mary). In all, 108 people saw her on March 25th, 1984.[2]

---

2. Odell, *Apparitions of Mary*, 266–67.

There is a backstory to this collective vision. Maria Esperanza Medrano de Bianchini, from Caracas, was one of those present on March 25th, 1984. From the age of five, Esperanza experienced numerous visions of Jesus, Mary, and others such as St. Thérèse of Lisieux throughout the course of her life. Ill with severe pneumonia at the age of twelve, in a response to prayer, Esperanza experienced a vision of the Virgin Mary that reportedly told her what medications she needed. Subsequently she obtained the medications and recovered.[3]

In June of 1974, Maria and her husband, Geo Bianchini, would purchase Finca Betania. On March 25th, 1976, Esperanza had a vision of the Blessed Virgin near the rock grotto, close to the exact location where more than one hundred would see her eight years later to the day. An enormous white cloud emanated from the farm that appeared to be on fire, like a candle. She was described thusly:

> And when she revealed herself, she went up to the top of the tree, and I saw she was beautiful, with her brown hair, dark brown, her eyes that were light brown, and she had very fine, very pretty eyebrows, tiny mouth, a nose very straight, and her complexion was so beautiful; it was skin that seemed like silk. It was bronzed. It was beautiful. Very young. Her hair was down to here, to her shoulders.[4]

Maria saw the apparition of the Virgin with outstretched hands from which light streamed, though she points out that "everything was (already) full of light."

> "My little daughter," the Virgin Mary told her, "tell my children of all races, of all nations, of all religions, that I love them. . . . I come to gather all of them to help them to go up to the high mountain of Mount Zion to my fertile land of Betania in these times so that they can be saved.
>
> "I love all of them—the youth, the innocent children, the beloved baby just born," the Virgin said. "To the youth I am directing myself so that they will really serve me and make me happy, so that they go to the foot of the cross and continue going . . . to save the world."
>
> Toward the end of the apparition, Mary spoke to Esperanza again. She said, "Little daughter, you are beholding me with my

---

3. Odell, *Apparitions of Mary*, 268–69.
4. Odell, *Apparitions of Mary*, 272.

hands outstretched with graces and wrapped in the splendor of
light to call all my children to conversion."[5]

Eighty people were present at the time of the apparition, including her family, but as with most Marian apparitions, this time only Maria saw the Blessed Virgin. Later that August, Maria again saw Mary, this time wearing a blue sash as had the Marian apparition that appeared in Lourdes, France. On March 25th, 1977, Mary's appearance was once again preceded by a bright light that again concerned at least one spectator that the farm was burning. As with the apparition from one year prior, none of those present with Maria saw the Virgin Mary emanate from the light as Maria did.[6]

One year later, March 25th, 1978, Maria's vision was yet again accompanied by a brilliant light that caused the perception that "the whole area appeared to be on fire" and "the sun began to gyrate, and everyone was shouting with emotion."[7] As for Maria, she had fallen to the ground during the vision and was subsequently raised into the air, reportedly tasked with "bringing the message of peace and reconciliation to all nations." Esperanza's apparent levitation was witnessed by her daughter Maria Garcia and her goddaughter Jacqueline. Both were extremely terrified.[8] Moreover, the collective vision that was to occur on March 25th, 1984, was foretold by Mary to Maria.

> Mary had promised Esperanza that many people would see wonders on March 25, 1984. And many did. Immediately, it was no longer a matter of private revelation for Señora Esperanza de Bianchini. On the other side of the world, on the same day, Pope John Paul II consecrated the world and Russia to the Immaculate Heart of Mary. The Act of Consecration was done in conjunction with all of the Catholic and Orthodox bishops of the world. According to Sister Lucia, the only visionary of Fátima still surviving then, this Act of Consecration finally fulfilled the request for consecration that Our Lady had made in 1917.[9]

---

5. Odell, *Apparitions of Mary*, 273–74.
6. Odell, *Apparitions of Mary*, 274–75.
7. Odell, *Apparitions of Mary*, 278.
8. Odell, *Apparitions of Mary*, 278.
9. Odell, *Apparitions of Mary*, 281.

It is worth noting that Maria endured other paranormal phenomena related to her calling.[10]

Pio Bello Ricardo was the bishop of the local Diocese of Los Teques. Until 1984, he had been reluctant to investigate the happenings at Finca Betania to adjudicate authenticity. However, after the collective vision, he headed the inquiry himself, obtaining the written testimonies from all who saw the Virgin Mary. Those that had been written by several agnostics and atheists were among the most persuasive testimonies.

> For three years, he gathered information about Betania. Reports of healings and conversions stacked up. Bishop Ricardo sent his findings and copies of statements from witnesses to Rome. Twice, he discussed Betania with Cardinal Joseph Ratzinger, the future Pope Benedict XVI. He also informed Pope John Paul II about events taking place in his diocese.
>
> In Betania, Bishop Ricardo later explained, the message of the Betania apparitions is quite simple. Peace and reconciliation! In a sense, these two crucial needs of the world are beyond words. And at Betania, he said, "Few people have had oral communication with the Blessed Mother, perhaps five percent. Say about twenty people from about one thousand to two thousand in total. . . . What has happened is a strengthening of faith here, conversion, growth of Christian life, frequency of receiving the sacraments, prayer, especially Mass and the Holy Rosary."[11]

As with Lourdes, pilgrims would find healing at Betania. On May 12th, 1986, Dr. Vinicio Arrieta, the director of the School of Medicine at the University of Zulia, was instantly cured of prostate cancer that had metastasized to the spine. He had been praying throughout the night and fell asleep on the ground in pouring rain. The following morning, Dr. Arrieta, along with his family and thousands of others, witnessed the sun turning green at its center and then descending upon the excited crowd. Dr. Arrieta felt that he was being cured as the heat pervaded his body, and this was confirmed with tests five days later. He had been treated prior to this with two rounds of chemotherapy.[12] It is worth noting that, at the time of this writing nearly four decades after this event, metastatic prostate

---

10. On fourteen occasions, a red rose formed on Esperanza's chest, reportedly causing her pain and embarrassment, appearing "as a tiny red bud, the beautiful and fragrant rose grew, flower and stem, in a matter of minutes." This process occurred under the observation of witnesses. See Odell, *Apparitions of Mary*, 281.

11. Odell, *Apparitions of Mary*, 282–83.

12. Odell, *Apparitions of Mary*, 283.

cancer is treatable with hormonal therapy, radiation, and chemotherapy, but is unfortunately still not curative.

As of 1987, five hundred cures had been reported at Betania. On November 21st of the same year, Bishop Ricardo declared that the Marian apparitions are "authentic and of a supernatural character." Our Lady, Reconciler of Peoples at Betania, was the fourth Marian apparition of the twentieth century to be approved as authentic by the Roman Catholic Church.[13]

---

13. Odell, *Apparitions of Mary*, 283.

12

The Miracle of the Sun in Fátima, Portugal

THREE SHEPHERD CHILDREN WERE occupied with the construction of a "house" made of rocks and a tangle of bushes as their sheep grazed nearby at the Cova da Iria, a piece of mountainous terrain just a couple of miles to the west of Fátima. A brilliant flash of light suddenly commanded their attention. Initially thinking it to be a bolt of lightning, they ran down a slope toward a four foot tall holm oak tree where they found that a luminous globe had settled at the top. Inside this brilliant sphere was a beautiful woman who claimed to be from heaven. Later this woman, ostensibly of celestial provenance, was identified as the Virgin Mary. Lucia dos Santos, then ten years old, would describe her as "a Lady of all white, more brilliant than the sun dispensing light, clearer and more intense than a crystal cup full of crystalline water penetrated by the rays of the most glaring sun."[1]

The vision occurred on May 13th, 1917. Lucia dos Santos was accompanied by her younger cousins, Francisco and Jacinta Marto, then nine and seven years old, respectively. Mary was to appear again to the three children on the thirteenth of each subsequent month, for a total of six appearances, until the final appearance on October 13th, at which time a miracle had been prophesied to occur. As knowledge of the apparitions spread to the public, crowds joined the seers at the time of the

1. Odell, *Apparitions of Mary*, 158.

appearances, culminating in a crowd of between fifty and one hundred thousand spectators on October 13th, 1917.

Lucia dos Santos was the only one of the three children who interacted with Mary and the crowds, though she was also seen and heard by Jacinta Marto, and seen but *not* heard by Francisco Marto. Other witnesses would see or hear effects of the Virgin's presence at the time of the appearances even though they did not actually see the apparition of Mary.[2]

Given the events that transpired in the months following the initial appearances, the sincerity of the three seers can scarcely be questioned. The children were ridiculed, even by family, especially Lucia. There were attempted bribes, such as offerings of jewelry, if they disclosed the secrets given them ostensibly by Mary. They were also subjected to interrogations by the local religious authorities and eventually by Arturo Santos, the county mayor. In fact, Santos had the children put in jail and threatened to throw them alive, one-by-one, into a cauldron of boiling oil if they did not reveal the secrets. Despite all this, the children did not disclose the secrets nor recant their visions.[3]

In addition to the perceived miraculous nature of the apparitions, several miracles are said to have been associated with these appearances. The Blessed Virgin is said to have predicted the early deaths of two of the seers, Jacinta and Francisco, who did in fact die during the influenza epidemic of 1919 and 1920, respectively. Also, Mary revealed three secrets to the children over the course of the six appearances. The first was a very brief, yet very frightening, vision of hell with demons and sinners seen in torment. The second was a prediction of the end of the Great War (World War I), but with a warning that another, even more deadly war would break out if people did not stop offending God. The third, not made public until May of 2000 by Pope John Paul II, is often interpreted, including by the pope himself, as a prediction of the assassination attempt against him on May 13th, 1981, in St. Peter's Square.[4]

On an evidentiary basis, there are some problems with accepting these predictions as accurate prophetic fulfillment. The predictions of the impending deaths of Jacinta and Francisco Marto, as well as that of the

---

2. Zimdars-Swartz, *Encountering Mary*, 79–80. This includes such reports as seeing a "grayish cloud" resting on an oak tree (where Mary was to appear), hearing a sound like a rocket taking off as she was leaving, and observing that the shoots atop the oak tree that had been standing straight up were bent toward the east after the appearance.

3. Zimdars-Swartz, *Encountering Mary*, 190–94.

4. Zimdars-Swartz, *Encountering Mary*, 298

end of World War I and the onset of World War II, were not recorded until after the fact, when Lucia had penned her four *Memoirs* between 1935 and 1941.[5] Furthermore, there are problems in the interpretation of the alleged prediction of the pope's assassination.[6] Also, Lucia reportedly predicted that the Great War would end on the day of the miracle of the sun, though this did not occur until thirteen months later.[7]

The miracle of the sun that occurred on October 13th, 1917, however, is another matter entirely. Around solar noon, when Mary was making her final appearance to the children, something magnificent did occur as predicted.

It had been an overcast morning as rain poured down relentlessly on the masses of people making their way up the mountain to Cova da Iria. Local military forces attempted to stop the people on their trek, but it was to no avail, as there were too many travelers determined to see what would transpire. The crowd was standing in mud and several inches of groundwater,[8] their clothes soaked through from the downpour, as they awaited the commencement of the last apparition to Lucia dos Santos, Jacinta Marto, and Francisco Marto.

Finally, the rain stopped and the clouds parted, at least enough for the crowd of tens of thousands of onlookers to see the sun. Only something was off. The sun appeared as a "gray disc" that could be gazed upon safely with the unaided eye. Very shortly after, the sun appeared to spin upon its axis while emitting a spectrum of colored rays, one color enveloped the earth and the heavens above, to eventually be replaced with another color on the visible light spectrum. Moreover, the sun was said to "dance" or "roll" or "zigzag" across the sky and even appeared to plummet close to the earth. The crowd was very frightened. Many thought it was the end of the world. Others were compelled to confess their sins aloud in response to the apocalyptic vision. The event occurred over a ten to fifteen minute time span, at the end of which the sun was instantly seen to be back in its expected place in the sky, no longer rolling or gyrating. Despite having been drenched by the rain just prior to the vision, those in the crowd discovered their clothing to be completely dry afterwards. Even the water that had accumulated on the ground had dried up.

5. Zimdars-Swartz, *Encountering Mary*, 198–200.
6. Nickell, *Science of Miracles*, 254–55.
7. Evans and Bartholomew, *Outbreak!*, 167.
8. According to Dominic Reis, who was present on that day, there were three inches of water on the ground before the vision occurred. See Haffert, *Witnesses*, 7.

THE MIRACLE OF THE SUN IN FÁTIMA, PORTUGAL   105

Moreover, this spectacle was seen by people from miles away, and stories were written about it in local newspapers.

I find it very difficult to explain the miracle of the sun on purely materialistic grounds. It is true that the weather conditions that day, heavy rain followed by the sudden appearance of the sun, were conducive for creating optical effects. Rainbows would not hardly have been surprising, but as far as I am aware, that entails the simultaneous production of all colors of the spectrum. The event at the Cova da Iria on that day produced a series of colorful deluges that encompassed everything upon the earth and the clouds in the sky. One eyewitness, Maria Teresa of Chainca, put it this way:

> The sky was covered with clouds and it rained much. We could not see the sun. Then suddenly, at noon, the clouds drew away and the sun appeared as if it were trembling. It seemed to come down. It began spinning like a fire-wheel in the pagan feasts. It stopped for a few minutes and again started rolling, perhaps in a diameter of more than a meter, while we could look at it as though it were the moon. Things all around turned into different colors.[9]

Not your typical rainbow experience, to put it mildly.

Some have conjectured that the crowds may have seen a sun dog (or mock sun, or parhelion). Sun dogs are "colored spots of light that develop due to the refraction of light through ice crystals" and "are located approximately twenty-two degrees either left, right, or both, from the sun, depending on where the ice crystals are present." Furthermore, sun dogs can present as colors on the spectrum, with red being on the inside (closest to the sun) and blue on the outside.[10]

There are at least a couple of problems with this hypothesis. First, sun dogs, in their most impressive manifestations, appear as an alternative light in the sky, as if there were two suns. However, the mock sun is fixed twenty-two degrees from the sun. In other words, from the point of view of a ground observer, sun dogs do not gyrate in the sky as the sun was seen to do at Fátima. Second, sun dogs typically precede precipitation rather than occurring just afterwards (like rainbows).[11] There are other problems that we will deal with presently.

---

9. Haffert, *Witnesses*, 44–45.
10. National Weather Service, "Halos, Sundogs." Accessed on 4/3/2022.
11. Garriss, "What Are Sun Dogs?" Accessed on 6/20/2025.

Nickell takes a multifactorial approach, suggesting optical effects may have been in play. He suggests the possibility of transient retinal distortion caused by staring at an intensely bright object, or "the effect of darting the eyes to and fro to avoid fixed gazing (thus combining image, afterimage, and movement)." Moreover, local meteorological factors could have been involved. For instance, the sun may have appeared as a silver disc because it was seen through a layer of thin clouds. Nickell goes on to suggest that atmospheric moisture and particulate matter such as dust may have produced a refraction effect on the incoming sunlight causing it to filter down to the crowd in various colors of the visible spectrum. He also correctly states that the conditions for suggestion or mass hysteria were in place as many in the crowd came expecting to see a miracle.[12]

At the end of the day, I do not find this constellation of purported explanations convincing. John Haffert deposed dozens of witnesses who were present at the miracle of the sun. The vast majority reported seeing essentially the same thing as described above, though there were a couple of important exceptions.[13] However, it is the impact and breadth of the event upon the witnesses that I find so compelling. A common theme across Haffert's depositions were respondents claiming that they thought the world was coming to an end. Believers and unbelievers alike served as witnesses, including those that did not expect to see a miracle.

> For example, we have the Baron of Alvaiazere, who carefully took all precautions outlined by Gustave le Bon in his *Psychology of the Crowd*. The Baron had not expected a miracle and wanted to be sure that he would not be the victim of suggestion. He died in 1955, and in a deposition to the Canonical Committee he stated, . . . "An indescribable impression overtook me I only know that I cried out: 'I believe! I believe! I believe!' And tears ran from my eyes, I was amazed, in ecstasy before the demonstration of Divine Power. . . . I converted in that moment."
>
> Doctor Garrett, a professor from the University of Coimbra, in detailed testimony describes that he feared some impairment to his retina, covered his eyes and turned in an opposite

---

12. Nickell, *Science of Miracles*, 251–52.

13. For instance, José Joaquim da Silva saw the sky become clear and indicated that everyone could safely gaze at the sun. Unlike the others, he did not see the sun plummet from the sky, though he stated that he felt that God had given many people a spectacular vision and testified that "they were saying that the world was going to end." Haffert, *Witnesses*, 67–68.

direction, opened his eyes again . . . and continued to see the miracle.

Several other men of science, who were actual witnesses, testified to the objective reality of the phenomenon and added that no natural explanation could be given.

Pio Sciatizzi, S. J., a scientist who published a critique of the Miracle in Rome, says: "Of the historic reality of this event there can be no doubt whatsoever. That it was outside and against known laws can be proved by certain simple scientific considerations." And he concludes:

"Given the indubitable reference to God, and the general context of the event, it seems that we must attribute to Him alone *the most obvious and colossal miracle of history.*"[14]

Also railing heavily against collective suggestion or mass hysteria is the fact that the miracle was seen by people at a distance from the Cova da Iria. According to Haffert, the miracle was visible across an area of about six hundred square miles. Doubtless many of these distant observers were aware that the solar phenomenon was anticipated to occur by a multitude on this day; they were probably just going about their daily lives at the time the spectacle demanded their attention. The impact on some of these distant observers was no less significant than that of the tens of thousands that were in the proximity of the seers at the time. One such distant observer, then a schoolboy, who would go on to become a priest, was with his brother in the village of Alburitel at the time. Father Lourenço gives the following testimony:

> I feel incapable of describing what I saw: I looked fixedly at the sun which seemed pale and did not hurt my eyes.
>
> Looking like a ball of snow, revolving on itself, it suddenly seemed to come down in a zigzag, menacing the earth. Terrified, I ran and hid myself among the people, who were weeping and expecting the end of the world at any moment. It was a crowd which had gathered outside our local village school and we had all left classes and run into the streets because of the cries and surprised shouts of men and women who were in front of the school when the miracle began.
>
> There was an unbeliever there who had spent the morning mocking the "simpletons" who had gone off to Fatima just to see an ordinary girl. He now seemed paralyzed, his eyes fixed on the

---

14. Haffert, *Witnesses*, 17, emphasis original.

sun. He began to tremble from head to foot, and lifting up his arms, fell on his knees in the mud, crying out to God.

But meanwhile the people continued to cry out and to weep, asking God to pardon their sins. We all ran to the two chapels in the village, which were soon filled to overflowing. During those long moments of the solar prodigy, objects around us turned all colors of the rainbow.... When the people realized that the danger was over, there was an explosion of joy.[15]

We have commented elsewhere that sometimes apparitional phenomena will change the physical environment. The miracle of the sun was no different in this regard. I first read about the miracle of the sun from a devotional source; hence, I initially figured the details about the ground and the inundated clothes worn by the crowd becoming dry were likely apocryphal. However, those details too appear to be part of the core event, as numerous of Haffert's depositions of eyewitnesses' attest.[16]

In closing, it bears mentioning that clearly the sun did not *actually* make the movements observed at Fátima. Astronomical observatories at the time did not report anything unusual, though this is not surprising. If the phenomena observed near Fátima reflected an astronomical reality, the sun's gravitational pull that keeps the solar system intact would have been traumatically disrupted, and life as we know it would have quickly ended. This was a collective vision. Nevertheless, that so many experienced essentially the same vision leads me to the conclusion that this vision was objective in nature, that is *not* hallucinatory, at least not at its core.[17]

CHARACTER OF MARIAN APPARITIONS

The Blessed Virgin Mary tends to be seen and/or heard only by the principal seer, or seers, even if large crowds happen to be present at the time. This was the case in Lourdes, Fátima, and Medjugorje. Interestingly, in these latter cases, the seer(s) may carry on long conversations with the apparition. In the collective visions of Knock and Betania, Venezuela, as well as the collective apparitions seen in 1968 in Zeitoun, Egypt, no conversations take place.

15. Haffert, *Witnesses*, 39–40.
16. Haffert, *Witnesses*, 88–91.
17. Such perceived differences in what seems to be fundamentally the same apparitional event is also found in some well-attested, secular apparitions. See again chapter 2, the Robert Bowes case.

Finally, what do we make of the healings that occur at these sites? Certainly, the placebo effect may be fairly invoked to explain some allegedly miraculous cures. However, an instantaneous cure of metastatic prostate cancer, proven with follow-up tests within five days, does not easily succumb to such explanations. Nor do many of the well-documented and highly scrutinized miracles at Lourdes, France, that have been accepted by the church as authentic.

ASSESSMENT OF RELIGIOUS APPARITIONS

Green and McCreery remark that collectively experienced apparitions appear to no more than two to eight people at once. They comment that apparitions will not, for instance, appear in crowded theaters.[18] Be that as it may, apparitions of Jesus did appear in a crowded church in Oakland, California, and were seen by groups as large as fifty and two hundred people. Similarly, the Blessed Virgin Mary appeared to more than one hundred people in Venezuela. The luminous apparition of Zeitoun, Egypt, that appeared numerous times over a Coptic Church and was widely interpreted to be the Blessed Virgin was seen by several thousand people simultaneously and by as many as one million people over a period of several years. The seers included Jews, Christians, and Muslims.[19] The miracle of the sun that accompanied Mary's final apparitional visitation to Lucia dos Santos and Francisco and Jacinta Marto in Fátima, Portugal was a remarkable visual spectacle witnessed by tens of thousands of people simultaneously.[20]

Such examples notwithstanding, apparitions of religious figures tend to appear mostly to individuals or very small groups, like their secular counterparts. Nevertheless, it behooves us to ask why such dramatic exceptions exist. The obvious explanation is the one accepted by most who directly experienced these apparitions. Jesus Christ and the Blessed Virgin Mary appeared to many because it was the will of God. Meanwhile,

---

18. Green and McCreery, *Apparitions*, 41.

19. See Zaki, *Before Our Eyes*, for a sympathetic overview of the Zeitoun apparitions. For a more skeptical take, cf. Nickell, *Weeping Icons*, "Mystery at Zeitoun," and Derr and Persinger, "Geophysical." For a more balanced treatment, see Allison, *Resurrection*, 294–300.

20. Religious apparitions do not hold a monopoly on being seen by large numbers of witnesses. Recall in chapter 8 that there have been apparitions produced at séances that were seen simultaneously by dozens of witnesses.

the experiences place an inviolable stamp of authenticity upon the underlying theologies that these apparitions and their messages represent.

As a theist, I take no exception to the possibility of divinely inspired visions, but is this the only option?[21] Recapping our findings in chapter 3, we have well-documented cases of apparitions having been produced by living agents, both deliberately and non-deliberately. Moreover, apparitions of the living may be seen collectively. We discussed one such deliberately-conjured apparition having been seen by two people at once.[22] Apparitions may be produced in times of emotional excitement and when the agents are in altered states of consciousness. If large groups of people with like-minded theological beliefs focus on widely adored religious icons, during times of prayer and especially in emotionally charged religious environments, is it possible that an agent or agents in the crowd may inadvertently project an impulse that results in an objective apparition appearing within the environment? Furthermore, on rare occasions, is it possible that others present may see this projected apparition?

As with so many phenomena discussed in this book, we cannot here move beyond the realm of conjecture. Be that as it may, in chapter 15 we will encounter some data and concepts that provide us with some substrate for such speculation.

---

21. Another paranormal explanation for Marian apparitions has been advanced by researchers in the UFO field. The parallels, especially those drawn between the Fátima visions and modern UFO encounters, I must admit are striking. Regarding parallels with Fátima, see Vallée, *Dimensions*, 22–25 and 227–38; Vallée, *Invisible*, 141–54 and Vallée, *Passport*, 11–13; Keel, *Trojan Horse*, 277–86; Fernandes and D'Armada, *Celestial*; Fernandes and D'Armada, *Heavenly Lights*; Fernandes et al., *Fátima Revisited*. On parallels with Knock, see Vallée, *Dimensions*, 178–81; Vallée, *Passport*, 130–33; for Zeitoun, see Keel, *Trojan Horse*, 290–92; on Lourdes see Vallée, *Dimensions*, 238–42; Vallée, *Invisible*, 154–57.

22. See chapter 3, the case "Fifth Experiment at a Distance of Nine Miles."

13

Assessing Apparitions as Subjective Phenomena

TO THIS POINT WE have surveyed several dozen documented cases of apparitional encounters, and this compendium could easily have been multiplied many times over from the primary sources. Such encounters include apparitions of still-living persons and apparent visitations of deceased loved ones to the aggrieved. Most occur spontaneously, but they can also be induced in apparition chambers and with EMDR. Apparitions sometimes convey information that could not have otherwise been knowable at the time to the percipient. Encounters occur mostly to individuals but there are scores of documented cases of apparitions appearing simultaneously to groups of two or more people. The data and evidence for apparitional encounters are very robust.

This begs the obvious questions, "What are we to make of all this? Do apparitions reflect reality? Are they truly objective manifestations or the result of objective stimuli, or are they explainable in other ways?" In what follows, I will discuss the matter of apparitions against the questions of fraud, exaggeration, folklore, hallucinations, and illusions.

APPARITIONS AS FRAUDULENT TALES

James L. Chaffin died in 1921. His entire estate was awarded to his third son based on the will he had drafted in 1905. Later, another of Mr. Chaffin's sons was reportedly visited by his deceased father in multiple dreams that ultimately revealed the location of a lost and more recent will. This new will divided the estate to all four sons in equal proportion and in time was accepted in court. A court ruling was ultimately unnecessary as the wife of the third son reached an agreement with the other sons on how to divvy Mr. Chaffin's estate (the third son had passed by the time of the discovery of the second will and the legal contestation).

For many years, the "Chaffin Will Case" served as a classic example of a paranormal transfer of information by an apparition. There was just one problem. Discovered later, a signature analysis of the two wills indicated that the signees were different people![1]

Being the highly unusual and extraordinary encounters that they are, I find it reasonable to view apparitional encounters through a critical lens, especially cases like this one where the "discovered" information served an ulterior motive. Fortunately, in most of the documented cases no obvious ulterior motive would be served for the percipient(s) to invent an apparitional encounter.[2] Authenticity must be assessed, I think, on a case-by-case basis and it would be careless for all such accounts to be uncritically accepted or dismissed. There are, however, other non-paranormal explanations that may be employed to explain some apparitional phenomena.

APPARITIONS AS THE RESULT OF EXAGGERATION OR FALSE MEMORIES

Could apparitions be the result of stories that "grow with the telling"? Consider the hypothetical situation of an observer who sees an unexplained shadow moving through the dusty attic of the new home he had just bought. He watches puzzled as this undefined shape glides over the attic floor for a few seconds and disappears into a dark space on the opposite side of the attic from where he is standing. The observer tells this strange story to several people over the course of several months (and eventually years), and in time, the shadow is described with more distinct features, and the time period over which it was seen grows from a few seconds to a few minutes or longer. As the story is told second, third, and

---

1. See Charman, *Telepathy*, 98–124, for a lengthy treatment of the case.

2. Though even in cases where percipients lack an obvious ulterior motive, caution is warranted before ruling out fraud as an explanation. See, e.g., the invented roadside ghost story spun by playwright Alfred Sutro that he initially claimed really happened. See Goss, *Phantom Hitch-Hikers*, 6–7.

fourth hand, the shadow is eventually "identified" with a man who once lived in that house before he died. The specter also spoke to the observer. Eventually this more defined specter, artificially but innocently created by the numerous retellings of the original story, tasked the observer with retrieving a family heirloom and giving it to his still-living son. Further, this specter accurately described where the heirloom may be recovered, in a brown jewelry box that is underneath a trapdoor in the main closet of the master bedroom (that the observer did not realize was there beforehand). Let us further suppose that the reality is very different. This observer did find the heirloom in the stated location and returned it to the man's son, but this had nothing to do with his shadowy encounter." He merely discovered the trapdoor and the jewelry box during Spring cleaning one year, the ghost story was merely spurious legend.

Most cases in the collections I have drawn from in this volume were documented in accordance with the direct testimony of the eyewitnesses rather than reliance on secondhand or thirdhand accounts. Frequently there are multiple eyewitnesses or corroborating witnesses who attested the apparitional encounters. SPR researchers would have sought the direct testimony of our hypothetical original observer or likely would not have accepted the case's authenticity. The next category of alternative explanations to apparitional phenomena will underline the importance of tracing a story back to the source(s) when possible.

APPARITIONS AS FOLKLORE

In Tompkinsville, Kentucky, at some undisclosed point in the past, two young men were driving along Meshack Road, on their way to a school dance, when they saw a young lady in a formal dress walking in the same direction they were traveling. Thinking the girl to have been stranded, they offered her a ride to the dance. She accepts the invitation, rides in the backseat, accompanies the two young men to the dance where they proceed to have an enjoyable evening. The young lady accepts a subsequent invitation by the young men to give her a ride home. Because it was raining, one of the young men lets her borrow his coat. The girl points out a small house along Meshack Road where she is dropped off. Several days later, one of the boys goes back to the house to retrieve his coat. An older woman answers the door and tells the boy that no young girl lives at the house, that she had a daughter once, but she was killed in an automobile accident along Meshack Road years earlier. The mystified young man then drives to a churchyard where he was told the young girl had been buried, shocked to discover that his coat was draped over her grave.³

I first heard this story one morning while listening to an episode of *Kentucky Sports Radio*, an astounding podcast that tracks University of Kentucky sports (among other things). I was surprised to discover later that this story finds widespread geographical analogy. Michael Goss, who researched the worldwide "Phantom Hitchhiker" phenomena, discovered four variant themes that are prevalent throughout the world.

1. Version A: The hitchhiker gives the driver an address, where the driver eventually learns that he had picked up a ghost.
2. Version B: The hitchhiker is an "old woman who prophesies disaster or the end of World War II." Upon subsequent inquiry she is likewise found to be deceased.
3. Version C: "Stories where a girl is met at some place of entertainment (e.g., a dance) instead of on the road; she leaves some token (often the overcoat she borrowed from the motorist) on her grave by way of corroborating the experience and her identity."
4. Version D: The hitchhiker is later to be identified as a local deity.⁴

Alan Brown writes regarding the Goss version C variant,

> The most famous Vanishing Hitchhiker variant is the story of Resurrection Mary, a young woman in a white dress who danced with young men at the Oh Henry Ballroom in Chicago and then asked them to take her home. The girl always vanished as the drivers approached Resurrection Cemetery on Archer Avenue.⁵

Evidently, the version C motif of the phantom hitchhiker theme was at some point appropriated for Meshack Road in Tompkinsville, Kentucky. This is not to say that there are not any phantom hitchhiker stories for which a respectable case for authenticity may be made. Michael Goss dissects several such cases which may have an authentic historical core, though later adorned with numerous inauthentic elements.⁶

---

3. Brown, *Haunted Kentucky*, 88–89.
4. Goss, *Phantom Hitch-Hikers*, 27.
5. Brown, *Haunted Kentucky*, 88.
6. See chapter 17 for consideration of one case I think is likely authentic.

APPARITIONS AS HALLUCINATIONS

Whether visual, auditory, tactile, and/or olfactory in nature, some of these experiences are potentially explainable as hallucinations. That is, subjective experiences that do not correspond to something (or someone) that exists in external reality nor results from the reception of an objectively real external stimulus.

Hallucinations are common symptoms of a wide range of medical disorders. Examples include hallucinogenic-recreational drug use like lysergic acid diethylamide (LSD) or psilocybin, withdrawal from substance abuse (e.g., alcohol), schizophrenia, and various forms of dementia (especially Parkinson's Dementia or Lewy Body Dementia). They also occur as side effects of some pain and anxiety medications like opioids and benzodiazepines, respectively. However, far from being confined to people diagnosed with relevant illnesses or who are taking certain medications, hallucinations can occur to anybody in certain contexts.

For instance, most people will experience sleep-related hallucinations at one time or another. Hypnogogic and hypnopompic hallucinations occur in the twilight state. The former occurs in the moment just before a person falls asleep, the latter in the moment just as a person is awakening. Sleep paralysis is characterized by the inability to move in the first moments upon awakening and is often accompanied by visual hallucinations.

Furthermore, type I false awakenings may account for some apparitional encounters. In a type I false awakening, a person apparently awakens in the usual environment. This may be followed by proceeding with the typical morning routine until at some point that person awakens again, this time for real. Could an apparition experienced in the context of a false awakening later be mistaken for having occurred after awakening? Speculative though it may be, this seems a plausible explanation in some cases.[7]

---

7. During the writing of this book, I experienced a rather uninteresting type I false awakening that did not involve an apparition. Having apparently awakened in my bed, the morning sunlight streaming through the venetian blinds of our sliding door, as usual, and all the bedroom furniture and television in their usual places, I reached over the right side of the bed for my phone to check the time. The phone was resting, as always, atop our pet stairs and, if memory serves accurately, plugged into its charger. The time on the phone was 10:01 a.m. (it was a day off). My memory of the dream is somewhat hazy after that. I recall waking up for real not long after that point into the exact same circumstances. Intrigued to compare the time of actual awakening with the time given me in the false awakening, I discovered that the actual time was 9:46 a.m. To

Since many case reports of apparitions occur to percipients while either asleep or nearly asleep, and often as they are just awakening, many undoubtedly are attributable to these phenomena. As always, each report should be assessed on its own merits (or lack thereof). In many cases, we will never know for certain.

Some paranormal occurrences may be reducible to fluctuations in local electromagnetic fields (EMFs) or that of the earth's geomagnetic field (GMF). It has been demonstrated that many haunt phenomena, such as feeling a sense of presence, subjective feelings of apprehension, apparitions, aberrant noises, unusual odors, and tactile sensations can be induced by fluctuating magnetic fields.[8] Through applied EMFs to the right temporal lobe of the brain of a middle-aged journalist, Michael Persinger was able to reproduce the same haunt phenomena that the journalist had earlier experienced in his dwelling. This consisted of "rushes of fear" followed by seeing the apparition towards the end of the experience.[9]

Other haunts in the field have similarly been diagnosed as being due to local perturbations in EMFs or the GMF.

> In one case a young man and woman, both of whom displayed elevated scores on the Roberts scale for temporal lobe sensitivity, reported suddenly awakening between 2:00 and 4:00 a.m. The man experienced an apparition moving through their bed. Both individuals experienced odd sounds (breathing), marked apprehension, and the feeling of a presence. Continuous monitoring of their electronically dense house revealed repeated transients of complex magnetic fields with peak strengths between 15 and 30 mG, similar to those that evoke the sensed presence in our experimental studies. The fields were generated by less than optimal grounding of the house.[10]

Persinger also relates the case of an adolescent woman who had been referred to see a psychiatrist after having seen an apparition and sensing a presence that produced tactile stimulation of an overtly sexualized nature. Over her left shoulder she would also sense the outline of a baby. These occurrences, which typically occurred between 2:00 and 4:00

---

my chagrin I had managed only to sleep in fifteen minutes less than the false awakening presaged.

8. Persinger and Koren, "Characteristics of Haunt Phenomena."
9. Persinger, "Neuropsychiatry," 518.
10. Persinger, "Neuropsychiatry," 518.

a.m., were interpreted by the young lady as having religious connotations. Upon investigation of her bedroom, however, it was found that an electronic clock was the culprit. The clock, situated just inches from her head as she slept, produced a "pulsed magnetic field whose structure was similar to those we employ to evoke the sensed presence in the laboratory."[11] Many haunted houses in modern times have been investigated, and the specific locations within these houses that exhibited the largest pockets of paranormal activity were revealed to have higher-than-average EMF or GMF fluctuations or problems with high ionic density.[12]

Of course, fluctuations in electromagnetic fields due to electronic devices or the earth's geomagnetic field are only one category of potential sources for hallucinatory (or illusory) activity. Environmental factors in certain houses, such as inadequate illumination, an overabundance of mirrors, the presence of Gothic paintings, or children's dolls may likewise invoke haunting sensations and/or hallucinations, particularly in sensitive individuals.[13]

Such factors account for some reports especially of haunting phenomena, yet the objective reality of some apparitions seen at haunted locations stands. Regardless of the source of hallucinatory activity, whether it is magnetic field fluctuations or the environment, apparitions that are experienced collectively by two or more persons cannot easily be explained in this way. In some cases, it may be that local disturbances in magnetic fields trigger sensory experiences of objectively produced paranormal phenomena, though this is speculative. In other words, perhaps the apparition is real in some cases, but it is visible to percipients who are exposed to these EMF or GMF perturbations.

It bears repeating that we cannot move beyond such educated yet speculative theories at the present time in explaining apparitional phenomena, be they hauntings or other types. I am optimistic this situation will change in time with more research combined with sufficient technological advancement, and as we increase our knowledge of the nature of reality.

---

11. Persinger, "Neuropsychiatry," 518.
12. See the discussion in Roll and Persinger, "Poltergeists and Haunts," 153–60.
13. See for instance Jawer et al., "Gestalt Influences."

APPARITIONS AS ILLUSIONS

While hallucinations are false sensory *perceptions* generated in the mind, illusions are false *interpretations* of real objects or stimuli. An example of someone experiencing an illusion would be one who sees an eagle with outstretched wings gliding across the sky and thinking it to be an airplane. The literature does demonstrate that, for example, every day household objects have also been mistaken for apparitions. Consider the following case.

MISS W.

> I was cautiously feeling for what I wanted when, partially turning around, I perceived at a short distance behind me the figure of a little old lady, sitting very sedately with her hands folded in her lap, holding a white pocket-handkerchief.[14]

Startled, having thought herself to be alone, all the other household inhabitants being left downstairs, Miss W. inquired of the identity of the unrecognized woman. Upon turning to face her, the lady disappeared. Being short-sighted, she thought her "eyes were playing tricks," then found that when she took up the same position as before the lady reappeared. More quickly turning and approaching the apparition produced the same result, the lady vanished. Each time she resumed the former position by a fireplace, the old lady reappeared.

> I moved my head slightly from side to side, and found that it did the same. I then went slowly backwards, keeping my head still until I again reached the place; when deliberately turning round the mystery was solved.
>
> A small, polished, mahogany stand near the window, which I used as a cupboard for various trifles, made the body of the figure, a piece of paper hanging from the partly-open door serving as the handkerchief; a vase on the top formed the head and head-dress, and the slanting light falling upon it, and the white curtain of the window completed the illusion. I destroyed and re-made the figure several times, and was surprised to find how distinct it appeared when the exact relative positions were maintained.[15]

---

14. Sidgwick et al., "Census," 95–96.
15. Sidgwick et al., "Census," 96.

Through a process of trial and error, Miss W. eventually discovered the cause of her apparition. How many apparitional reports are the result of similar illusions for which such a discovery process was not undertaken? It is especially plausible that some of those involving only one sense, in this case the visual sense, may be explainable as illusion. This is particularly true when apparitions are seen in conditions of poor visibility, such as in rooms that are dimly lit or by percipients with visual impairment.[16] Numerous examples of apparitions that were demonstrated to be illusions, such as the one above, are detailed in the "Census of Hallucinations".[17]

CRYPTOMNESIA

During hypnosis, a subject channeled information from a discarnate entity that claimed to be Blanche Poynings, a member of the royal court of King Richard II. Specific details, even including some proper names of those associated with her life, proved to be accurate upon subsequent investigation. Did this episode furnish proof of the conscious survival of bodily death? As it turns out, no. The investigator, G. L. Dickinson, further probed the subject for potential "normal" sources of information and hit paydirt. Through use of a planchette, the subject mentioned a novel published in 1892—*Countess Maud*, written by Emily Holt—that had contained the relevant details of Blanche Poynings's life. The subject later "recalled having read the book, or at least having examined it" when she was twelve years of age. During the investigation, the hypnotized subject was twenty five years old, the information to that point having lain dormant within her mind for about thirteen years.[18]

Cryptomnesia should be considered in cases where information is otherwise ostensibly gained through supernormal means such as telepathy. A hasty conclusion in this case would have prematurely concluded that a deceased member of the royal court of King Richard II was communicating via a hypnotized subject. This is a relevant consideration

---

16. Sidgwick et al., "Census," 96.

17. The discussion in Sidgwick et al., "Census," 94–112, is helpful. Goss in *Phantom Hitch-Hikers*, 71–73, details another instructive example, of three young men on the roadside in Essex, UK, in 1977, "their heads and upper bodies swaddled against the drizzle with towels and squash-shirts," initially being mistaken by two eighteen year old motorists for a "ghostly tableau of monkishly-cowled figures posed in a country lane."

18. Stevenson, "Cryptomnesia and Parapsychology," 9–10.

in cases of alleged reincarnation, particularly in the matter of past life memories, and it could be plausibly used in some apparition cases to explain what otherwise seems to be a supernormal transfer of information.

14

Apparitions and the Fantasy Prone Personality

INITIALLY, I HAD PLANNED to include discussion of the Fantasy Prone Personality (FPP) as a section in the previous chapter. However, for reasons that will become clear, this phenomenon, I think, serves as something of a bridge between non-paranormal and paranormal explanations of apparitions, and I would suggest other anomalous experiences as well. As such, I felt this topic was worthy of its own chapter.

Psychology researchers Theodore Barber and Sheryl Wilson conducted interviews of twenty-seven women who were "excellent hypnotic subjects" and twenty-five women who were on the low, medium, and medium-high end of the hypnotic susceptibility range. The interviews focused on the subjects' memories in childhood and adulthood as well as their history of psychic and fantasy experiences. They incidentally discovered that, with a single exception, "the excellent hypnotic subjects had a profound fantasy life, their fantasies were often 'as real as real' (hallucinatory), and their involvement in fantasy played an important role in producing their superb hypnotic performance."[1]

---

1. Wilson and Barber, "Fantasy Prone," 340–41. Of note, the women in both groups were mostly highly educated. Only two of the women had not attended college, one was a MD (psychiatrist), one had a PhD (psychologist), four were PhD candidates in psychology, nineteen had bachelor's or master's degrees, ten of those credentialed in psychology or counseling, and another twenty-five were college students. Ages ranged between nineteen and sixty-three, with a mean age of twenty-eight. Hypnotic responsiveness was measured through administration of numerous instruments, such

Those in the "excellent hypnotic-responsiveness" group (i.e., with FPP) often shared the following characteristics.

1. As children, the FPP group lived in a make-believe world "much or most of the time." As adults, 92 percent in the FPP group estimated that they were engaged in fantasy more than half the time. They also tend to put aside a special place and special times for fantasizing, including spending entire weekends in fantasy.

2. All in the FPP group who, as children, had played with stuffed animals or dolls believed that they were alive, lived independent lives, and had distinctive personalities and feelings.

3. As children, almost all in the FPP group believed in elves, fairies, guardian angels, leprechauns, and tree spirits and carried the conviction that they had seen, heard, and/or played with them. Most interestingly, "with few exceptions," their belief in the reality of these creatures continued into adulthood to some extent.

4. The majority of the FPP group (58 percent) spent "a large part of their childhood" playing with imaginary friends compared with just 8 percent in the comparison group.

5. As children, and often as adults, those in the FPP group commonly claimed that they would "become" a character in a fictional book. One identified with the character Wendy in *Peter Pan*. Having read the book, she subsequently had "exciting adventures daily (as Wendy) with Peter and the other children; they became her imaginary companions and, she says, they were as real as real children."

6. Those in the FPP group (except two) pretended to be someone else during childhood (such as an animal, a princess, an orphan, or even a fairytale character such as Cinderella), and would become so absorbed in the role that they literally felt they had become that character. This role would often spill into their daily lives well beyond the actual play periods.

7. Almost all people in the FPP group "have very vivid sexual fantasies that they experience 'as real as real' with all the sights, sounds, smells, emotions, feelings, and physical sensations." In fact, 75

---

as the Creative Imagination Scale, the Barber Suggestibility Scale, and the Memory, Imagining, and Creativity Interview Schedule. See Wilson and Barber, "Fantasy Prone," 341–45, for details.

APPARITIONS AND THE FANTASY PRONE PERSONALITY 123

percent reported that the fantasies are so realistic that they produce orgasms. The authors note that one person (of twenty-five) in the comparison group also experienced this.

8. Among those in the FPP group, fantasizing was considered an essential part of their lives on par with eating and sleeping. Even pondering the question of what life would be like without fantasy was met with great duress. "The typical reaction . . . was an expression of disbelief that they were being asked to consider such a dreadful prospect." Many claimed it would be akin to losing one of their senses, such as going blind. Some stated that they would simply cease to have a purpose, or they might as well be dead.

9. Those in the FPP group experienced their fantasies "as real as real" in all five sensory modalities. Sixty-five percent even experienced the visual aspect of their fantasies with as much intensity as with their eyes open. The other 35 percent would only experience the visual aspects of the fantasy world with the same intensity when their eyes were closed.

10. The fantasy world created by those in the FPP group is just as real to them as the ordinary world; in fact, several said, "Compared with their fantasy, reality becomes a pale copy" and in some cases they "feel that their fantasy world is real, and that the actual world is a fantasy." Eighty-five percent in the FPP group claimed to confuse the memories formed in their fantasies with memories of actual events.

11. In all cases in the FPP group (and none in the comparison group), the fantasies are self-propelling. "As they describe it, they 'set the stage,' that is, they begin with certain characters, settings, or themes, and then sit back and watch the drama unfold." They feel as if they are taking part in an entertaining motion picture.

12. The difficulty that those with FPP have in untangling the real, ordinary world from fantasy can create dangerous situations. In one case, when she was eleven years old, one of the FPP subjects was fantasizing of walking with her pet lamb in an imaginary meadow. "As she was concentrating on stepping with deliberately high steps through the tall grass, she was startled out of her fantasy world by the sounds of automobile horns. She was shocked to find herself surrounded by heavy traffic in the middle of a busy street. She

recalls how she instantly decided always to maintain some awareness of her surroundings whenever she was in any potentially dangerous situation." Moreover, for 70 percent of those in the FPP group, particularly those who experience the vivid fantasy imagery with their eyes open as well as closed, driving can be a problem. For instance, they may hallucinate a child or an animal running out in front of the car if they think about it beforehand. This risk may be mitigated by focusing on the mechanics of driving, even to the point that they will "carry on a continuous verbal monologue such as 'I'm now approaching an intersection, there's a lot of traffic, slow down, be ready to stop, and so on.'" Other strategies mentioned by the authors for promoting safety are imagining a protective halo of light around the car or imagining that four small angels, one for each corner of the car, accompanies her on the trip.

13. The vast majority in the FPP group (96 percent), and only one person in the comparison group (4 percent) produce very vivid memories of their childhood and can often recall past experiences in similarly vivid ways, as if they were there again literally reliving the past with all five sensory modalities.

14. Ninety-two percent in the FPP group (versus 16 percent in the comparison group) thought themselves to be "psychic or sensitive" and think that they experience telepathy and precognition.

15. Among the FPP group, 88 percent report having experienced out-of-body experiences vs. 8 percent for the comparison group.

16. Common among the FPP group (50 percent) was the experience of automatic writing, that is "the feeling that someone was using them to write a poem, song, or message." The implication is that this writing originated from a higher intelligence or a spirit. By contrast, 8 percent in the comparison group experienced automatic writing.

17. Six of the twenty-seven in the FPP group had religious visions that were "the most impactful and memorable experiences of their lives." None in the comparison group experienced such impactful religious visions. This includes one who claimed to have a vision of the Virgin Mary at eight years of age. Several others had visions or heard the voice of God, while another "saw the full face of Buddha" and heard the statement, "I am the voice of god."

18. Over two-thirds in the FPP group (and none in the comparison group) felt that they had the gift of healing, that during "close interaction they feel that they transmit energy and health to the sick or injured."

19. Nearly three quarters of the FPP group (73 percent), compared with 16 percent in the comparison groups, reported encounters with ghosts or apparitions.[2]

Barber and Wilson state that about 4 percent of the population are fantasy prone.[3] The reason that most of us are unaware that this phenomenon exists is that, for obvious reasons, people with these abilities tend to be secretive about it, even to the point where they do not inform their spouses about it.[4] Importantly, most of those with FPP are well-adjusted socially, do not suffer from psychopathology, and tend to lead normal lives.[5]

Stuffed animals with distinctive personalities that lead independent lives. A young girl transforming herself into a Disney character. Vivid landscapes of all varieties generated by the imagination. I marvel at the abilities of those capable of such mental feats. Their minds are like a virtual reality maker capable of creating worlds that engage all senses, limited only by their respective imaginations. No wonder one of Barber and Wilson's interviewees could state,

> It's being anything you can be, could be, or are. It's possibilities made possible. It's soaring, thrilling, living. [Who is] to say what's happening right now is reality? Fantasy is your own private world. You set the stage. You make it. It's being godlike. Anything you believe, if you believe it, it's true.[6]

No matter how real these things may seem to the fantasizers, they are still to be relegated to the realm of fantasy. Though we have seen the line between the ordinary and fantasy worlds blurred at times for the fantasizers, they would ultimately agree with this. However, as points 14–19 in our list indicate, those with FPP, disproportionately to the rest of the population, see apparitions, have religious visions, experience OBEs,

---

2. Wilson and Barber, "Fantasy Prone," 345–64.
3. Wilson and Barber, "Fantasy Prone," 368.
4. Wilson and Barber, "Fantasy Prone," 365–66.
5. Wilson and Barber, "Fantasy Prone," 379.
6. Wilson and Barber, "Fantasy Prone," 352.

administer psychic healings, and have episodes of automatic writing. Are these merely fantasy as well?

FANTASY-PRONE PERSONALITY AND TRANSLIMINALITY

As we have seen, the line between reality and fantasy is not necessarily easy for fantasizers to discern. If a driver with FPP can fabricate the existence of a young child running in front of her car, causing her to act as if the child is real (perhaps to the point of slamming on the breaks), then that same person can also fabricate an apparition and mistake it for an objectively real entity. Inevitably, FPP has implications for explaining some apparitional phenomena in a non-paranormal way.

Nevertheless, as with other explanations we have considered thus far, FPP cannot explain the whole gamut of apparition reports. Only about 4 percent of the population fall under the category of FPP. However, at least 10 percent of people claim to have experienced apparitions at one time or another. A spate of studies on bereavement across numerous cultures since the 1970s has consistently demonstrated that at least 50 percent of those in grief experience afterdeath communications (ADCs) in some form, most commonly a sense of presence or apparitions.[7] More importantly, FPP does not explain most cases of collectively experienced phenomena or those which impart information gleaned in a supernormal manner.

Barber and Wilson's research article hints at numerous points where their interviewees may have obtained information in a supernormal way. For instance, several of them claimed to correctly predict in advance serious illnesses and deaths of close friends and family members. Two claimed to always know beforehand where they would find a vacant parking place even in very large and crowded lots. One also seriously claimed to have correctly predicted the winner of the Kentucky Derby for ten years running up to the time of the interview, though she did not cash in on this ability lest she "use her gift inappropriately."[8] At age four, one had been very ill and claimed to have an out-of-body experience (OBE) where she was sitting atop her bedroom door. When her father came into the room, she claimed to see for the first time a small bald spot on the

---

7. See appendix A.
8. Wilson and Barber, "Fantasy Prone," 359.

back of his head. When she saw him unsuccessfully try to arouse her from sleep, she "fell back" into her body and excitedly told him what had happened. The authors did contact her parents who confirmed the event, though assumed she was simply delirious from her fever.[9]

Those with FPP commonly report striking physical effects that accompany certain suggestive stimuli. They are more likely to become physically ill after consuming food they thought, incorrectly, to have been spoiled. Also, when believing, incorrectly, to have been contaminated with lice, they develop a relentless itch. More interestingly, one interviewee informed the authors that she had found a neighbor's pet frog that had escaped and, having "remembered that she had been told that frogs cause warts," subsequently did have a wart develop on her hand that proved highly resistant to treatment. Thirteen of twenty-two of the fantasizers who were asked (60 percent) reported having had a false pregnancy (pseudocyesis) at least one time. Aside from merely believing themselves to have been pregnant, they experienced many of the typical symptoms such as amenorrhea (the cessation of menstruation), breast changes, abdominal enlargement, morning sickness, unusual cravings, and even felt "fetal movements." Two of them even went to have abortions, though no fetus had been found when examined. In the others, the symptoms resolved shortly after receiving negative pregnancy tests. Effectively only one woman in the comparison group had comparable symptoms of false pregnancy as those in the FPP group.[10]

I will make the preliminary conclusion that there is a correlation between people with FPP and high transliminality, that is, the sensitivity of a person to experiencing paranormal phenomena, including but certainly not limited to apparitions. Those with FPP were "discovered" by the authors because of their being excellent hypnotic candidates. A deep state of hypnosis is an altered state of consciousness, into which those with FPP easily enter. The creation of vivid fantasy worlds where the perceiver is literally able to disregard ordinary space and time is likewise an altered state of consciousness. As we have seen, such altered states facilitate paranormal phenomena.[11]

---

9. Wilson and Barber, "Fantasy Prone," 361.
10. Wilson and Barber, "Fantasy Prone," 358–59.
11. The full discussion in Wilson and Barber, "Fantasy Prone," 373–79, is helpful.

15

Assessing Apparitions as Objective Phenomena

DESPITE THE PROBLEMS THAT the prospects of fraud, exaggeration, hallucinations, illusions and cryptomnesia present, many apparitional encounters resist being reduced to these categories. Below is a list of the broad lines of evidence we have encountered in the case reports which support the objectivity of many apparitional experiences.

1. A disproportionate number of apparitions are crisis apparitions. In the vast majority, the percipient does not realize the person appearing has died or is experiencing some other form of extreme circumstance.

2. In experimental settings, apparitions have been produced deliberately. Most often they are seen by percipients who were not informed beforehand.

3. Percipients have claimed the crucial aid of apparitions in accompanying them in, and in some cases ostensibly rescuing them from, life-threatening situations.

4. Apparitions of the deceased have been reported by people on their deathbeds who were unaware at the time that the person appearing to them had died.

5. In a similar vein, most transitional apparitions are representative of deceased relatives or religious figures rather than "phantasms of

the living." Furthermore, transitional apparitions tend to be seen by the dying when in more lucid, coherent states, and they frequently have a next-world focus. This contrasts with hallucinations of a this-world purpose that are frequently incoherent, and more often occur in the setting of the administration of mind-altering drugs, uremia, some form of neuropathology, or other conditions commonly associated with confusion.[1]

6. Many well-documented cases are collective; that is, the apparitions are seen by multiple percipients.

7. Veridical (supernormal) information transfer often will occur in the context of apparitional experiences. Often, an unrecognized apparition will later be identified by the percipient from a photograph. In some cases, apparitions will come with the explicit purpose of informing percipients of specific information, such as the location of hidden money.

8. On rare occasion, apparitions will ostensibly alter the environment in which they appear.

9. Despite being independently reported for the most part, some categories of apparitions produce cases with very similar characteristics. Most reunion apparitions, for instance, tend to be very simple, restrained accounts that occur for the purpose of delivering a message of reassurance or to convey information about retrieving a lost item. Well-authenticated hauntings likewise exhibit very stereotypical characteristics.

For these reasons I find it difficult to classify all reported apparitions under the categories presented in chapter 13. Does this prove that some ghost reports represent authentic glimpses of spirits visiting from the great beyond? Or are their other considerations?

APPARITIONS AS PARANORMAL (PSI) PHENOMENA

The potential mechanisms for apparitional phenomena I discuss in this chapter will be eschewed by scientific materialists (i.e., physicalists) no less than the possibility that consciousness survives bodily death. Be that as it may, I think such avenues of thought are skeptics' best hope

---

1. Osis and Haraldsson, *Hour of Death*, 57–77.

of avoiding the prospect of postmortem survival. What I am suggesting here is something of a rarely tread upon middle ground between those with religious or spiritual beliefs on the one hand and physicalists on the other. Perhaps the objective reality of apparitions may be affirmed without necessarily resorting to the conclusion that they are conscious spirits returned from the realm of the dead.

Researchers, most robustly in the late nineteenth and early twentieth centuries, have amassed a wealth of documentary evidence supporting the authenticity of psi phenomena such as telepathy and psychokinesis. While counterintuitive, evidence of this in nature will be illustrated presently. I suspect a great many readers will have already encountered psi phenomena in their lives, even if it was not initially appreciated for what it was at the time.

PSI IN HISTORY

Comparative religions scholar and modern-day icon of psychical research Jeffrey Kripal once aptly wrote, "Forget Hollywood. Forget the comic books. Superpowers have been with us for millennia, and they are *real* in the simple sense that people experience them all the time and have reported their effects throughout history."[2]

Evidence of supernormal abilities has not emerged merely in recent centuries. Powers of telepathy/extrasensory perception (ESP), psychokinesis (PK), precognition, and supernormal bodily manifestations are documented in the mystical traditions associated with Hinduism, Buddhism, Sufism, Judaism, Christianity, various forms of shamanism across the world, and even the philosophical tradition of Neoplatonism. The value of the evidence is mixed though there are more than ample reasons to accept that authentic psi occurs across the various cultural and religious traditions.[3] The best documentary evidence for psi within a religious tradition, however, is to be found in Catholic Tradition of the saints.

Catholic hagiography is replete with accounts of saints levitating, psychokinesis (especially in conjunction with communion), the reception of stigmata, bodily transformation, and a period of bodily incorruptibility after death. Many accounts are likely fictional or, at best, greatly

---

2. Strieber and Kripal, *Super Natural*, 5, emphasis original.

3. See Kelly and Grosso, "Mystical," 495–575; Murphy, *Future*; Kelly and Whicher, "*Siddhis*," 315–48; Shaw, "Neoplatonism," 275–314.

exaggerated, while some are very well-attested. Authentic cases of psi in the lives of some Catholic saints are supported broadly by several lines of evidence. First, many purported cases were observed repeatedly and by many witnesses deemed credible, and this often included skeptical or hostile witnesses. Second, the canonization and beatification of saints were very rigorous processes that often would last years, sometimes decades. Evidence was sifted carefully. Witnesses were deposed. There was even a *promotor fidei* (promoter of the faith) or devil's advocate appointed to cases who was responsible for challenging the evidence of purported miracles. Third, frequently because of privacy concerns or even a sense of embarrassment about the purported psi phenomena, those who manifested psi went to great lengths in attempts of *concealing* the phenomena rather than wishing to draw attention to it.[4]

Gifted mediums and other subjects of modern accounts would experience psi during an ecstatic trance or some other altered state of consciousness or while in a state of absorption. This is true of the meditative traditions and those under the influence of psychedelic substances.[5]

STIGMATA OF CRUCIFIXION AND HYPNOTIC SUGGESTION

> According to Dr. Coomes's account, a certain Mrs. Stuckenborg seems to have bled from spontaneously formed stigmata on every Friday since the beginning of June. There are wounds on the hands and feet, a wound on the side (from whence issues a watery exudation tinged with blood), a cross on the forehead, a large cross and a heart on the chest, and the letters I. H. S. on the right shoulder. From three to six every Friday there is profound trance, with superficial anesthesia, but much convulsive movement and manifestation of inward pain. If we may rely on Dr. Coomes's account, which seems a careful one, simulation is quite out of the question. The patient seems to desire neither money nor notoriety. She is a devout Catholic, but does not talk about religion; and complains much of the pain and exhaustion due to the wounds and the convulsive trance.[6]

4. On discussion and evidence, see Kelly and Grosso, "Mystical," 528–30; Murphy, *Future*, 478–526; Thurston, *Mysticism*, is the magisterial work on the subject, the product of painstaking analyses of the voluminous primary sources.

5. On psi and psychedelics, see Luke and Spowers, *DMT Entity Encounters*.

6. Myers, *Human Personality I*, 495.

This case of stigmata took place in Louisville, Kentucky and was reported initially in the *Courier-Journal* on December 7th, 1891. Dr. Hodgson, an investigator for the SPR, attempted on two occasions to meet Mrs. Stuckenborg, but was restricted from doing so by local Roman Catholic authorities. Hodgson was, however, able to meet with Dr. Coomes along with one or two other medical personnel who had witnessed the case. After his investigation, "there seemed no doubt of its genuineness."[7]

Since the thirteenth century, hundreds of stigmata cases have been reported, though perhaps as few as fifty with adequate testimony.[8] Are these miraculous events? Perhaps. But they may also reflect a well-known, albeit supernormal manifestation of the subliminal mind. Stigmata will, to varying extents, emulate the wounds of crucifixion and scourging that Jesus suffered, including puncture marks on the palms or wrists, sometimes marks on the forehead, back, and shoulders that correspond to the crown of thorns and the lashings, and even on occasion bloody tears. The "wounds" are sometimes simply red marks or may be characterized by actual bleeding, sometimes emanating from unbroken skin. As with the case quoted above, the marks appear periodically and at regular times, especially on Fridays, and may repeat on a weekly basis for months to years. Importantly, the appearance of the lesions occurs most often when the subject is in a trance, a state of ecstasy, or some other altered state of consciousness. Most mysteriously of all, the marks, regardless of their severity, will disappear rapidly without leaving evidence of their prior presence (such as scars) and are never accompanied by inflammation, infection, or sepsis.[9]

The power of hypnotic suggestion demonstrates the abilities of the subconscious, or subliminal self. Around the turn of the twentieth century, SPR researcher Frederic W. H. Myers detailed numerous examples that seem to border on the supernatural in his massive, two-volume posthumous work, *Human Personality and Its Survival of Bodily Death*. The more recent, meticulously researched *Irreducible Mind: Toward a Psychology for the 21st Century* edited by Edward Kelly et al. pays homage to Myers's important work and serves as a modern update to the enormous literature that exists on the relevant topics.

The various authors in this important volume address a wide range of fascinating topics related to consciousness, including such phenomena

---

7. Myers, *Human Personality I*, 495.
8. Kelly, "Psychophysiological," 152.
9. Kelly, "Psychophysiological," 153.

as sudden uprushes of inspiration and genius, motor and sensory automatisms, near-death experiences, and mystical experiences. Collectively, to my mind these authors convincingly demonstrate the failure of scientific materialism to account for the data. The comprehensive case for consciousness existing independently of the human brain made by these authors, along with the litany of others over the past century and a half or so, particularly the SPR researchers, is impressive.

Hypnotism involves the deliberate induction of an altered state of consciousness, usually in one person by another, typically for therapeutic purposes. Myers details many cases where people were cured of a diverse array of diseases, frequently in cases that proved refractory to conventional medical therapies available at the time.[10]

Related I think to stigmata, Myers details several cases where various skin manifestations are produced by hypnotic induction. In Santa Barbara, California, 1885, Dr. M. H. Biggs whispered to a hypnotized (or "magnetised," as he calls it in the original work) woman that she would repeatedly develop a red cross on the upper part of her chest, but only on Fridays, and in the induction process pressed a cross made of rock crystal onto the spot where the impression was later to appear. He also suggested to her that the Latin words "*Sancta*" and "*Crucis*" would appear above and underneath this cross, respectively. Sure enough, on a later date he found a pink cross on the skin where he had placed the cross of rock crystal. Subsequently suggesting to her while magnetized that the cross would appear every Friday for four months, this indeed repeated for a period of roughly that length of time. As the end of the specified period drew near, the cross would appear each Friday but grew paler every time. Furthermore, part of the letter "S" did appear above the cross, but nothing more. The full words "*Sancta*" and "*Crucis*" that had been suggested otherwise failed to materialize. Several witnesses to the appearance of the cross are listed in the account.[11]

One highly suggestible subject Mdlle. Ilma S. who had been cured of melancholy (depression) via hypnosis suffered a severe wound after a medical student had placed a pair of scissors on her chest, suggesting to her that the scissors were scalding hot, though this was not the case. The wound took two months to heal. Dr. Krafft-Ebing later suggested certain

10. Myers, *Human Personality I*, 437–564; Playfair, *Magic*. For more modern examples, see Alex Tanous et al., *Psi in Psychotherapy*.
11. Myers, *Human Personality I*, 493–94.

shapes should appear upon her skin, specifically the letter "K," which did in fact develop gradually yet painlessly over the course of about two and a half months, at the specified site, on the back between the shoulder blades. Even more curiously, Mdlle. Ilma S., who had no feeling on her right side, would under hypnosis develop symmetric yet reversed lesions that were impressed upon her *left* side. A Dr. Jendrássik pressed an object representing the letter "K" on her left shoulder, suggesting to her that the object was hot. Hours later the K did appear, but it was on the right shoulder. More intriguingly, the letter K that appeared was not in the exact shape of the one impressed upon her left shoulder; rather it was a capital K but in the form of "another person's handwriting."[12]

More recently in 1990, Anna Maria T., an Italian Catholic woman, first experienced stigmata at the age of 64. Different from most who experience stigmata, Anna would not enter a trance-like state at the time the lesions would appear. However, the stigmata were initiated on an occasion when she was praying. She experienced a vision of Jesus approach her and take her by the hands. "Red rounded blotches" that resembled burns, that sometimes would blister but would not bleed, appeared on her palms on the first Friday of each month, lasting two or three days prior to disappearing without leaving scars. According to Williams, this continued regularly for at least nine years, up to the publication of Anna's story.[13]

> She was closely followed by the author for five months, during which time color and infrared photographs were taken, various physiological reactions measured, and psychological tests (MMPI and Rorschach) administered. Measurements and photographs were made on days when the stigmata were present as well as on days when they were not. Physiological measurements showed differences in temperature, blood flow, and electrodermal response between the stigmatic areas and surrounding skin, as well as differences between the days when stigmata were present and "control" days when they were not. The psychological tests showed no signs of psychopathology, including low scores on the hysteria scale. She did have a high score on the schizophrenia scale of the MMPI, but her high scores were primarily attributable to items about experiences that the American Psychiatric Association now considers non-pathological, such as religious and mystical visions.[14]

12. Myers, *Human Personality I*, 495–96.
13. Kelly, "Psychophysiological," 154.
14. Kelly, "Psychophysiological," 154–55.

In the case of a German girl designated as Elizabeth K., we have an instance of stigmata being deliberately produced through the medium of hypnosis. She had reported feeling intense pain in her hands and feet after attending a lecture on Jesus' crucifixion on Good Friday in 1932. Elizabeth K. had frequently, and for several years, been treated for hysteria with hypnotic therapy. After reporting the pain at the time of the lecture, her hypnotist, Lechler, suggested to her that she would have a dream the same night of nails being driven into her hands and feet. The following day she did have red and swollen wounds at the specified sites, with the skin even a little open. At that point Lechler disclosed the hypnotic suggestion he had given her the day before, and this time with her consent, suggested that the wounds should become deeper, also that she would produce bloody tears. These suggestions likewise proved successful. At subsequent sessions he produced actual bleeding from the lesions of the hand and feet as well as at other specified locations like her forehead and shoulder. The forehead lesions were in the shape of triangles, corresponding to shapes that thorns might make. Furthermore, after each hypnotic induction that followed the initial one, she was kept under constant surveillance, presumably to rule out the possibility that the wounds were self-inflicted.[15]

THE COLLECTIVE EFFECTS OF HALLUCINOGENIC DRUGS

Substances such as N,N-Dimethyltryptamine (DMT), ayahuasca, lysergic acid diethylamide (LSD), and psilocybin are used in many cultures, particularly by priests and shamans, for the purposes of inducing healings and mystical visions. As we have touched upon elsewhere, hallucinations are produced in the mind of a single individual. Two or more people may simultaneously hallucinate when expectation and emotional excitement are present, but frequently the content of the individual experiences is markedly different.

However, the experiences of transpersonal psychologist Jorge N. Ferrer suggest that these substances may sometimes give the conscious mind glimpses into some objective "subconscious realm" rather than producing merely false sensory experiences. During his stay in a Peruvian jungle near Iquitos in 2008, Ferrer ingested ayahuasca and "was struck by the vision of a number of non-physical entities (animal, human, and

---

15. Kelly, "Psychophysiological," 159.

other-than-human) wandering in the *maloca* (traditional ceremony shed)." During the vision, he perceived an "energetic thread of white light" emanate from the mouth of the healer that was singing a healing song. Upon further observation, he discovered that this energetic thread was attached to humanoid-shaped entities that he describes as nonphysical that were entering into the shed. These entities had a head, body, arms, and legs but were taller than humans and seemed to be comprised only of "a fuzzy white light that concealed any identifiable traits beyond their general form."

These "astral doctors," what they are called by the indigenous people, would move about the space, "situating themselves in front of the ceremony's participants and extending their arms to make contact with specific areas of participants' bodies, especially the heart and the vital center."[16] Ferrer relates his experience when the astral doctors reached him.

> When my turn arrived, their contact resulted in dramatically tangible energetic adjustments of incredible finesse in those centers, accompanied by feelings of deeply healing, profound gratitude, and instinctive trust in the benevolent nature of the entities. This experience led to a new understanding of the healing power of (at least that particular) ayahuasca ceremony as emerging from the complex interplay of the medicine, the healer, the *icaro*, and the astral doctors.[17]

The most interesting aspect of this testimony is that the healer also, when asked the next morning by Ferrer, corroborated the presence of the astral doctors at the ceremony.[18]

> Overall, this procedure struck me as remarkably similar to the scientific emphasis on public observation and replicability with one (arguably huge) difference—these healers were discussing entities that scientific naturalism would consider fictitiously supernatural.[19]

In 1990, Ferrer participated in a wachuma ceremony in Urubamba, Peru. In this ceremony, extracts from the San Pedro cactus, common in numerous South American countries, were used to produce healing

---

16. Ferrer, *Participation*, 64.
17. Ferrer, *Participation*, 64–65.
18. Ferrer, *Participation*, 65.
19. Ferrer, *Participation*, 65.

visions. Ferrer claims that, several hours into the experience, he saw what he describes as complex "energetic spiderwebs" that would react to his physical contact. Amidst the experience, he was able to confirm with other participants, including a young American woman who was drinking San Pedro for the first time and Victoria the healer, that they were also seeing the red spiderwebs.

> The red spiderwebs marked the beginning of nearly two hours of breathtaking external visionary experiences (I later titled the entire episode "Harry Potter Meets the Matrix")—blue and green energies curatively entering my body, contact with benevolent Indigenous spirits, and perceptions of energy vortices of diverse colors in the room, some of which stemmed from Victoria's "power objects."[20]

Ferrer states that San Pedro leaves one's "critical capacities" intact, which allowed him to keep on his "researcher hat" during the vision. He repeatedly and painstakingly confirmed with both co-participants that they were seeing and experiencing the same visions. When he asked specifically what they were seeing as he pointed out a particular space, he notes that, without exception, "they accurately described the color, shape, and directional movements of the various energetic fields I was seeing."[21]

Ferrer concluded from this that "San Pedro allowed human sight to perceive or enact subtle energetic dimensions of reality."[22]

Ferrer's conclusion seems inescapable to me. Collective hallucination, if we define hallucination as a "false sensory experience," clearly does not explain what is occurring here. However, another speculative option may be available if one wishes to avoid the premise that the psychedelic agents unveiled a world of benevolent spiritual entities.

Cultural factors clearly play crucial roles in the apparitional dramas created. Like Ferrer's astral doctors, supernormal healings are appropriately accompanied by apparitions of doctors in nonindigenous communities. This is particularly true in Iceland where it is common for people to seek cures from doctors on the other side.[23] Consider the following case.

---

20. Ferrer, *Participation*, 65.
21. Ferrer, *Participation*, 65–66.
22. Ferrer, *Participation*, 66.
23. See Haraldsson, *Departed*, 165–72.

PER REQUEST

A man who suffered from chronic back pain was working on the freighter Fjallfoss after it had returned from America. His condition worsened shortly after launch. Feeling so poorly one night that he had initially decided to forfeit his shift, he was laying in bed when two doctors dressed in white entered his cabin and asked to examine him. While he replied that he had made no such request, the doctors told him, "We are going to operate on you." The man protested that he was not aware that his particular ailment was amenable to an operation and that he could not be bedridden beyond 4 o'clock, when his next shift began. The doctors assured him that he would not be bedridden and could work the following day as long as he was cautious and did not lift heavy objects. The man felt the doctors' hands on his back and felt no pain. They then informed him that the operation had ended and then disappeared out the door. Expeditiously, the man jumped out of the bed, opened the door, and saw only darkness. Inquiring of the man on duty where the two doctors went, he was told that there were no doctors present. The man said that as he had jumped from the bed—despite having been practically unable to move beforehand—he felt no pain nor discomfort anywhere. Furthermore, he was "completely healthy and have had no problem since," though he had suffered for this issue for some fifteen years previous and was often confined to bed.[24]

Often, the cures sought from deceased doctors are obtained through the intercession of mediums.[25] Two-thirds of those visiting spiritual healers were also being treated by physicians. Forty percent of the patients believed they had experienced full recovery; 32 percent partial recovery; 28 percent no recovery. Of those cured, 30 percent attributed the success to the spirit doctor from the other side, and another 30 percent attributed the cure to prayer.[26]

Could it be that Ferrer's astral doctors and the apparitional doctors in Iceland were produced by the subliminal minds of the healers and patients? In the collective case, could it be that Ferrer and others present saw similar imagery because their minds were entangled with that of the healers? Perhaps the psychedelic agents utilized facilitate such experiences.

24. Haraldsson, *Departed*, 166–67.
25. Haraldsson, *Departed*, 169.
26. Haraldsson, *Departed*, 169.

TELEPATHY

Telepathy is the transference of thoughts or ideas, or images in the case of apparitional phenomena, from person to person (and possibly from one individual or group to another individual or group). In chapter 2, we considered apparitions representing people that appear during times of crisis, particularly around the time of death. A disproportionate number of cases in the literature are crisis apparitions, and the impeccable timing of such occurrences transcends what we would expect if coincidental. Similarly, as was demonstrated in chapter 3, there are case reports of apparitions that have been produced intentionally and unintentionally by living agents. These apparitions are often seen by percipients who are a considerable distance from the physical location of the agent conjuring it.

Given the characteristics of these apparitional categories, I find myself in agreement with the consensus of psychical researchers that we are dealing with evidence of telepathy. Consider the following disturbing crisis case.

GUNSHOT FROM A DISTANCE

> In 1973, Deborah had a 21-year-old son who had been deployed to Vietnam. According to Deborah, "I woke up one morning around 2 a.m. feeling like I had been punched in the head. I was covered in sweat, had a terrible headache, and felt blood gushing down my face. I couldn't breathe and was gasping for air as if choking, I felt as if my lungs were filling with water or sludge, so I went to the bathroom to try and cough up the substance. I was overwhelmed with feelings of fear, sadness, and anger. Feeling weak, I sat down on the bathroom floor while crying."[27]

At the exact time that this was occurring, she heard the voice of her son saying, "Tell my mom I love her. . . . Please tell her I love her." Nearly instantaneously, Deborah's horrifying symptoms completely resolved. She got up from the floor and examined herself in the mirror, finding no evidence of head trauma or marks that could account for the symptoms. One week after the episode, she was notified that her son had died by a gunshot wound to the chest and catastrophic trauma to the head. The

---

27. Massullo, *Ghost*, ch. 4, para. 33.

time of his death was the same time that Deborah had experienced the traumatic symptoms.[28]

In this case, Deborah experienced auditory and extremely unpleasant tactile phenomena, but not visual phenomena. Also, the agent apparently projected these sensations while undergoing experiences that evoke extreme emotional reactions, as in the case of crisis apparitions. Lastly, the percipient, Deborah, was asleep when she received this most unpleasant message from her son. States of high absorption or relaxation seem to be prerequisite for experiencing psi effects. Louisa Rhine performed a study based on a collection of 169 cases like the above, practically all of which were firsthand reports.[29]

TELEPATHY IN ANIMALS

Interestingly, telepathic ability does not seem to be confined to humans. The following tragic case provides a good example of telepathic information transfer from canine to human.

OLD BOB

> On the night of Saturday, July 9 [1904], I went to bed about 12.30, and suffered from what I took to be a nightmare. I was awakened by my wife's voice calling to me from her own bed upon the other side of the room. As I awoke, the nightmare itself, which had been long and vivid, faded from my brain. All I could remember of it was a sense of awful oppression and of desperate and terrified struggling for life such as the act of drowning would probably involve. But between the time that I heard my wife's voice and the time that my consciousness answered to it, or so it seemed to me, I had another dream. I dreamed that a black retriever dog, a most amiable and intelligent beast named Bob, which was the property of my eldest daughter, was lying on its side among brushwood, or rough growth of some sort, by water. My own personality in some mysterious way seemed to me to be arising from the body of the dog, which I knew quite surely to be Bob and no other, so much so that my head was against his head, which was lifted up at an unnatural angle. In my vision the

---

28. Massullo, *Ghost*, ch. 4, para. 33.
29. Rhine, "Psychosomatic Psi."

dog was trying to speak to me in words, and, failing, transmitted to my mind in an undefined fashion the knowledge that it was dying. Then everything vanished, and I woke to hear my wife asking me why on earth I was making those horrible and weird noises. I replied that I had had a nightmare about a fearful struggle, and that I had dreamed that old Bob was in a dreadful way, and was trying to talk to me and to tell me about it.[30]

Sadly, Rider Haggard's nightmare emulated what Old Bob had suffered in his dying moments. Old Bob was found dead shortly after Rider's vivid nightmare. Old Bob's collar had been discovered by railway men on an openwork bridge. It was surmised that he had been hit by a train which had knocked him to the water below, where he ultimately drowned.[31] Rupert Sheldrake has amassed a trove of evidence that supports the contention that animals may exhibit telepathic ability.[32]

PSI AND APPARITIONS

In this chapter, we have seen evidence from the annals of psychical research of psi, in the form of psychokinesis, being used in altered states to produce stigmata of crucifixion. Moreover, apparent miraculous healings have been performed while under hypnosis. Evidence has been presented of apparitions being successfully produced, or at least summoned, while in altered states, including under the influence of psychedelic drugs, that were accompanied by healing. Finally, two non-visual cases of influence from a distance were detailed that are best explained by telepathy.

The upshot of that this data, along with the evidence of materialized entities produced in séances,[33] is that a good case can be made for the hypothesis that apparitions may be produced, in certain circumstances, by telepathy and psychokinesis. This will be important to keep in mind as we proceed.

---

30. "L. 1139 Dream," *JSPR* 11, 278.
31. "L. 1139 Dream," *JSPR* 11, 279–80.
32. Sheldrake, *Dogs*.
33. See chapter 8.

16

Apparitions, Super-Psi and the Question of Survival

THE BELIEF THAT DECEASED loved ones are enjoying heavenly bliss while looking out for us from the great beyond is comforting. Countless millions have experienced the presence of lost family and friends, sometimes even seeing, hearing, and touching them. In this volume, especially chapters 5–8, considerable evidence from eyewitness case reports has been presented that would argue strongly for the premise that consciousness survives bodily death. Credible reports of collectively experienced apparitions, along with the supernormal delivery of information in the context of these encounters, would seem to provide especially powerful evidence for this belief. On the face of it, the concept of life after death is not merely an ungrounded hope. As it turns out, our religious texts seem to be correct on at least this one crucial point.

Disinclined to believe that it can all be explained away by often gratuitous assertions of deception and misperception, the concept of survival after death once seemed to me happily inescapable. Still, deep beneath the data there lurks a menacing hobgoblin that resists efforts to exorcise it. That hobgoblin is known as super-psi, and it makes a living by throwing wrenches into what appears to be the obvious interpretation of messages apparently from the great beyond, including apparitions of the dead.

Super-psi is a blanket term for the most extreme or impressive manifestations of psi phenomena that occur in nature, some of which

APPARITIONS, SUPER-PSI AND THE QUESTION OF SURVIVAL

we considered in the last chapter.[1] On this theory, crisis apparitions and apparitions produced by the living result from telepathic and/or psychokinetic impulses. Hauntings are memory traces left upon objects or dwellings. Apparitions representing the entity that left those imprints behind on an object or environment may manifest if a sensitive enough person, or another conscious entity such as a dog, happens to be nearby. These categories of apparitions, covered in chapters 2–4, are not usually conscious. They are merely shades of those that they represent. I believe super-psi adequately accounts for these categories.

What about apparitions that rescue sailors caught in a storm at sea, or those that appear to comfort the terminally ill or spouses in grief? Are they of a different provenance? The appearance of a deceased person emanates from the deceased person, whether the apparition is conscious or it was created by a telepathic impulse. Or so the logic goes. This once seemed to me a very straightforward conclusion.

Numerous curveballs have been thrown my way over the course of this research. Some of these curveballs managed to change the trajectory of where I thought this project was ultimately headed. However, the apparition produced by Wesermann, considered in chapter 3, was the most impactful.[2] To summarize briefly, Wesermann successfully produced a waking apparition to two participants, a Lieutenant N. who was the target percipient, along with another person who happened to be with him at the time and place. This apparition was of a woman who had been deceased for five years.

Closing Tyrrell's book, where I encountered this case for the first time, I reflected on the information for most of that evening, coming to an abrupt realization that it was a gamechanger. That night, I felt as if I had just swallowed Morpheus's red pill. Like Neo, but admittedly in far less dramatic fashion, my view of reality had been irrevocably altered and there was no going back. This case begged a vexing question.

ARE ALL APPARITIONS PRODUCED BY THE LIVING?

There is a specific haunting case that I think punctuates the question. The father of a young lady had initially given his blessing for her to get

---

1. See Braude, *Immortal*, 10–23, for a good summary of the problems presented by super-psi within psychical research.
2. See the section titled "Fifth Experiment at a Distance of Nine Miles."

married, and then withdrew it. His wife, the mother, while on her death bed, asked him to reconsider. Initially, he did not grant this last request. Then the hauntings ensued. He received visits from her every morning at 4:00 a.m., which was the hour that she had died! The apparition always spoke of the couple and wore the same dress and cap she wore when she had supposedly uttered, "If I die before your father renews his consent, I shall haunt him till he does." The father was unaware of this until much later when one of his other daughters told him about it, after he had told her and her husband about the hauntings. He eventually renewed his consent, and at that point the visitations immediately stopped.[3]

Typical haunting? Or could it be that the apparition of the mother was produced non-deliberately by her husband, perhaps guilt-ridden from not yielding his blessing for the marriage? Another possibility is that the married daughter produced the apparition non-deliberately, the idea catalyzed by the mother's claim that she would haunt her surviving husband if he did not consent to the marriage. The background information of this case, along with the fact that the haunting apparition stopped after the father renewed his blessing, suggests that the appearances of the mother may have been apparitions generated by a living person.

Tyrrell relates other hauntings that were probably produced by living agents. An apparition of the recently deceased wife of "Mr. S." was seen numerous times by at least five different witnesses, and there were multiple collective appearances. The appearances continued for about one and a half years until Mr. S. remarried and left the house. The reprieve from the haunting lasted about five months, recurring when Mr. S. returned for a visit.[4]

---

3. Tyrrell, *Apparitions*, 145–46.

4. Tyrrell, *Apparitions*, 145. Tyrrell comments, "It seems here that the ghost haunts the house, like an ordinary ghost, yet the haunting centres about a person, as with a crisis-apparition." See also Case 52 in Tyrrell's collection, where haunting phenomena center around a particular cook at a house in Worcestershire. While in this latter case no apparition was reported, there were unexplained noises, disembodied footsteps, and disturbing tactile phenomena, including the feeling of a hand being placed around the throat and a principle being pushed by an invisible force. It was enough to "terrify the domestic staff." After the cook left the house, one of the principles wrote to the investigator that "since Mrs. E. (the cook) has gone on the 12th inst., we have had 'peace, perfect peace' as far as ghosts are concerned." Notably, the same cook had reportedly admitted that "something of the kind had happened in houses where she had been before." Tyrrell, *Apparitions*, 144–45. Then there are hauntings where the apparitions of initially unrecognized persons are later discovered by percipients to match that of still-living persons who eventually come for a visit. See Evans, "Ghost Experience," 45–46, for a striking example of the "You are our ghost!" phenomena. See also Bennett,

APPARITIONS, SUPER-PSI AND THE QUESTION OF SURVIVAL   145

Bereavement apparitions bring comfort and even psychological healing to countless numbers of grief-stricken people. Dr. Allan Botkin uses EMDR to produce such apparitions in veterans suffering from PTSD and achieves therapeutic outcomes that border on the miraculous. In the end, are these simply tricks of the mind, even though they are oftentimes elaborate? I am not sure this possibility can be ruled out.

What of those apparitions that convey information not obtainable through normal means? Again, super-psi has an answer. This information can in theory be retrieved from any conscious being. Some go as far as to suggest that information from every event that has ever taken place in history is stored in electromagnetic fields or some other heretofore undiscovered space. Just as we can turn the dial of a radio or flip channels on our streaming devices to tune in to thousands of different sources of information or entertainment, those experiencing (projecting?) apparitions can likewise tap into psi fields to obtain previously unknown information. Some, especially mediums, have demonstrated "secondary centers of consciousness" that somehow manage to retrieve information, or exhibit knowledge, of which the medium's primary personality was unaware.[5] For instance, sometimes mediums will speak languages that they have not learned or studied when entranced.

A person who exhibits signs of spirit possession may likewise be explainable through super-psi. For example, a secondary center of consciousness within a person with dissociative identity disorder, being closer to the subliminal stream of consciousness, would also be the aspect of personality more likely to manifest psi. We know from the mystical literature there are well-evidenced cases in history of levitations, amplifications of physical strength, telepathy, and of course psychokinesis, which may manifest as a poltergeist. Could it be that people ostensibly possessed, with or without exhibiting such paranormal abilities, are manifesting an alternative stream of consciousness deep within their respective personalities?[6]

What about the apparitions of religious figures who frequently render miraculous healings to their percipients? Abundant evidence exists to support the contention that the placebo effect is real.[7] The baseline

---

Haunted Houses, 337–45.

    5. See Crabtree, "Automatism," 354–61.

    6. See Braude, *First Person Plural*, where this possibility is explored.

    7. See Dispenza, *You are the Placebo*; Beauregard and O'Leary, *Spiritual Brain*. Good articles also appear in peer-reviewed medical journals. See Benedetti et al., "Conscious

placebo effect that exists in the medical literature would not explain some of the well-evidenced healings that are documented to have occurred at religious shrines or in the context of the appearances of religious apparitions. However, there is evidence that, in the right conditions, this baseline placebo effect may be amplified to produce unexpected and dramatic outcomes. If a person's subliminal consciousness may create an apparition of an entirely different person, then perhaps a person may create an apparition of a religious figure or even a fictional character. What better way would there be for a subconscious mind to affect physical healing than to simultaneously produce the apparition of a healer, whether it be a religious figure or the image of a doctor? If we combine the subliminal projection of a religious healer with the subliminal mind's innate ability to provide dramatic forms of bodily healing, such events are explainable via super-psi. We have demonstrated that both kinds of events occur in nature. Is it too great a stretch to suggest that both an apparition and a healing, in an appropriately dramatic context, may be created by the subliminal mind?

Obviously, these possibilities do not *require* these interpretations. However, I think in most cases these alternative interpretations are plausible. In such cases, the occurrence of apparitions of the dead or of religious figures as evidence for consciousness surviving bodily death is diminished.

I mention the complicated matter of super-psi for its heuristic value. In my opinion, super-psi often provides more plausible "solutions" for those wishing to avoid the conclusion that consciousness survives bodily death than do the usual explanations we have discussed in chapter 13. However, at the end of the day, I believe the survival hypothesis to be superior to super-psi. Some of the cases of apparitions require very convoluted, multifaceted, and *ad hoc* explanations if we lean exclusively on super-psi. The straightforward explanation may be the best one in such cases.[8]

Expectation"; Benedetti et al., "How Placebos Change"; Colloca and Barsky, "Placebo and Nocebo Effects"; Hróbjartsson and Gøtzsche, "Powerless"; Kaptchuk and Miller, "Placebo Effects"; Rossettini et al., "Context." Duffin, *Medical Miracles,* is also helpful.

8. One case from chapter 7 where I think the survival hypothesis is significantly superior to the super-psi hypothesis is the one described in the section *"I've left something inside that wall"—Charles's and Jean's Experiences.* The ostensible agent, Murphy, appeared to his old friend Charles in a dream multiple times even though they had been estranged for some time prior to Murphy's death. Charles seems to me an odd candidate for the visitation on the super-psi hypothesis. See Braude, *Immortal,* for a very comprehensive and balanced treatment of the issues involved regarding the "survival vs super-psi" debate.

Nevertheless, it is probable that some apparitions across all the categories we have considered are produced by living agents. Apparitions may certainly be produced deliberately and non-deliberately by living agents and be witnessed by multiple percipients. Can multiple agents produce apparitions of the living? Given the evidence we have for the former, accepting the latter does not seem to be a huge leap in logic. It is to this possibility that we now turn.

17

Apparitions as Expressions of the Collective Unconscious

PHILIP WAS BORN IN 1624, a cavalier who served under Charles II. His infidelity with a gypsy girl led Philip's wife to accuse her of witchcraft. Philip's mistress was burned at the stake. The tragedy led Philip to take his own life at the age of thirty. Researchers for the Toronto Society for Psychical Research performed a series of séances to contact Philip's spirit. There were eight participants in all, and after repeated attempts they were eventually successful. Strange sounds and other poltergeist-like phenomena were produced in response to questions and requests. This included knockings on fixed objects (raps), mysterious table movements, and lights flickering on a nearby panel. All these things occurred and could not be easily explained by normal causation.

Moreover, there was intelligent communication between Philip and the eight people that summoned his spirit. A series of raps—one rap for "yes," two raps for "no"—were communicated to the group in response to inquiries. The information received conformed well to Philip's biographical information. When requested to provide further evidence, Philip even caused a series of raps to occur upstairs where George Owen was present (the séance room was downstairs) and even at the dwelling of a participant who was ill and had to stay home on the night in question.[1]

This case would seem to provide strong evidence of postmortem survival if it were not for one pesky detail. The character of Philip and the

1. Roll and Persinger, "Poltergeists and Haunts," 153.

corresponding biography were completely fabricated by the Toronto SPR and those involved in "summoning" him. This is a further demonstration that psi phenomena are producible through the concentrated and deliberate efforts of a group of people. More importantly for our purposes, it shows that mere *ideas* may, in a manner of speaking, be brought to life.[2]

Clinical psychologist Kenneth Batcheldor hosted numerous séances that were successful in producing psychokinetic activity, particularly involving table tilting. Psychical researcher Guy Lyon Playfair was a participant and relates some of the astonishing things that occurred.[3] Playfair writes, "Batcheldor reckons that almost anybody can produce PK who really believes and decides that it is possible."[4]

In chilling fashion, Batcheldor spells out the implications of the reality of human-mediated psychokinesis, specifically regarding Ouija boards and equivalent.

> It could certainly explain some of the problems that can arise after playing with Ouija boards. As many children and quite a few adults now know, you can start by putting your fingers on an upturned glass, watch in surprise as it moves from letter to letter and begins to spell out intelligent messages, and then find things getting out of control.
>
> "As soon as it spells something a bit strange, you get frightened, and then you're in trouble," Batcheldor explained. "The main dangers of dabbling with psychic forces is that if you get frightened of them, you shape them into some frightening event—you create what you're frightened of. If you know this, and exercise some control over not getting unduly frightened, by constantly reminding yourself that you're creating this stuff by PK, and it's going to do what you believe, you can keep things under control. I don't allow my sitters to talk about apparitions of the devil or anything like that. We don't know what we might create if we start thinking along those lines.[5]

---

2. For similar accounts of poltergeist/psychokinesis in an experimental setting, see the discussion on the Society for Research on Rapport and Telekinesis (SORRAT) in McClenon, "Sociological," 74–79. Hilary Evans's full discussion on "Experimental Entities" is instructive regarding deliberately conjured apparitions. See Evans, *Visions, Apparitions, Alien Visitors*, 173–243, especially the chapter on "Thought-Forms" on pp. 216–22. See also chapter 3 of this volume.

3. Playfair, *Magic*, 176–88.

4. Playfair, *Magic*, 185.

5. Playfair, *Magic*, 182–83.

George Tyrrell said apparitions were sensory expressions of "idea-patterns," customarily formed from the midlevel personality (i.e., subliminal consciousness) of both agent and percipient (the "producers"). While the agent produces the idea that is to be conveyed, most often unintentionally, the percipient's subliminal consciousness also has a role to play in modifying the incoming information and presenting it to the conscious mind as a sensory expression.[6] He further speculates on the possibility of collective idea patterns, suggesting that they may arise from popular traditions, such as of the god Pan, fairies in Celtic lands, appearances of the devil, saints, the Blessed Virgin Mary, and witches on brooms in the Middle Ages, and the Flying Dutchman.[7]

Given the preponderance of cases where such idea patterns are experienced in much the same way by multiple percipients, the ideas projected may be experienced not only by targeted percipients but also perhaps by sensitive bystanders. Is this impulse delivered in some way to a particular place, or environment, as some of the data would seem to demand? Or is the process thoroughly mental? Perhaps we can invoke the concept of quantum entanglement to understand how collectively experienced apparitions are possible.[8] This would, I think, be particularly helpful in understanding Dr. Allan Botkin's collectively induced after-death communications (IADCs), where another present in the room may see (inwardly) the same unfolding drama as the patient.

Collective idea patterns lend credence to Carl Gustav Jung's "collective unconscious" where archetypal images are passed on through countless generations by heredity.[9] We have already seen how haunted houses share very similar, almost predictable characteristics, as do near-death experiences and bereavement apparitions. Essentially the same may be said for certain entities, such as encounters with ghosts, angels, and demons.[10]

Furthermore, culture shapes the content of apparitional experiences. For example, unlike in modern times, common within medieval

---

6. See chapter 2.
7. Tyrrell, *Apparitions*, 147–48.
8. See appendix B.
9. Jung, *Collected Works*, 42–53.
10. Common claims associated with sleep paralysis comes to mind, including people seeing grotesque, frightening incubi sitting on their chests. Similar encounters with the Old Hag are transcultural, see especially Hufford, *Terror*; also Evans, "Ghost Experience," 53–54, and Allison, *Mystery*, 21–26. On encounters with evil entities and demons, see Allison, *Mystery*, 38–46; on encounters with angels, Allison, *Mystery*, 73–98.

Christendom was the motif of distressing apparitions of the deceased suffering in purgatory.[11] It is surely no coincidence that a predominant concern among the faithful at that time involved the application of prayer and the paying of indulgences to diminish the suffering of deceased loved ones. Contrarily, as was demonstrated in chapter 7, reunion apparitions today are mostly comforting. Viewing the paranormal world through the lens of idea patterns or Jungian archetypes could also potentially explain well-attested and more versatile cases of entity encounters typically assigned to the realm of folklore. In this light, it is worth mentioning that there is considerable evidence that writers and their audiences will not uncommonly, and most of the time inadvertently, produce apparitions of fictional creations.[12]

Supernormal healings are also frequently accompanied by visions of doctors or religious icons, the content and interpretation of which tend to be dependent upon the percipient's culture. Across cultures, transitional and rescue apparitions sometimes represent deceased loved ones or religious figures. Christians may see angels or Jesus. Hindus may see deities associated with Hinduism or other figures such as Yamdoots.[13] In times of trouble or oppression, Catholics will sometimes experience apparitions of the Blessed Virgin Mary, some of which have received international acclaim replete with shrines where people continue to experience supernormal healings.[14]

11. Finucane, *Ghosts*, 49–86. See p. 71,"Many reports of apparitions, then, emphasized Church teachings about avoiding damnation or escaping from purgatory."

12. See Cutchin, *Fourth Wall Phantoms*, and Ramesh, *Embodied Imaginations*.

13. Yamdoots are messengers of Yamaraj, the god of death, that come to collect the souls of the dying.

14. I ran across a couple of interesting stories that effectively combine a Marian apparition within the construct of the phantom hitchhiker motif.

Two Muslim doctors encountered a "young lady walking along the road in the hot desert sun" as they journeyed from Alexandria, Egypt towards Cairo. The young lady was dressed as a nun. The doctors offered her a ride and she accepted. Along the way, the young lady questioned them about the Virgin Mary sightings in Zeitoun. Eventually realizing that Zeitoun was her destination, they drove her there. Upon arrival, they started for the car door to let the young lady out. People standing around the car at the time reportedly saw a dove fly from it. As for the young lady, she had vanished and could not be found. The author notes that four people he knows confirm this story, one of them a "very holy priest" who knew the two doctors very well.

In the second story, a nun carrying a Bible was picked up by a truck carrying forty passengers travelling from a church at St. Abu Seifen in Alexandria to St. Bishoi in the Natroun Valley to fulfill the wishes of deceased architect Kathy Kapel Khalil to baptize her daughter Mary in a coventry. Interestingly, along the way, the nun declined an offer for a drink of water but did peal an orange and gave it to a child. Upon arrival at the

I do not think the culturally-tuned content of these apparitions is coincidental. However, in emphasizing this cultural overlay I am by no means arguing for the subjectivity of said events. Quite the contrary. However, it does lend credence to the possibility that, in at least some cases, the agent of these apparitional dramas may be human rather than divine, angelic, or demonic.

Perhaps this is also why some religious apparitions greatly eclipse their secular counterparts in terms of the number of percipients. With countless millions of people paying homage to Jesus Christ and the Blessed Virgin Mary, is it more likely that like-minded individuals will share in seeing an objectively produced apparition? In communities where collective prayer is ceaselessly performed in the names of Jesus and Mary, does this make the production of their apparitions more likely to be of human agency? This theory would be consistent with the fact that the apparition of Jesus in Oakland, California, was identified with the famous Warner Sallman's *Head of Christ* and why the apparition of Mary in Betania, Venezuela, resembled the apparition that appeared to Bernadette Soubirous in Lourdes.

Consider phantom hitchhikers. The great majority of such tales are anecdotal at best and rarely are traceable to eyewitnesses. Nevertheless, phantom hitchhikers have been around for a while, even predating the invention of automobiles by centuries. This motif is so globally ubiquitous that Michael Goss was able to classify the encounters under four general templates in terms of how the narratives unfold.[15] Nevertheless, there are some well evidenced phantom hitchhiker encounters. Hilary Evans provides one such example from France.

> On 20 May 1981, four young people aged between twenty-five and seventeen were returning from the beach to their home town of Montpellier in southern France. It was some time after 11 p.m. The two young men were in front, their girlfriends behind. Quite soon after starting the journey, they saw a woman standing by the roadside, apparently thumbing a lift: she was dressed in white and wore a headscarf. Though he did not usually stop for hitchhikers, and though the car was full, Lionel, the driver, said that they could not let a woman stand alone on the roadside at that hour of night. He stopped beside the woman and told her they

---

coventry, the nun stood in front of the group, raised her hand, and said, "Peace." A bright light was then said to appear, and the nun disappeared. The passengers interpreted this figure to be the Blessed Virgin Mary. Zaki, *Before Our Eyes*, 134–35, 141–42.

15. See chapter 13.

were headed for Montpellier: she said nothing, but nodded her head. Then, because it was a two-door car, the other young man got out, and one of the girls, so that the woman could get in: she sat between the two girls in the middle of the back seat, and could now be seen to be a woman in her fifties.

Not a word had been spoken so far, but suddenly, after travelling some distance, the passenger cried out, so loudly as to drown the car radio, "Look out for the turns, look out for the turns!" She gesticulated with her right hand and added, "You're risking death."

All of them gazed intently at the road as if an imminent danger really did threaten. Lionel slowed down as he negotiated the bend. Then the two girls screamed: their fellow-passenger had abruptly vanished.[16]

The four pulled the car over and looked around for the hitchhiker but found nothing. They reported the incident to the Montpellier police. While initially skeptical of the young quartet, the police eventually became convinced by their apparent sincerity and fear.[17]

I surmise that the subliminal mind(s) of Lionel or one of the other passengers (or a combination of two or more of them?) produced the apparition, using the phantom hitchhiker motif to avert danger. Could it have been an act of precognition that pending disaster awaited when they arrived at that bend in the road? Notably, after the apparition spoke, Lionel and the other passengers became more alert and slowed the vehicle. We can only speculate on the how and why and whether an actual motor vehicle crash was prevented.

As we proceed, the evidence of psi produced by groups must be kept in mind as we interpret the postmortem appearances of the Lubavitcher Rebbe and Jesus Christ.

---

16. Evans, *Visions, Apparitions, Alien Visitors*, 160.

17. Evans, *Visions, Apparitions, Alien Visitors*, 160. The author intimates in another source that a Commissaire Lopez led the police investigation. See Evans, "Ghost Experience," 51–52.

18

Menachem Mendel Schneerson
The Lubavitcher Rebbe

HIS FOLLOWERS THOUGHT HIM to be the long-awaited Messiah and redeemer of Israel. This charismatic rabbi demonstrated unsurpassed theological insight and even performed miracles. Abruptly his followers' hopes were quashed by his unexpected death. Yet these hopes found renewal partly based upon interpretations of ancient Scripture and centuries of religious tradition. Followers to this day speak of his being raised from the dead. Many still seek his intercession through ritual and prayer. Some claim that he has appeared to them alive.

Yes, the similarities to Jesus are striking. Journalist Sue Fishkoff gives a brief account of one yeshiva student that believed Rabbi Schneerson to still be alive. Despite praying and citing Jewish liturgy at Schneerson's grave site, the student claimed that the Rebbe was never placed inside of the coffin: "I didn't look in the box. Did you look in the box?"[1]

THE REBBE AS MESSIAH

The Lubavitch movement originated from the White Russian city of the same name (Lubavitch) and was based at that location from 1815 to 1917. After World War II, the leadership moved to the United States and eventually headquartered in Brooklyn, New York, at 770 Eastern Parkway in

---

1. Fishkoff, *Rebbe's Army*, ch. 14, para. 43.

Crown Heights. Commonly referred to simply as "770," it is there that Schneerson served as the movement's leader from 1951 until his death in 1994. This mystical Jewish sect is also identified by the name "Chabad," which is an acronym meaning "Wisdom, Understanding, and Knowledge," based on a conflation of the three terms in the Hebrew language (*Chochmah, Binah, Da'at*). The movement's leader, or "Rebbe," means a teacher/expositor of Jewish sacred texts.[2] There have been seven Rebbes since Chabad's existence, Schneerson being the seventh and last one (to date no successor has been appointed).

By any measure, the Rebbe was an exceptional leader. Rabbi Schneerson was considered by some as "the most well-known rabbi since Moses Maimonides."[3] As of 2016, his outreach movement to fellow Jews had established Chabad Houses in forty-eight states and in eighty countries.[4] Schneerson was posthumously awarded the Congressional Gold Medal in 1994, the only rabbi and only the second clergymen to receive this honor. The Rebbe was a highly respected and influential figure even among prominent politicians of his day, including civil rights hero and congressman John Lewis and former Speaker of the House Newt Gingrich.[5] In 1982, President Ronald Regan wrote a letter to the Rebbe in honor of his eightieth birthday.[6]

Unfortunately, Schneerson suffered a stroke in 1992 and was paralyzed for the remainder of his life. He died of further complications of this in 1994. Already before his death, there was hope inside the movement that the Rebbe would be revealed as Messiah of Israel. The incapacitating stroke the Rebbe suffered in 1992 merely escalated the urgency and frequency of claims that he was Moshiach (Messiah). Unable to speak at this point, he could no longer refute the claims that were being made by the messianic faction of Lubavitch Hasidism. Fishkoff writes:

> Signs outside Lubavitch homes and offices, bumper stickers, billboards, and full-page ads in major newspapers proclaimed the aged, infirmed Chabad leader to be the long-awaited Messiah. Some Lubavitchers would sleep with their clothes laid out on the bed, so they would be ready to greet the Messiah should he arrive when they were sleeping. . . . Whenever Schneerson

---

2. Telushkin, *Rebbe*, 516n4.
3. Telushkin, *Rebbe*, 4.
4. Telushkin, *Rebbe*, 12.
5. Telushkin, *Rebbe*, 3.
6. Telushkin, *Rebbe*, 3–4.

appeared in his synagogue, Lubavitchers began singing *yechi adoneinu,* "Long live our Rebbe, our master, teacher, and king Messiah, forever and ever," taking his half-conscious nods as indications of his approval.

Movement leaders tried to quash these public displays, but their efforts were hampered by their own ambivalence: If Jewish tradition holds that a potential Messiah is born in every generation, then who in this generation, they asked, was more fitting for the title than the Luba-vitcher Rebbe?[7]

As the Rebbe lay in a coma in his last months of life in Beth Israel Medical Center in Manhattan, vigils were kept around the hospital by Hasidic "Messianic hopefuls" while the media "ran daily, sometimes hourly, reports on his health, seeking out young, grief-crazed Chabadniks eager to talk about how Schneerson would soon rise from his sickbed and lead them all to Jerusalem to rebuild the holy Temple."[8]

Messianic claims did not end after the Rebbe passed away on June 12th, 1994. Thousands of Lubavitchers the world over came to Crown Heights for the funeral. As the funeral procession moved down Eastern Parkway, most mourned while others were in a state of jubilation, singing and dancing with tambourines in anticipation that the Rebbe would rise from the dead.[9] On the day of the funeral, some of his followers refused to perform *kria,* the ritualistic ripping of one's clothing at the time of death of a family member or teacher. To this day, when referencing the Rebbe, the Lubavitcher Messianists will not use the standard formulaic expressions of one that has died (such as *"zichrono livrakha,"* or "may his memory be a blessing") whether in written statements or on monuments. Unlike the tens of thousands of others that make pilgrimages to the Rebbe's gravesite every year, especially to observe his *yahrtzeit* (the anniversary of death), the Messianists will do neither.[10]

THE ONGOING BELIEF THAT THE REBBE IS STILL ALIVE

As with Jesus, the Rebbe has followers who believe him to be the Messiah. While the overt belief in the Rebbe's messianic status constitutes a

---

7. Fishkoff, *Rebbe's Army,* ch. 14, paras. 16–17.
8. Fishkoff, *Rebbe's Army,* ch. 14, para. 22.
9. Fishkoff, *Rebbe's Army,* ch. 14, para. 23.
10. Telushkin, *Rebbe,* 420–21.

substantial minority within Chabad, there are a few that go further in attributing divine status to the Rebbe.[11] Perhaps most interestingly, some Messianists claim that he is still alive.

Chabad leadership generally denounced unambiguous messianic claims for the Rebbe:

> In 1998, the Central Committee of Chabad-Lubavitch Rabbis in the United States and Canada, Chabad's central rabbinic body, issued a statement denouncing this kind of messianism: "Belief in the coming of the Moshiach and awaiting his imminent arrival is a basic tenet of the Jewish faith. It is clear, however, that conjecture as to the possible identity of Moshiach is not part of the basic tenet of Judaism. . . . The preoccupation with identifying the Rebbe as Moshiach is clearly contrary to the Rebbe's wishes."[12]

Major Chabad organizations such as Agudas Chasidei Chabad and Merkos L'Inyonei Chinuch, and most of the emissaries of the Lubavitch movement (i.e., shluchim) antagonized trumpeting the belief that the Rebbe was the Messiah. Officially, the Hasidic leadership in both Israel and the US stands in opposition to such "overt messianist propaganda." The shluchim remain less influenced by such messianic belief than the general population in certain Lubavitch strongholds such as in Israel and Brooklyn.[13]

In 1993, Agudas Chasidei Chabad, the umbrella organization and central leadership body of the Lubavitch movement, tried to defuse the messianic fervor. Fishkoff notes, however, that the "decentralization that gives Chabad emissaries their maneuverability" made such defusing a difficult task. The director of Lubavitch Youth International and head of the *International Campaign to Bring Moshiach*, Rabbi Shmuel Butman, was one of the more vocal members of the messianic faction. Through private funding, Butman had hired his own board of directors not accountable to Agudas Chasidei Chabad.[14]

> Through the spring of 1993, a surrealistic situation prevailed, whereby Butman sat in his Crown Heights office, sending out messianic proclamations on 770 Eastern Parkway letterhead, while Agudas Chassidei Chabad staffers sent out counterfaxes

11. This is, per Simon Dein, a very small minority view among Lubavitchers; see Dein, *Prophecy*, ch. 4, paras. 11–14.
12. Fishkoff, *Rebbe's Army*, ch. 4, para. 27.
13. Dein, *Prophecy*, ch. 4, para. 1.
14. Fishkoff, *Rebbe's Army*, ch. 14, para. 20.

warning reporters and Jewish organizations to ignore all communications emanating from 770 not issued by themselves.[15]

Fishkoff explains that the question of whether a Lubavitcher is or is not a Messianist (or Moshichist) is "not a black-and-white question" but "more a sliding spectrum of belief." One on extreme, there is a small percentage of Lubavitchers who cautiously, and not in front of mixed company and definitely not to the media, claim that the Rebbe is *not* the Messiah. There are others who are ambivalent on the question. They admit that the Rebbe is dead, but leave open the possibility that the Rebbe could at some point prove to be the Messiah. Per Fishkoff, this is the majority position of Lubavitcher leaders and emissaries (shluchim). There are others that agree that the Rebbe is dead, but adamantly believe that he will be revealed as Messiah at a future time. Finally, on the other extreme, some claim the Rebbe to be Messiah *and* believe that he remains alive.[16]

Clearly many Lubavitchers are hopeful that the Rebbe will ultimately prove to be the Messiah, perhaps culminating in God raising him from the dead, but this has yet to occur, at least in the minds of the vast majority of the Rebbe's followers. Only a small minority of his worldwide community believe him to still be alive in some sense.

For those Lubavitchers who believe the Rebbe to be alive, different terms are often employed to describe his current state of existence. Some apply resurrection language while others refer to the Rebbe's "occultation" or "concealment."[17]

The Rebbe's grave is visited by many thousands of Lubavitchers annually. This is common in Hasidism as followers come seeking prayerful intercession in such practical matters as finance, health, and fertility. Additionally, as of 2011, about one thousand faxed requests are sent each day from those "hoping that the Rebbe's spirit will intercede on his or her behalf in heaven."[18] One of the Rebbe's assistants collects the faxed messages, delivers them, reads the requests aloud before dropping them atop a note pile that is more than twelve inches high and covers the area of the gravesite, about eight foot square.[19]

Curiously many Messianists engage in similar practices.

15. Fishkoff, *Rebbe's Army*, ch. 4, para. 21.
16. Fishkoff, *Rebbe's Army*, ch. 14, para. 4, emphasis added.
17. Dein, *Prophecy*, ch. 4, para. 35.
18. Dein, *Prophecy*, ch. 6, para. 45.
19. Dein, *Prophecy*, ch. 6, para. 45.

Paradoxically, although they maintain that the Rebbe is alive, some messianists regularly visit the Rebbe's grave to communicate with him and ask for his intercession. Many vehemently deny that he lies there, and do not visit the *Ohel*. . . .

One Lubavitch adherent explained this paradox:

"Terms like living and dead do not easily apply to a *tzadik*. They are not ordinary people. It is possible for the Rebbe to be alive and dead. It is not logical but there is no contradiction. Yes we hold that the Rebbe is alive, but his physical body is in the *Ohel* and his spirit is there. The Rebbe can be in many places at once both spiritually and physically. His soul is in Gan Eden (Heaven) but manifests itself in the physical world. We cannot understand this. What is important is that we are connected to him."[20]

The doctrine of *histalkus* in Hasidism is the belief that "a spiritual leader is even more powerful following his physical death."[21] The soul of a saint who experiences *histalkus* does not exit the physical body nor the physical world. Rather, it still is present within them, but exists in a more transcendent position.[22]

Rabbi Schneerson is not thought to be unique in this regard among Lubavitchers. Similar beliefs are held about Schneerson's predecessor, Yosef Yitzchak Schneersohn, the sixth Rebbe,[23] the Old Testament Patriarch Jacob,[24] and King David.[25]

In Chabad, the world is understood as both an illusion constructed by God and at the same time the state of existence that is really *real*. As such, some of the Rebbe's followers applied these conceptual elements to the Rebbe himself, understanding him to be both hidden yet somehow revealed simultaneously.[26] From the time of his apparent death, the Third of Tammuz, Messianists are no longer able to see the Rebbe in the physical sense, and yet, paradoxically, he remains alive; "it is only to our eyes that he is concealed." This day is known by some in the Lubavitch movement as the "day of concealment" or the "last test." The Rebbe is

---

20. Dein, *Prophecy*, ch. 6, paras. 41–42.
21. Dein, *Prophecy*, ch. 3, para. 1.
22. Dein, *Prophecy*, ch. 3, para. 40.
23. Dein, *Prophecy*, ch. 3, paras. 38–45.
24. Dein, *Prophecy*, ch. 7, paras. 4, 7–9.
25. Dein, *Prophecy*, ch. 7, para. 20.
26. Dein, *Prophecy*, ch. 3, para. 19.

here though he cannot be seen, just as God is here with us but cannot be seen with the eyes.[27]

Referring to Beis Menachem, a messianic sect in Stamford Hill, England, Dein writes, "They argue that the Rebbe is 'alive' in the literal sense but that we cannot yet see him. The problem lies with his followers who need to open their eyes, not their physical eyes, but their spiritual eyes, in order to see him."[28] Meshichists think of the Rebbe as alive, but invisible to our "eyes of flesh." Yet, in the end he will be revealed by God to be alive and well, and properly coronated as the Messiah of Israel.

To summarize, built upon a foundation of Hasidic Jewish epistemology, Messianic Lubavitchers believe in two simultaneous realities regarding the Rebbe's death and current state of being. The reality we see with our (physical) eyes is the one where the Rebbe died and is interred in a grave in Crown Heights, though as we will discuss presently there is some variability in belief here among Messianists. The other is the true and spiritual reality. This reality is unseen, or hidden, until God reveals it. Here the Rebbe is still alive, yet concealed to the more-mundane, physical reality that we all currently experience.

Dein further writes regarding the belief that the Rebbe is alive:

> Almost everyone I interviewed in Beis Menachem claimed that the Rebbe was alive, but sometimes it was impossible to clarify what they meant by this and whether the term related to the physical or spiritual. A few questioned the opinion of the doctors who certified him as dead and stated that their diagnosis might have been wrong. Additionally some spoke of the Rebbe as being in his grave but having his physical body intact and not decomposing since he was a "righteous person."[29]

As we have also seen, it appears that some Messianists believe the Rebbe's body would not be found at all if his grave were to be disinterred. Perhaps most intriguingly, some Messianists also claim to have experienced the Rebbe alive since well after his death. That is the subject of the next chapter.

---

27. Dein, *Prophecy*, ch. 4, para. 38.
28. Dein, *Prophecy*, ch. 7, para. 6.
29. Dein, *Prophecy*, ch. 7, para. 11.

19

Apparitions of the Rebbe

CONTRARY TO CHRISTIANITY, POSTMORTEM appearances of the Rebbe to Messianists were not foundational to the belief that he is still alive. Further, such appearances do not seem to play a central, or even prominent, role in Lubavitch Messianism. However, there have been scores of reported appearances of the Rebbe since his death. Anthropologist Yoram Bilu interviewed ten Messianists who saw the Rebbe in the period from 2008–2010, which is roughly fifteen years after the Rebbe had died.[1] Overall he amassed seventy-six reports of appearances of the Rebbe that had taken place between 1994 and 2010, 75 percent of which occurred in the latter half of that time frame.[2] Roughly two-thirds of the seers are men and that includes some children (13 percent, mostly boys). While some of the seers are well-known rabbis, most are "rank-and-file Hasidim." Interestingly, seers are disproportionately represented from recent immigrants to Chabad, those likely to be particularly enthusiastic members. There are also some cases of appearances to non-Chabadniks, including to nonobservant Jews.[3] Although most appearances occur once to a single individual, there are some cases where the Rebbe appears more than once, at different times, to the same individual.[4] Finally,

---

1. Bilu, "King," 99.

2. Bilu, "King," 101. In his later publication, Bilu puts the number of reports at "about eighty." Bilu, *More Than Ever*, 146.

3. Bilu, "King," 101.

4. Rabbi Schlomo Zalman Landa, in an interview, disclosed that he had encountered the Rebbe six times. Also, these encounters are "but the tip of the iceberg—such

there are rare instances of collective appearances of the Rebbe, usually to two individuals at once, though there is one documented appearance of the Rebbe to seven women at once at 770 during the Jewish holiday of Shemini Atzeret in 2005.[5]

The sightings tended to be brief, lasting anywhere from a few seconds to a couple of minutes, some were accompanied by "a short message or command or a few words of encouragement." Only a couple of accounts indicate that the Rebbe's message evolved into "an elaborate discourse." While most of the Rebbe's appearances occur at 770 and other Chabad Houses, frequently in the context of ecstatic atmospheres on Jewish holidays and festivals, about one-third of appearances occur in more mundane settings. These other settings are variable, including at people's homes, schools, hospitals, courthouses, on public transportation, open fields, and even out at sea and in forests. Appearances of the Rebbe have been reported in diverse places including Australia, France, India, Vietnam, and Egypt's Sinai Peninsula. However, most appearances of the Rebbe occur in the United States, almost exclusively at 770, and somewhat fewer appearances in various locations in Israel.[6]

For the appearances outside of ritualized contexts, "most of them are triggered by severe distress and sometimes life-or-death situations."[7] Bilu details three examples.

1. A girl was in a field when she was assaulted by a snake. Panicked, she shouted, "Rebbe, save me!" The Rebbe immediately appeared and with urgency told her to strangle the snake, which she did.

2. Palestinians were shooting at a public bus bound to Beitar Illit from Jerusalem. The Rebbe appeared in front of one of the passengers and pulled her down to the bottom of the bus. She was spared, but unfortunately the girl sitting next to her was killed.

3. A diver nearly drowned as he suffered from a condition called nitrogen narcosis.[8] Upon recovery, he recalled being saved by two figures that brought him to the water's surface. One of them, his

---

apparitions are common occurrences in his life." Bilu, *More than Ever*, 147.

5. Bilu, *More Than Ever*, 148.
6. Bilu, *More Than Ever*, 148.
7. Bilu, *More Than Ever*, 160.
8. Nitrogen narcosis occurs when divers breath compressed air, typically at depths of one hundred feet or more. This can affect muscle and cognitive function, potentially even leading to a loss of consciousness.

friend, insisted that he was alone in saving him. However, days later the diver saw the Rebbe in a photograph, recognizing him as the other man present that had pulled him from the depths.[9]

Other appearances of the Rebbe were catalyzed by those suffering from severe illness, undergoing economic crises, and in the context of lost loved ones.[10] There are two controversial reports of the Rebbe having been possibly captured on film. The Rebbe, his back to the camera, was seen in a photograph of a young boy originally taken in 2004 at 770. Reportedly no apparition was seen in real-time, but the image appeared only after the photo had been developed.[11]

Two years later, Schneerson was said by some to have been captured on video courtesy of a visitor to 770 and his cell phone. In a ritual setting, the video captured the "path" that formed by parting Hasidim prior to the prayer service to "make way for the Rebbe." The camera "caught a low figure with a white beard striding energetically toward the Holy Ark between the dancing and singing Hasidim on each side."[12] The video is reportedly of poor quality and the image appears for merely a split second. Regardless, it was interpreted by some Meshichists as proof that the Rebbe is alive.[13]

Messianists relentlessly plead with the Rebbe to reveal himself from his concealment, maintaining the belief that his absence is similar in nature to Moses's forty days of absence while on Mt. Sinai.[14] Bilu postulates that a combination of expectation, emotional arousal, and environmental factors create a milieu that is conducive to apparitions. The ritual settings themselves account for the first two, while the rich panoply of "icons, traces, and mimetic practices of embodiment" in Lubavitch Messianism accounts for the third.[15] Bilu writes,

> Widespread circulation of the Rabbi's pictures in messianic Habad and beyond is unprecedented in the Jewish world. Impressive portraits of the Rabbi, with his long flowing white beard and piercing blue eyes, adorn posters, signposts, books, magazines, charity boxes, clocks and watches, ritual cups,

9. Bilu, *More Than Ever*, 160–61.
10. Bilu, *More Than Ever*, 161.
11. Bilu, *More Than Ever*, 155.
12. Bilu, *More Than Ever*, 156.
13. Bilu, *More Than Ever*, 156.
14. Bilu, "King," 104.
15. Bilu, "King," 104–11.

key-binders, visa cards, medallions, and much more. . . . After 1994, this visual repertory became a major resource for making the absent Rabbi present and visible.[16]

In addition to portraits, video clips of the Rebbe's prior Hasidic gatherings play during the religious festivals at 770 as well as other Chabad houses. Visualization techniques are also practiced widely by Hasidim. Schneerson entreated his followers to visualize the prior leader of Chabad, Rabbi Yosef Yitzhak, when seeking intercession, including when visiting his tomb. More intriguingly, without explicitly identifying who the Messiah is, he urged them to create in their minds an image of the Messiah on festive occasions and holidays while performing a ritual called "The Messiah's Dance." In such contexts some followers visualized the Rebbe dancing alongside them. Not surprisingly, some of the apparitions reported by Messianists after his death were of the Rabbi dancing with them.[17]

While none of the interviewees indicate that visualization of the Rebbe in the mind's eye directly evolved into an externalized apparition, Bilu argues that such visualization practices may have served as "sensory prompts" from which many of the apparitions potentially occurred. Many of the apparition reports are similar in terms of positions and postures that the Rebbe takes in popular pictures at 770. Twenty-nine of the fifty-seven apparitions reported in the anthology, *Lifko'ah et Ha-Einayim* (*To Open the Eyes*), were in the likeness of pictures of Schneerson at 770.[18]

The Rebbe's pictures are also thought to possess curative properties. The portraits' miraculous power emanates from elaborate rituals designed to invoke a visual reciprocity between Schneerson and the petitioner. A petitioner suffering from a health problem might be encouraged to stand within close proximity of one of the portraits at 770, praise the Rebbe as King-Messiah, and recite passages of scripture while in a state of absorption (i.e., an altered mental state). There were three instances in which auditory messages from the Rebbe were heard to emanate directly from the portraits during such rituals.[19]

Likewise creating a milieu from which visions may spring, the Messianists continue to celebrate elaborate rituals (particularly on Sabbath, prayer days, and Jewish holidays) in which the Rebbe is "made to still

16. Bilu, "King," 104.
17. Bilu, "King," 105–6.
18. Bilu, "King," 106–7.
19. Bilu, "King," 106.

participate" in the same ways he would have when he was still alive. Referring to this phenomenon as "Mimetic Practices of Embodiment," Bilu details several specific examples.

> To convey the assertion that the Rabbi is still among the community, the structured daily routine that dominated the site until 1994 is meticulously reproduced. Most vivid in this system are rituals that act as sensory prompts "placing" the Rabbi in the same times and places where his past presence was most strongly felt. This is most evident in the three daily prayers conducted in the big study hall (*Zal Ha-Gaddol*) serving as synagogue. Just as the prayer is about to begin, a young *yeshiva* student reaches the podium on which the Rabbi used to pray in front of the congregants. He rolls the carpet over the podium and then exposes the covered armchair of the Rabbi and his "stander" (pulpit). . . . Ready to accept the King–Messiah, the congregants lift their eyes and gaze at the stairs descending from the Rabbi's office on the second floor. Then they split to create a clear path (*shvil*) leading to the podium. . . . The same Hasidic song that welcomed the approaching Rabbi in the past is excitedly reiterated today. Following the prayer, the carpet is unrolled, the armchair and stander covered, and the congregants accompany with song and dance the Rabbi's presumed exit.[20]

Bilu details other rituals in which the Rebbe is symbolically made to participate.[21]

The religious milieu in which Lubavitch Messianism operates is one ensconced within a rich tapestry of iconography. It is also charged by elaborate rituals and ecstatic experiences in which the Rebbe is still made to participate, if only symbolically. Add to this the intense desire of some Hasidim to catch a glimpse into that concealed reality in which their leader is still alive, it is not surprising that reported sightings have occurred.[22]

APPEARANCES OF THE REBBE IN DREAMS

Many of the Rebbe's followers also claim to see him in dreams, and some people interpret these dreams as objectively real. There are more than

---

20. Bilu, "King," 110.
21. Bilu, "King," 110–11.
22. The entire discussion in Bilu, *More Than Ever*, 149–57, is helpful. Also see pp. 74–97 and 98–134 of the same volume.

sixty such reports in *Sichat Hage'ulah*. As with apparitions seen in the waking state, in about 25 percent of these there is a connection between the dream and a picture of the Rebbe. Sometimes the Rebbe is recognized as the subject of the dream by pictures seen of him beforehand. There are other cases when the Rebbe is recognized from a photograph seen *after* the dream, however.[23]

Bilu says that "dreams that relate to the appearance of the Rebbe stress the splendor of his countenance," focusing frequently "on his white beard and piercing eyes." He has appeared in dreams wearing a crown on his head, sitting on a cloud, and surrounded by a halo of light, all highlighting his messianic status.[24] The Rebbe can also appear in more of an antagonistic role, demanding such things as strict Sabbath observance or telling a thief to return his ill-gotten gain.[25]

One example is worthy of quoting. The subject is an American from the Satmar Hasidic community who was serving a prison sentence.

> On the last day of the eight-day Pesach holiday, he was perturbed because he had no wine and *matzah* left to observe the Hasidic custom of the "Messiah's Meal" on the night after the last day of the holiday. Anxious and depressed, he fell asleep and saw himself at an audience with the Rebbe. The Rebbe turned to him and commanded him to say "*Lechayim*," "To life," as Jews customarily say when they drink. He said that he could not say it because the prison authorities had refused to supply him with wine. The Rebbe said: "You must be happy, you have nothing to worry about, the *matzot* and wine are on their way to you." When the Hasid woke up, a prison guard came into his cell and, to the man's astonishment, gave him wine and *matzot*. She explained that a "rabbi" had come to her in a dream and told her that "there is a Jew here who needs *matzot* and wine." She wondered how she would obtain the items, and the Rebbe responded: "The *matzot* are in the prison pantry and the wine in the refrigerator nearby."[26]

Afterwards the man showed the prison guard pictures of prominent spiritual leaders inside Chabad and she identified the Rebbe without

---

23. Bilu, *More Than Ever*, 136.
24. Bilu, *More Than Ever*, 139.
25. Bilu, *More Than Ever*, 139–40.
26. Bilu, *More Than Ever*, 144.

hesitation as the rabbi that had appeared in her dream.[27] This story is remarkable for several reasons. First, the Hasid's dream accurately presaged a very improbable solution to a problem. Second, somebody outside of the Hasidic community experienced an apparition of the Rebbe in a dream that she only later identified from a photograph. Third, veridical information was transferred, namely the location of where *matzot* and wine could be found.

ASSESSMENT OF THE REBBE'S POSTMORTEM APPEARANCES

Undeniably, the multi-faceted variety of appearances of the Rebbe to some of his followers, and to some who were not followers, holds tremendous value to those that experienced them. To be respectful to the seers, I wish to note at the outset that I am not in a position to adjudicate on the question of whether the experiences were merely subjective experiences (hallucinations or "sensory overrides," to use Bilu's term), objective apparitions, and/or actual appearances of Menachem Mendel Schneerson. However, as has been done for centuries with the post-resurrection accounts of Jesus, it behooves us to speculate on the possibilities.

To put the matter succinctly, through the religious environments created especially by the rich iconography (replete with pictures, paintings, videos, etc.), practices of visualization and absorption, and the mimetic practices described above, the Messianists frequently, and with a vast number of opportunities given the thousands of participants involved over the years, place themselves in positions to experience subjective visions of the Rebbe. Combined with the emotional excitement and the sense of expectation present, the prerequisites for mass hallucinations are satisfied in some cases where two or more people claim to have seen the Rebbe. This explanation seems especially plausible in the many cases where the appearances resemble the Rebbe's position and posture as seen in pictures displayed at 770. However, for those collective appearances reported where the Rebbe appears at the same time and location in space—and especially when he was perceived to look the same to the seers, and to have spoken the same words—this is more consistent with an objective event rather than group hallucinations. That is, those appearances do

---

27. Bilu, *More Than Ever*, 144.

correspond to something occurring in the external world, however this might be explained. More on this presently.

We briefly considered appearances of the Rebbe to a young girl who was attacked by a snake, the passenger on the bus that was under gunfire, and the diver who almost drowned. These appearances are strikingly similar in nature to rescue apparitions. We have considered more than a few of these in chapter 5. One might reasonably propose, as an alternative to positing objective appearances of the Rebbe, that these appearances are projections of the percipients' subconscious minds. We have evidence from case reports that some can project apparitions of themselves and even of others, deliberately and non-deliberately, and that a problem or crisis may be an occasion for which this might occur.[28] This is theoretically a plausible explanation for the young girl who was attacked by the snake and the man taking gunfire on the bus. It is more difficult to apply this explanation to the diver that nearly drowned, however, since he was not familiar with the Rebbe until recognizing him in a photograph a few days later.

What are we to make of the photograph and the brief video footage that many Lubavitchers attribute as evidence of the Rebbe briefly breaking into the physical world for an appearance? The photograph shows a man resembling the Rebbe as seen from behind. Presumably, there are others who may attend 770 who resemble the Rebbe, particularly with only the benefit of a backside view. It is difficult for me to do more than speculate. Regardless, as we only have a backside view, I do not think that this apparition can be classified as evidential. As for the video, I have not been able to see it for myself. Yoram Bilu refers to it as brief and of poor quality. I will simply note that there have been other situations where paranormal phenomena have been possibly captured on film and video. As one might expect, the matter is controversial.[29]

Some of the apparitions of the Rebbe that occur in dreams are, in my estimation, the most difficult to account for without positing a

---

28. See chapter 3.

29. See Massullo, *Ghost*, ch. 2, paras. 7–8, for an example of audio footage of a phantasm picked up on a Talkboy recording device in the 1990s; See Arcangel, *Afterlife*, 157–61, in which the author consulted with someone who had expertise in photography regarding a ghostly image of Jenny Vanckhoven's son Tim, who appeared on a photograph. Cavendish, *Myth*, 1098–99, prints three very old photographs allegedly depicting ghosts. Cf. Nickell, *Science of Ghosts*, ch. 38, and Nickell, "Phantoms, Frauds, or Fantasies?" 220–22, regarding ghostly images produced through fraud and other non-paranormal mechanisms.

supernormal explanation. The case of the Hasid receiving his wine and *matzot* for Pesach in the context of serving a prison sentence resists such naturalistic reduction. At minimum, I think we are dealing with a paranormal transfer of information, both in terms of the non-Hasid having a dream of somebody she recognized only later from a photograph along with having learned the location of the needed wine and *matzot*. The literature on the "nonreligious" categories of apparitions is replete with such cases of apparitions later identified by photographs.[30]

In summary, more than sixty dream cases and roughly eighty reports of apparitional phenomena of the Lubavitcher Rebbe have been published since his death (as of the time of this writing). These appearances have served multiple purposes from matters relating to childbirth, finance, and observing Jewish holy days. Most cases are in charged religious environments, but there are numerous cases of apparitions occurring in mundane contexts. In the religious environments, there are numerous examples of collective visions. There are also recurring visions. In one well known instance, that of Rabbi Landa, the Rebbe appeared to him six times over a lengthy period. We have seen at least three examples of rescue apparitions involving the Rebbe. Moreover, as with many of the secular apparition cases we have considered, a good case can be made for veridical information transfer in a few of the Rebbe's appearances. Finally, it is worth noting that the Rebbe has appeared to multiple people not within the Hasidic Jewish community, two of whom did not know who he was until later seeing a picture of him. One of these was in a dream, the other as a rescue apparition.

Whatever we are to conclude from this, all the Rebbe's appearances and the phenomena related to them do find analogy within the copiously documented literature on apparitions. While I would speculate that most of the reported apparitions of the Rebbe were subjective hallucinations, I do believe that a substantial minority of them were likely objectively real apparitions. This data adds a very intriguing dimension to the already robust evidence of paranormal phenomena, or psi, that has been documented over the course of the past 150 years by psychical researchers.

Now we turn to the reported appearance traditions of Jesus Christ to followers shortly after his crucifixion. What may be gleaned from these traditions and are they reducible to general apparitional phenomena?

---

30. For four such cases, see Bennett, *Haunted Houses*, 40–48, 90–93, and 114–16.

20

The Resurrection of Jesus Christ

REGARDING THE SOURCE MATERIAL for Jesus' post-resurrection appearances, we are disadvantaged in a major way compared with what we have for other phenomena discussed in this book. Much of our best evidence for apparitions comes from direct interviews with the seers. The meticulous investigators who comprised the early Society for Psychical Research often examined well-evidenced apparition cases with a high level of scrutiny and with a premium placed on eyewitness testimony. Yoram Bilu personally interviewed numerous witnesses of apparitions of the Lubavitcher Rebbe. Thanks to the efforts of John Haffert and others, we have depositions of more than thirty people who were present at the Cova da Iria in Fátima, Portugal, when the miracle of the sun occurred.[1] For the Marian apparition at Knock, Ireland, depositions of fifteen of the seers were conducted less than three months after the fact and were published in books less than one year afterwards.

Outside of Saul of Tarsus, who became known as the apostle Paul, we have no undisputed direct testimony of Jesus' postmortem appearances. Even in Paul's case we are given no details of the appearance(s). Specific information about what took place during these initial encounters comes mostly from the Gospels of Matthew, Luke, and John. And what historically reliable information these narratives contain is a highly controversial matter.

---

1. While these interviews were conducted more than forty years after the fact, imagine the excitement that would be generated if we had something comparable for the disciples of Jesus regarding the post-resurrection appearances.

Nevertheless, the situation is far from hopeless. I think there is good reason to believe the post-resurrection narratives in the canonical Gospels convey essentially reliable information. This will be explicated presently. In what follows, we will evaluate the postmortem appearances of Jesus Christ through the lens of the apparitional categories and other psi phenomena we have considered in earlier chapters.

SOURCE DATA FOR JESUS' EARLIEST POSTMORTEM APPEARANCES

In his undisputed letters, the apostle Paul confirms that he persecuted the early Church.[2] In 1 Cor, Paul writes that he had seen the risen Jesus,[3] the implication being that his conversion to Christianity was the result of Jesus' post-resurrection appearance to him. The details of Paul's experience and his conversion are narrated by Luke.[4]

In 1 Cor 15:3–7, Paul lists post-resurrection appearances of Jesus to other individuals and groups including to Cephas (Peter), to "the Twelve," to a group of more than five hundred of Jesus' earliest male and female followers, and to a wider group of apostles ("all the apostles"). Intriguingly per this tradition, Jesus also appeared alive to his half-brother James, a very prominent early church leader who is generally thought to have been a skeptic prior to his experiencing this post-resurrection appearance. Virtually all New Testament scholars across the ideological spectrum agree that Paul here reproduced oral tradition that originated from Jesus' earliest followers shortly after the genesis of the church.[5]

Of course, the list of appearances in 1 Cor 15 was not exhaustive of early Christian claims. According to the post-resurrection narratives in the canonical Gospels, Jesus appeared to Mary Magdalene and possibly to at least one other woman simultaneously before appearing to any of the disciples.[6] He also appeared to two other male disciples collectively, including Cleopas, on the road from Jerusalem to Emmaus.[7]

---

2. Gal 1:13, 23; Phil 3:6; 1 Cor 15:9.

3. 1 Cor 9:1; 15:8.

4. Acts 9, 22, and 26.

5. See Allison, *Resurrection*, 37–44; Licona, *Resurrection*, 222–35; Habermas, *Risen*, 17–19; more recently Habermas, *Evidences*, 481–84 and 499–503.

6. John 20:11–18; Matt 28:8–10.

7. Luke 24:13–35.

While controversy exists to what degree, if any, the Gospel narratives are to be considered historically reliable, taking them at face value would indicate that the appearances of Jesus are physical in nature and occur within mundane contexts. The appearances of Jesus in the Gospels of Matthew, Luke, and John all indicate that Jesus was touched. He also engaged in theological instruction and discourse, as such carried on lengthy conversations, consumed bread and fish, cooked fish, and even directed the disciples, who were fishing on a boat at the time, to yet another miraculous catch. Paul likewise appears to understand resurrection to involve the corpse.

To the best of our knowledge, none of Jesus' followers believed he would be raised from the dead prior to experiencing the initial postmortem appearances.[8] There is certainly no indication that any members of Jesus' inner circle believed this would occur until Jesus appeared alive to them on Easter Sunday.[9] However, the foundation of the church's rejuvenated belief in Jesus' messiahship was his vindication by resurrection, which in turn was authenticated by the post-resurrection appearances.[10]

HISTORICITY OF JESUS' POST-RESURRECTION APPEARANCES IN THE GOSPELS

While the early and apostolic origin of the material in 1 Cor 15:1–8 is generally beyond dispute in scholarly circles, this is not the case for the appearances narrated in the Gospels. Some very conservative New Testament scholars accept the historicity of almost all the content found within the various narratives while those on the other end of the scholarly spectrum find therein little-to-nothing of historical value. Most scholars fall somewhere in between these two extremes.

An adequate defense of the Gospels' post-resurrection narratives would require a book of its own. In what follows I will summarize in cursory fashion why I believe that these narratives are substantially accurate regarding what happened on Easter Sunday and beyond.[11] This will,

---

8. This despite Jesus' predictions of vindication after death; see for instance Mark 8:31. For a detailed treatment of the historicity of Jesus' predictions of death and vindication, see Habermas, *Evidences*, 797–802; Licona, *Resurrection*, 284–301, and Kendall, "Passion," 51–80.

9. See Luke 24:13–49.

10. See Acts 2:32.

11. Note that I do agree with the scholarly consensus that the longer ending of Mark

I think, be helpful to extract data that needs to be considered when we compare Jesus' postmortem encounters with his disciples to the general phenomena of apparitional encounters.

Michael Licona points out that Jesus' post-resurrection appearances find multiple attestation from 1 Cor 15, the early speeches in Acts, which likely represent summaries of early apostolic preaching,[12] the four canonical Gospels,[13] Clement of Rome, and possibly the first-century Jewish historian, Flavius Josephus, an unsympathetic source.[14]

Somewhat more controversially, the authors of the post-resurrection narratives in the Gospels appear to draw upon multiple traditions. The narratives in the Gospels of Matthew, Luke, and John overlap in some key areas while diverging in important ways. Each evangelist narrates post-resurrection appearances that are unique to his own Gospel. The appearances occur in different locations and circumstances. Moreover, there are some differences in the accounts that make it difficult to harmonize them into a single coherent narrative. While these differences are no friend to some views of biblical inerrancy, they are suggestive of multiple, at least partially independent traditions.[15]

N. T. Wright has cogently argued that the post-resurrection narratives are likely based upon very early traditions on the following grounds:

1. The prominence of women in the accounts, the significance of which we will discuss presently.

2. The relative dearth of Old Testament Scriptural allusions and embroidery in the accounts that we find very frequently elsewhere in the New Testament.

3. The absence of future hope in the narratives, such as an explicit connection of Jesus' resurrection to salvation or believers' future resurrection.[16]

(vv. 16:9–20 in modern translations) is inauthentic and that the original author ended his Gospel at v. 16:8 or, if not, the original ending has been lost. See Metzger, *Textual Commentary*, 102–7.

12. See Dunn, *Beginning*, 87–98, where this is persuasively demonstrated.

13. Although Mark does not narrate post-resurrection appearances, he expresses awareness of them. See Mark 14:28; 16:7.

14. See Licona, "Criteria of Authenticity," 301–2.

15. So Ladd, *Believe*, 93–94.

16. This is distinct from what we find in much of the early Christian traditions and literature. The post-resurrection narratives espouse a primitive atonement theology. We find Jesus commissioning the disciples to preach the resurrection for forgiveness of sins

4. The mundane nature of Jesus' appearances is not what one would expect given the extant Jewish literature at the time of resurrection hope.[17]

Several New Testament authors seem to differentiate the post-resurrection encounters of Jesus to those who were to become apostles from these subsequent visions of Jesus that were experienced by some early Christians.[18] For Luke, the dividing line seems to be drawn at the time of Jesus' ascension.[19] Admittedly this dividing line gets murky when including the appearance to Paul on a par with the appearances of Jesus before his ascension.[20]

Gerd Lüdemann believes that this differentiation was invented by the leaders of the early church essentially for political purposes.[21] In order to maintain an authoritative, apostolic stature, only these initial appearances of Jesus counted to that end. Nevertheless, I find the reason implicit to the Gospel narratives to be a better explanation for this differentiation. Prior to his ascension, Jesus did appear in these mundane circumstances, demonstrating in convincing ways that he was alive again in a body that had continuity with the one that had died, yet had properties that made it somehow different, and somehow enhanced. If Jesus did appear in the way he was said to have in the Gospels, the reason to differentiate these appearances from those that occurred later in church history is obvious.

If we have multiple, early independent traditions represented in the Gospel post-resurrection narratives, our confidence in the basic historicity of the narrated content that multiple Gospels have in common is increased. In all four Gospels, women find Jesus' tomb to be empty on

---

which in its first-century context need mean no more than national covenant restoration.

17. Wright, *Resurrection*, 599–608. Drawing on the fourth point, the portrait of Jesus in these narratives is especially curious on the premise that the narratives were fabricated for apologetic purposes, as they describe a person who the early church believed was the messiah, the Son of Man of Dan 7, divinity incarnate who was exalted to the right hand of God, and who did appear in a majestic, glorious form in visions to at least certain individuals in early church history. See Acts 7:55–56; Rev 1:9–18. For exposition of this point see Kendall, "Vindication," 153–61, and O'Connell, "Collective," 93–105.

18. 1 Cor 9:1; 15:8.

19. Acts 1:9–11.

20. In 1 Cor 15:8, Paul says "last of all" that Jesus appeared to him.

21. "Many people have seen Jesus and have had experiences of Jesus, but the church had to put a stop to these experiences. In other words, when we talk about resurrection witnesses, and who is an apostle and so forth, these are determinations made by the Jerusalem church, which had to define its own authority vis-à-vis other conflicting stories." Lüdemann, "First Rebuttal," 55.

Easter Sunday. They are instructed by one or two angels to inform Jesus' disciples that he has risen. Mark knows about post-resurrection appearances of Jesus to his disciples in Galilee.[22] We find narratives of post-resurrection appearances of Jesus in Galilee in Matthew and John.[23] Jesus appears to disciples in Jerusalem in both Luke and John.[24] Percipients of the risen Jesus are apparently able to touch him in Matthew, Luke, and John; and in at least Luke and John, Jesus invites them to test his corporeality.[25] In both Luke and John, Jesus shares a meal with the disciples, and even is said to have cooked fish and bread in the latter.[26] As such, he would have left physical changes in the environment as a result of his actions at the time of appearing. Complex conversational exchanges are implied, if not narrated in significant detail, in all three Gospels. Finally, it is worth pointing out that in each Gospel, Jesus appears in ordinary spacetime and is apparently perceived with ordinary vision collectively by all that are present at the time. In other words, Jesus does *not* appear from another dimension against some other-worldly or heavenly backdrop as he does in some of the visions that Christians experienced later in the history of the church. Each of these aspects of Jesus' post-resurrection appearances are multiply attested, and this increases the probability of authenticity.

The narratives also contain features that would have proved embarrassing to the disciples and early church. This would argue against fabrication. That women were the first to both discover the empty tomb and see the risen Jesus in all the narratives is highly unlikely to have been invented. First-century Roman and Jewish cultures did not value the testimony of women in legal matters or in matters of religious revelation. This skepticism is manifested by Jesus' disciples when they first hear the women's report of discovering the empty tomb and their encounter with the angels that inform them that he has risen.[27]

---

22. Mark 14:28; 16:7.

23. Matt 28:16–20; John 21.

24. Luke 24:36–48; John 20:19–23, 26–29; on the probability of appearances in both Galilee and Jerusalem, see Wedderburn, *Beyond*, 53–56.

25. Luke 24:39; John 20:27.

26. Luke 24:41–43; John 21:9–13.

27. Luke 24:11; on credibility in general, see Bauckham, *Gospel Women*, 268–77. Robert Conner is skeptical of the historicity of the empty tomb, but his discussion of the scandalous nature of the women's central involvement in the narrative seems to unwittingly support the apologetic argument. Conner, *Ghost Story*, ch. 4.

For similar reasons, the disciples' fear of the authorities and initial doubts of these reports was unlikely to have been fabricated. According to Luke, even when Jesus first appears collectively to the disciples, they were frightened and initially thought him to be a spirit.[28] Then of course there is the famous "Doubting Thomas" episode that was said to have occurred one week after Jesus' initial appearance to the disciples.[29] One may argue that these doubts were used to set the stage for apologetic purposes, prompting Jesus to prove his corporeality by, for instance, consuming bread and fish and inviting the disciples to touch him.[30] However, the motif of doubt could just as easily have been a stumbling block to evangelism and was unnecessary to invent in order to furnish proofs of Jesus' physical resurrection. In this author's opinion, the most likely explanation for the inclusion of this motif is that this accurately reflects the disciples' initial reaction to the event. If the initial doubts were present, and if Jesus did appear bodily to the disciples after his resurrection, it seems natural that he would want to demonstrate his physicality.

GOSPEL AUTHORSHIP AND EYEWITNESSES

While one may plausibly argue that we are dealing with early, multiply attested traditions within these narratives, I am of the persuasion that eyewitness testimony lies closely behind their composition. Originally the Gospels did not circulate with the authors' names being contained within the documents, as was true of nearly all the extant biographies composed during that era.[31] Furthermore, many scholars doubt the traditional authorial ascriptions. Nevertheless, traditional authorship is supported unanimously by the earliest external sources we have for

---

28. Luke 24:36–37.

29. John 20:26–29.

30. Allison accepts the historicity of the doubt motif, also that the Gospels likely preserve a memory of Jesus' appearances being solid, as with many apparitions, though leans more skeptical of the historicity of Jesus' overt demonstrations of his physicality. Allison, *Resurrection*, 205–6, 229.

31. Hengel argues persuasively that it is unlikely that the Gospels circulated anonymously for a long period of time amongst the early Christian communities. Hengel, *Four Gospels*, 53–56. In a similar vein, see Bauckham, *Eyewitnesses*, 536–37.

Matthew,[32] Mark,[33] and Luke.[34] Most of the earliest external sources attribute authorship of John's Gospel to John the son of Zebedee, though this is not unanimous.[35] For most ancient documents we do not have the comparatively early and robust authorial attestation that we have for the four Gospels.[36]

Based on the consensus of our earliest sources, I think Mark's Gospel is primarily based on the testimony of the apostle Peter.[37] Fortunately, I seem to be in good company.[38] Luke, not an apostle, claims to have conducted a careful investigation of testimony that had been passed down by the original eyewitnesses.[39] On the most natural understanding of the so-called "we passages" in Acts, there is reason to believe that he was in a good position to do so. First, he was probably a travelling companion of the apostle Paul. More speculatively, based on the evidence from Acts,

---

32. Davies and Allison, *Saint Matthew*, 7–17.

33. See France, *Mark*, 36–38, on the unanimity of the earliest sources not only of Markan authorship but also that he derived his Gospel from the teaching of the apostle Peter. Joel Marcus's analysis makes a good case for traditional authorship by John Mark, but he rejects a Petrine connection. Marcus, *Mark*, 15–24.

34. Fitzmyer, *Luke*, 36–40.

35. Other possible authors of the Fourth Gospel include John the Presbyter (another disciple, not one of the Twelve), Lazarus, and John Mark, who is traditionally ascribed authorship of the Second Gospel. Raymond Brown, *John*, lxxxviii–xcviii, contains a helpful survey of the early evidence and discussion of the various possibilities. Bauckham, *Eyewitnesses*, 412–70, argues for John the Presbyter as author.

36. More than two centuries passed from the time the second-century classical historian Tacitus wrote his *Annals* before finding direct confirmation by an external source. See Holding, *Trusting*, 140–41. The situation is dramatically better for each of the four Gospels; see Holding, *Trusting*, chs. 15–18. Similar is the attestation for the classical biographer Plutarch who likely wrote his *Lives* in the early second century: "The best source attesting Plutarch's authorship is the Lamprias Catalogue, written more than a century and perhaps more than two centuries after Plutarch's death. Additionally, it is falsely attributed to Plutarch's son. Still, no one questions Plutarchan authorship." Licona, "Reliable."

37. In addition to the unanimous external testimony, strong indicators within the Gospel itself are highly suggestive of a connection between Mark and the apostle Peter. See Hengel, *Four Gospels*, 78–89, and Bauckham, *Eyewitnesses*, 509–36.

38. In his unpublished MA thesis "The Modern-Day Scholarly Opinion of the Dating of Mark's Gospel," Joshua Pelletier surveyed the views of more than two hundred critical scholars writing between 1965–2016 regarding Markan authority, finding that a substantial majority favors the traditional view of Markan authorship. Furthermore, a majority also favored the traditional view that the apostle Peter was Mark's chief source. See Habermas, *Evidences*, 777–78.

39. Luke 1:1–4.

he may have resided in Judea for about two years.[40] If so, this would have given the author of the Third Gospel more than ample opportunity to talk directly to many eyewitnesses of Jesus' sayings and deeds, and other relevant events found in his Gospel. Whether or not the author of John's Gospel was the son of Zebedee or if the "Beloved Disciple" is someone else entirely, we have good reason to believe that the content originates from a well-connected Jewish author, even if not one of the Twelve.[41]

The matter of Matthew is complicated. The earliest sources indicate that the apostle Matthew penned his Gospel first in Aramaic (Hebrew) prior to the composition of Mark's Gospel. The version of Matthew we have now was originally written in Greek and it is widely believed that Mark served as one of the main sources.[42] However, if Matthew used Mark, which is probable, this precludes the existence of an Aramaic Gospel of Matthew that is substantially like the later Greek version. The current scholarly consensus rejects the view that the Greek version of Matthew (that we now have) could have been a translation of an underlying Aramaic Gospel.[43]

Doing justice to the unanimous early evidence, my best speculation entails Matthew having originally penned a primitive, albeit very different, form of his Gospel in Aramaic. Perhaps this is limited only to the material peculiar to his Gospel ("M") or perhaps he authored something like Q.[44] A later author, likely with Matthew's direct stamp of authority, translated and incorporated this material, compiling it with edited material found in Mark, to compose the Greek, canonical version we now have. This admittedly speculative theory would seem to place me somewhere in Craig Keener's proximity on Matthean authorship.[45]

40. Keener, *Acts Commentary 3*, 394–428.

41. John 21:24. Even if the author was a separate disciple named John, John Mark, or Lazarus rather than John the son of Zebedee, the author would have been in a good position to collect and convey accurate historical testimony, and this contention has widespread scholarly support. See Habermas, *Evidences*, 859–63.

42. See Licona, *Contradicted*, 30–41, for an accessible discussion of why scholars generally prefer Markan priority.

43. Though this view has not gone unquestioned, see Davies and Allison, *Saint Matthew*, 12.

44. Q, short for *Quelle* (meaning "source" in German) is a hypothetical source that most scholars believe was used by Matthew and Luke to compose their respective Gospels. Q material is the material common to Matthew and Luke that is *not* found in Mark.

45. "I am therefore presently inclined to accept the possibility of Matthean authorship on some level, although with admitted uncertainty. Perhaps the most probable scenario that incorporates the best of all the currently available evidence is the presence

Establishing that eyewitness testimony likely underlies the Gospel content only takes us so far, as even eyewitness testimony can be unreliable. Psychological studies have demonstrated that memory can in some instances be imperfect. Richard Bauckham addresses this at length and how it may affect the accuracy of the Gospel testimony in his *Jesus and the Eyewitnesses*.

A comprehensive treatment of this subject would require a detour into how traditions are transmitted in oral societies (of which the one in question was) and how specifically the early church utilized safeguards to preserve the accuracy of its own traditions. Fortunately, this has been done by Bauckham and others at length. What we will consider briefly here are the characteristics of events that are, if present, more likely to make them memorable and how a few of them relate to the Gospels.

Drawing from psychological studies of recollective memory, Bauckham discusses nine factors that are more likely to render an event more memorable:

1. Unique or unusual event
2. Salient or consequential event
3. An event in which a person is emotionally involved
4. Vivid imagery
5. Irrelevant detail
6. Point of view
7. Dating of the event
8. Gist and details
9. Frequent rehearsal

Bauckham discusses each of these factors generally and subsequently how each is pertinent to the Gospels.[46] While all nine may be relevant in some sense to the New Testament narratives, three of the above factors in particular stand out as especially important in application to the post-resurrection accounts.

---

of at least a significant deposit of Matthean tradition in this Gospel, edited by the sort of Matthean school scholars have often suggested (though I believe the final product is the work of a single author, not a 'committee')." Keener, *Matthew*, "Authorship," para. 5.

46. Bauckham, *Eyewitnesses*, 331–46.

1. *Unique or unusual event*: Bauckham points out that "most of the Gospel narratives recount events that we would ordinarily regard as 'memorable' because of their often unique, often unusual, often surprising characteristics."[47] Doubtless, events surrounding the resurrection would be the apogee of said unusual or unique events for all involved.

2. *Salient or consequential event*: It would be difficult to understate the salience of Jesus' post-resurrection encounters to all that experienced them (and to a large extent those that heard the stories and converted as a result). For the disciples, this was the most consequential event of their lives.[48]

3. *Frequent rehearsal*: By practical necessity, the post-resurrection appearances would have been told and retold hundreds of times by the percipients from an extremely early point and down to matters of detail. At the absolute latest, the apostles would have had to recite these stories from the first day of evangelism (according to Luke, this was at Pentecost, which was about fifty days after Jesus' crucifixion and ten days after his ascension). Anyone outside of the movement who had not seen the risen Jesus would have doubtless inquired of such details before devoting their allegiance to a crucified Messiah. As such, these stories would likely have acquired a fixed form early on.

Bauckham writes regarding frequent rehearsal that it "would have the effect of preserving an eyewitness's story very much as he or she first remembered and reported it."[49] He further writes,

> The eyewitnesses who remembered the events of the history of Jesus were remembering inherently very memorable events, unusual events that would have impressed themselves on the memory, events of key significance for those who remembered them, landmark or life-changing events for them in many cases,

---

47. Bauckham, *Eyewitnesses*, 341.

48. These first two factors can be tested on a personal level. Do you remember where you were and what you were doing when you first learned of the 9/11 terrorist attacks? Your wedding day? I do. For those of you with children, what about the day they were born? I remember the specific circumstances (where I was, who I was with, etc.) when my Kentucky Wildcats won the 1996, 1998, and 2012 NCAA Tournaments, also in 2015 when tragedy struck and my team's bid for a historic 40-0 run was cut short in the national semifinals.

49. Bauckham, *Eyewitnesses*, 345–46.

and their memories would have been reinforced and stabilized by frequent rehearsal, beginning soon after the event.[50]

While Bauckham was referring to Gospel events more generally, his comments apply more forcefully to the resurrection than probably any other event or saying narrated in the Gospels.[51]

Reflecting Bauckham's point, Dale Allison summarizes the implications well.

> It is, to my mind, wholly implausible that early Christians would have been content with bare assertions devoid of concrete illustration or vivid detail. Were there no story-tellers until Matthew, Mark, Luke, and John showed up? First Corinthians 15:3–8 is skeletal, a bare-bones outline. It begs for more. How did Christ die, and why? Who buried him, and why? And in what way exactly did Jesus "appear" to people? Did such questions not interest anybody?
>
> ... Such a conclusion would be consistent with my claim, made earlier, that old appearance narratives probably lie behind 1 Cor 15:3–8, for if the traditions in the Gospels are not the descendants of those narratives, where did they all go? Did the original stories simply disappear, to be replaced by a new batch of tales of a wholly different character? Is it not intrinsically more likely that the narratives known to us, with their parallels in first-hand reports of apparitions, were outgrowths of more primitive narratives? I myself am emboldened by relevant parallels to reckon with more historical memory in the canonical Easter stories, or rather more memory in some of their repeated motifs, than I otherwise would.[52]

In summary, the likely proximity of the Gospel authors to eyewitness testimony, multiply attested motifs, numerous characteristics within the narratives that point to general authenticity, along with the inherent memorability of the events narrated lead me to believe that we are at least generally on solid historical ground when reading the post-resurrection narratives.[53] From this I conclude that the appearances of Jesus to the disciples involved the following:

50. Bauckham, *Eyewitnesses*, 346.

51. See Keener, *Christobiography*, 401–502, for more on eyewitness testimony/reliability of Gospel oral traditions.

52. Allison, *Resurrection*, 41, 226.

53. For a thorough argument supporting the basic reliability of the post-resurrection narratives in the Gospels and Acts, see Habermas, *Evidences*, 751–907.

1. Multiple collective appearances to groups of between at least two to twelve people in multiple locales.
2. Jesus ostensibly was seen with ordinary sight in everyday contexts and circumstances.
3. His body appeared to be overtly physical but with enhanced properties such as the ability to appear and disappear at will. While he was the same person as before, there seems to have been something different about his new body that altered his physical appearance to a degree.
4. Contrary to what may have been expected, Jesus' resurrection body was not luminous, nor did he appear against a heavenly backdrop.
5. These appearances often involved complex conversations between him and the disciples.
6. The appearances were multisensory in nature. Specifically, they consisted of visual, auditory, and tactile phenomena. Importantly, Jesus was capable of being actively touched by the percipients, not just the other way around.
7. At least some of Jesus' appearances would have inevitably left marks on the environment in which he appeared.

21

Jesus' Appearances
Resurrection or a Compilation of Apparitions' "Greatest Hits"?

SOME APPARITIONS APPROXIMATE ACTUAL human behavior better than others. The percipients may see an apparition in a dream or while awake. An apparition manifests visually by definition but may also be experienced in one or more of the other senses: auditory, tactile, and/or olfactory. Here we have mostly focused on manifestations that occur visually to the percipient, but many of the documented cases include non-visual encounters. Some paranormal experiences may not invoke any of the usual five senses, but rather create a "sense of presence" by or for the percipient.

Most apparitions studied and reported in the annals of psychical research do not talk, and if they do, it is usually one short phrase or sentence, and the communication often is done telepathically. In certain rare cases, apparitions will engage in protracted conversations with percipients. Apparitions will sometimes touch percipients. However, it is only on rare occasion that a percipient is successful when attempting to actively touch an apparition. Multiple percipients may see an apparition simultaneously, while some are only visible to one or some present within a group at the time of the appearance. Regarding some of the apparitions that are perceived collectively, the seers' experiences may differ to some degree. Finally, it is a rare, but not unheard of, event when the environment is changed by an apparition, especially if it is one that occurs spontaneously.

Put another way, some apparitions (along with other non-visual paranormal manifestations), seem to get through better than others. Remarkable though they are, compared with the characteristics of their real-life counterparts, apparitions exhibit obvious imperfections that give them away as such. Percipients can invariably differentiate apparitional experiences from interactions with real people, though the correct interpretation may only be made later. A perfect apparition would in theory never be detected as an apparition.

According to the Gospel narratives, Jesus' postmortem appearances do share some things in common with apparitional encounters. The most obvious commonality is Jesus' ability to suddenly appear and disappear. In the Gospel of John, Jesus unexpectedly materializes inside of a locked room where his disciples are hiding from the authorities. In the Gospel of Luke, Jesus is said to disappear after he breaks bread during his appearance to Cleopas and his companion disciple. Also consistent with most of the non-induced apparitional encounters we find in the literature, most of Jesus' appearances in the Gospels were unexpected.

The lack of expectation on the part of the percipients is a death knell for the hallucinations theory but it is consistent with objective apparitions. If the Gospels are substantially accurate portrayals of what occurred on the first Easter Sunday and the few weeks after that date, then Jesus' appearances would serve as something of a greatest hits compilation of what we find in the apparitions literature.

Assuming the postmortem appearances of Jesus to be *spontaneously* occurring apparitional encounters, we have in them a constellation of the most remarkable properties found in the literature on spontaneous apparitional encounters. According to the Gospels and 1 Cor 15, Jesus' appearances were: 1) recurrent; 2) perceived by groups; 3) included a "mass sighting"; 4) tactile (i.e., could be touched); 5) capable of changing the environment; 6) found within a variety of contexts and locations; 7) capable of carrying out lengthy conversations. When we sweep the net broadly across the entire spectrum of apparitional categories, well-evidenced apparitions can match all of these characteristics. Here are some examples of non-religious apparitions' greatest hits when we consider each item on the list in isolation.

1. *Recurrent*: By definition, any well-evidenced haunting matches this characteristic. The Samuel Bull apparition and the Morton Ghost come to mind, though there are others.

2. *Perceived by groups*: The Samuel Bull apparition was seen often and by as many as nine family members simultaneously, while Captain Towns and the St. Petersburg, Russia, crisis case were seen by eight and seven people, respectively, though the latter was also seen by a dog.

3. *Mass sighting*: At what number of percipients a group appearance can be labeled a sighting of mass proportion is admittedly arbitrary. Be that as it may, I will put that number at twenty. I am not aware of any spontaneous, "secularized" cases in the psychical literature that is even halfway to that number (though see below regarding religious apparitions; also mass sightings of apparitions have been produced in séances, see chapter 8).

4. *Tactile*: This occurs in a substantial minority of cases, as high as 13 percent according to some surveys. This number may be inflated somewhat because the surveys often include vague phenomena as tactile. such as cold sensations. However, spontaneous apparitions are often resistant to being touched when the percipient attempts to initiate, though this does occur on rare occasion. See the German Knight case from chapter 4.

5. *Changing the environment*: The apparition of Dadaji consumed half a biscuit and smoked part of a cigarette. After the apparition disappeared, the half biscuit was gone and the partially-smoked cigarette was still burning.

6. *Variety of contexts and locations*: This is a relatively rare characteristic though, as with tactile cases, there are examples of this in the psychical literature. We have noted that there are some rare crisis apparitions in which this has occurred. There are also some bereavement apparitions and, surprisingly, rare hauntings in the psychical literature that fulfill this characteristic (see below). Such travelling apparitions seem to be connected to a certain person.

7. *Lengthy conversations*: We noted a crisis apparition that occurred during the Boer War that met this characteristic. Raymond Moody had a lengthy conversation with his deceased, paternal

grandmother after attempting to induce an apparition of his *maternal* grandmother.

Thus for most aspects of Jesus' postmortem encounters with the disciples, we find parallels in the apparition literature. What may not be immediately obvious, however, is that in order to construct a matrix through which to understand Jesus' post-resurrection appearances to his disciples as apparitions, we have to draw from a rich tapestry of cases that have occurred over the past 150 years in different countries on several continents, different contexts, with differing levels of evidence, and that have occurred across numerous apparitional categories. In these circumstances, said matrix is only constructed with considerable difficulty. Let's unpack this with some brief discussion of some of the aforementioned cases.

We pointed out that haunting apparitions like the Morton Ghost and the Samuel Bull case were recurrent. The Samuel Bull apparition was also tactile, as it would touch his dying wife on the forehead before disappearing. However, there were no lengthy conversations, just a single word ("Jane") was said to have been uttered on one occasion. Both the Morton Ghost and Samuel Bull appeared in the same location, traversing identical paths each time they appeared.[1] They were both seen by multiple percipients simultaneously, or at least within a very tight timeframe. Samuel Bull was seen by as many as nine percipients at once. Finally, neither of these haunting apparitions were said to make lasting changes on the material environment. Of the thousands of apparitional cases published over the course of a century and a half of psychical research, these two cases are among the most remarkable, yet they check only three of the seven boxes.

When percipients attempt to initiate the touch of an apparition, they are usually unsuccessful. Contrast this to the Gospel data. Not only do Jesus' disciples initiate the touch, but are even invited to do so. In this characteristic some of Jesus' appearances may be compared with the Valerie Dudley case where she successfully embraces the apparition of her deceased father.[2] Yet, this was a single-witness case that does not fulfill

---

1. There are exceptional cases of haunting apparitions that make appearances in multiple locations. See Bennett, *Haunted Houses*, 244–49. In 1871 in a house in West Brompton, London, UK, a gray, shadowy apparition was seen over time by five independent witnesses. The family moved to another house in the same neighborhood in 1877, and the haunting phenomena, including sightings of this same shadowy apparition, resumed in 1879. See also the two cases discussed in chapter 16 of this book. Also, Green and McCreery, *Apparitions*, 63–65, narrate a couple of cases of traveling ghost cats.

2. See Arcangel, *Afterlife*, 44–47.

any of the other six aspects of Jesus' postmortem encounters that we find in the Gospels.

Dr. Raymond Moody's lengthy encounter with his deceased grandmother shortly after emerging from the psychomanteum and the Boer War crisis case involved complex conversation. It is notable that Moody's apparition was an induced apparition, even if the apparition that eventually materialized was of the "wrong" grandmother. We will discuss the ramifications of induced apparitions just below. For now, it is worth noting that neither Moody's encounter nor the Boer War crisis case shared any of the other six aspects of the appearances of Jesus to his disciples.

It is unusual for spontaneously-occurring apparitions to leave behind physical evidence of their presence in a place. Sometimes doors may open or other apparent changes to the environment occur during an apparitional encounter, only for the percipient to discover that everything is back the way it was prior when the encounter ends. Green and McCreery discuss a couple of exceptions. One involves an apparition that opens the blind of a window which stays open after the encounter. In the other case a candle/night-light is extinguished during the encounter.[3] Jesus' encounters with his disciples would likely have left behind physical evidence of his having been present (such as cooked fish, consumed fish, bread, etc.). Similarly, Dadaji's deliberately produced apparition left behind changes to the environment and was perceived by multiple percipients. This remarkable case of bilocation checks two to four of the seven boxes.[4]

Michael Perry studied the annals of psychical literature and wrote about the correspondences between Jesus' postmortem appearances and apparitions in 1959. His comments then mirror my current thoughts on the subject, even with another two-thirds of a century having elapsed since he wrote.

> The first thing to say is that there are some striking similarities between the Christophanies and apparitional cases. This in itself suggests that each may have something to tell us about the other. All the same, it remains true that the overall scale of the Resurrection appearances is far greater than that of modern cases.

3. Green and McCreery, *Apparitions*, 207–10.

4. The Dadaji apparition communicated with a percipient, but it was through sign language rather than apparent voice phonation. It also apparently successfully retrieved a glass of tea from the percipient.

Unless we are to assume that the records are exaggerations, this makes us pause. To find parallels for all the aspects of the Resurrection appearances, we have had to ransack the literature of parapsychology and build up a composite picture from the most striking aspects of a number of cases.[5]

More promising than these more "secularized" apparitions are the apparitions of the Blessed Virgin Mary, some of which manage to check most of the seven boxes. The Marian apparition at Fátima was seen by a group of three children recurrently, on the thirteenth of every month for a period of six months. Notably, however, nobody else saw her, even when there were thousands of others present. While there were no mass sightings of Mary on October 13th, 1917, tens of thousands witnessed the miracle of the sun. The apparition did have complex conversations with one of the children (Lucia Dos Santos), though notably Fernando Marta saw her, but could not hear what was said. These apparitions changed the environment, as the apparition of Mary would descend upon a tree branch which would be seen to bend. Also, the miracle of the sun dried the rain-drenched grounds in a matter of minutes.

The apparitional tableau at Knock was seen by fifteen witnesses, but it was not recurrent and did not converse with the percipients, nor did the tableau produce lasting changes upon the environment and occurred at only one location. The apparition at Betania, Venezuela, was seen by more than one hundred people, was recurrent over the course of a single day, was predicted in advance to Maria Esperanza, but occurred in only one location and did not converse with percipients. The Marian apparitions at Zeitoun, Egypt, in 1966–68, were recurrent, seen by groups, sometimes which numbered in the thousands. Most apparitions were seen at the Coptic church, but there may have been others that occurred within that general vicinity.

Importantly, these four Marian apparitions occurred in four different countries on three different continents in the context of different geopolitical contexts, over a time period of nearly one hundred years, and upon the foundation of global Marian adoration that had lasted centuries beforehand. In my judgment, however one may wish to interpret them, all of them rest upon strong evidential grounds.

If the Gospel post-resurrection appearance traditions are substantially accurate, Jesus' postmortem encounters with the disciples are either

---

5. Perry, *Easter Enigma*, 188.

indicative of bodily resurrection or a series of apparitional encounters that embodied the rarest and most impressive characteristics of spontaneously-occurring apparitional experiences. If the latter, the apparitions were so realistic that the disciples concluded that he had been raised from the dead in the sense that all righteous Jews longed for at a future time when God would set all the wrongs to right and restore creation back to perfect order.

CAVEAT #1: FORTY DAYS OF APPEARANCES

The sheer number, magnitude, and effects of Jesus' multiple appearances can rightfully be deemed impressive evidence against reducing them to apparitional phenomena. However, the evidential impact is diluted depending upon the timeframe involved. We are in good scholarly company in believing the Gospel data that the appearances started just days within Jesus' death by crucifixion.[6] However, when did the appearances stop? As discussed in the prior chapter, some New Testament authors indicate that these initial appearances were different from the later visions of Jesus experienced by the early church. Luke places the dividing line at the time of the ascension, forty days after the crucifixion.[7]

If this is correct, Jesus' appearances manifested our seven characteristics over a period of less than seven weeks. That they started just days after his death is also crucial. Reunion apparitions may occur within days of a person's death as well, but they are more likely to occur weeks to months later.[8] Haunting apparitions tend to manifest months to years later. Religious apparitions tend to occur anytime between months to centuries later.

How do the apparitions of the Lubavitcher Rebbe stack up in this regard? The compendium of apparitions surveyed in chapter 19 includes manifestations within dreams, visual appearances to individuals and groups while in the awake state, rescue apparitions, apparitions that were later identified with a photograph, and at least a series of recurrent apparitions to Rabbi Landa. Overall, Yoram Bilu has collected over one hundred such appearances. However, this compilation includes appearances

6. Habermas, *Evidences*, 437–79.

7. Acts 1:2.

8. Dewi Rees writes, "Usually these experiences do not come soon after death; they are not part of the immediate grief process and are more likely to occur many weeks or months later." Rees, *Eternity*, ch. 10, para. 1.

over a period of sixteen years (1994–2010), three-fourths of which occurred after 2003, more than a decade after the Rebbe's death.

Of course, I would be remiss not to remind the reader that apparitions of Jesus have never stopped occurring from before the time of New Testament composition to the present, as we discuss and provide references for in chapter 9. There have undoubtedly been countless thousands of these since the genesis of the church, which is why I think accepting Luke's short time period for these pre-ascension appearances is vital to the validity of the argument being made in this chapter. The upshot is that the early church thought that these pre-ascension encounters with the risen Jesus were somehow distinct from the later visions and apparitions. I contend that is because the pre-ascension appearances were undeniably physical encounters with Jesus in a reanimated body.

CAVEAT #2: APPARITIONS THAT ARE DELIBERATELY PRODUCED OR INDUCED

Dadaji deliberately produced an apparition of himself that changed the physical environment. His contemporary Sathya Sai Baba may have achieved similar exploits during episodes of bilocation, as did paranormal researchers Andrew and Eileen Landau.[9] What these cases have in common is that they were apparitions produced by the living, and were mostly deliberate.

Materialized persons who appear at séances may also carry out lengthy conversations. They are also often overtly physical, in some cases may be actively touched by percipients, and may make lasting changes upon the environment. As we discussed in chapter 8, they are also often seen by large groups of people. These exceptional considerations have to be borne in mind as we assess Jesus' postmortem encounters in the next chapter.

CAVEAT #3: ARE THE GOSPEL ACCOUNTS OF THE RESURRECTION RELIABLE?

The argument made here also assumes that the post-resurrection accounts in Matthew, Luke, and John are substantially accurate. In the last chapter, it was demonstrated why I believe this to be the case, but it is

9. See chapter 3. We give more examples in the next chapter.

important to keep in mind that the reliability of the accounts is a very controversial matter.

In the following chapter, we will assess the ability of apparitions to command explanatory power regarding Jesus' resurrection based on three different sets of assumptions on the reliability of our sources.

22

Apparitions as an Alternative Explanation to Jesus' Resurrection

REITERATING WHAT I SAID in the introduction, I do believe that Jesus was raised bodily from the dead and subsequently appeared to his disciples. As intriguing and as metaphysically challenging as this project has been in crucial ways, I maintain that this is the best explanation for the rise of the early church. However, here I wish to play *advocatus diaboli* and speculate on how the robust phenomena of apparitional encounters might be employed to postulate an alternative theory to bodily resurrection.

As such, well-evidenced apparitional reports, when considered broadly as a collective phenomenon, perform many of the same tasks as the risen Jesus does in the oral tradition preserved in 1 Cor 15 and the Gospels. Complicating matters, which New Testament data is accepted as authentic, along with how it is best interpreted, is controversial. Perhaps it is not going too far to suggest that every scholar across the theological spectrum that has studied Jesus' resurrection will differ at least somewhere in the minutiae, if not on key data points.

Whatever one concludes regarding what happened on the first Easter Sunday will largely depend on one's biases and horizons.[1] It is hardly surprising that Christian New Testament scholars, especially conservative ones, tend to find more historical value in the Gospels (including the post-resurrection narratives) than their more skeptical scholarly

---

1. Horizons are the lenses through which the scholar or historian sees the world. Licona, *Resurrection*, 31–62.

counterparts. The reader will likewise not find it shocking that I tend to agree more with the conservative scholars. As such, for reasons I have discussed in chapter 20, I believe we have reasonably accurate historical summaries of what occurred in the Gospel post-resurrection narratives.

There I made the case for what I think can be accepted as historical characteristics of Jesus' postmortem encounters. To what extent one treats the material in the Gospels as historical will enable one to make certain theories about Easter more or less plausible. In what follows, I will analyze the "Apparitional Hypothesis" (AH) as a paranormal (but not supernatural) alternative theory to Jesus' resurrection under three different scenarios. In the first scenario, I will assume the only reliable information we have of Jesus' resurrection comes from the creed in 1 Cor 15, since this material is very widely accepted to be early and authentic across the scholarly spectrum. In the second scenario, I will evaluate AH in the light of 1 Cor 15 and the assumption that the empty tomb is historical. In the third scenario, I will evaluate AH based on what I think, for reasons espoused in chapter 20, may be deemed historical from the Gospel materials.

SCENARIO 1: APPARITIONAL HYPOTHESIS IN THE LIGHT OF 1 COR 15

In 1 Cor 15:3–8 we have three appearances of Jesus to individuals (Cephas, James, and Paul) and three group appearances (to the Twelve, the five hundred, and "all the apostles"). In drawing our data solely from the information in this creed, we do not know the location(s) of the appearances nor the time frame nor any details of Jesus' appearances or actions, if there were actions. This ambiguity invites the possibility of understanding these group appearances as simultaneous hallucinations. We will consider that possibility first.

WERE JESUS' POST-RESURRECTION APPEARANCES COLLECTIVE HALLUCINATIONS?

Also called mass hallucinations, we are here considering the possibility of the appearances as purely subjective phenomena that is occurring merely within the mind or minds of the percipients in the absence of an objective impulse or stimulus. We considered this as a plausible explanation in accounting for some of the Rebbe's collective appearances to followers, especially those occurring in charged, religious environments. Can we find some traction here for explaining Jesus' collective appearances as well?

Expectation and emotional excitement are prerequisites for the occurrence of collective hallucinations. This makes sense because of the unlikelihood that two or more people would spontaneously, and simultaneously, have a hallucination without an actual stimulus. Furthermore, the hallucinations would have to be quite similar in content if they are to be mistaken by the percipients as having experienced the same, objective event. As a result, it is not surprising that the content of collective hallucinations may differ markedly.

Jake O'Connell's work on this proves instructive. I will briefly summarize a couple of the case reports he details.

1. In San Martin de Manzaneda on April 20th, 1903, a priest was imparting a message on Isaiah and the forgiveness of Christ when a mass hallucination occurred regarding the Eucharist that was on display during the sermon. Some in the audience reportedly saw the Eucharist replaced in space with Christ, as a child, with his arms outstretched. Some saw his heart bleeding while some saw him holding his hand to stop the bleeding. Others saw the monstrance illuminated. Some saw nothing.[2]

2. In Bojano, Italy, on March 22nd, 1888, two ladies in search of lost sheep became terrified by a vision that began with seeing light emanating from fissures in rocks. After investigation, they saw a young, beautiful lady who was disheveled and appeared to be bleeding from seven sword wounds. After word got out, large crowds started visiting the site and many had visions. Many saw the Blessed Virgin Mary in traditional forms, such as Our Lady of Mount Carmel, Our Lady, the Queen of the Holy Rosary, Our Lady of Dolores, Our Lady of Loreto, and the Mother of Sorrows. Others saw various saints including Saint Michael, Saint Anthony, Saint Joseph, and Saint Sebastian. Still others saw the face of Jesus. Others did not see anything. More than seven hundred people experienced apparitions at different times, some of which were interviewed as part of the local bishop's investigation, which was eventually reported to the pope.[3]

---

2. O'Connell, "Collective," 78.

3. O'Connell, "Collective," 78–79. Note that the hallucinations and (subjective?) apparitions that resulted from the initial vision of the two women. This initial vision,

O'Connell presents these along with several other cases, then summarizes the characteristics that are common to collective hallucinations:

1. Visions are expected.
2. Extreme stress is present, evidenced in part by fainting on the part of some percipients.
3. Not everyone present sees a vision.
4. The percipients see the visions differently.
5. The vision does not carry on a conversation.[4]

Mass hallucinations also occur outside of Christian contexts. On July 29th, 1992, around 11:00 p.m., a litany of visions was seen in the sky by about two hundred students at the Hishammuddin Secondary Islamic School in Klang, State of Selangor, Malaysia. For example, the word "Allah" was seen in Arabic Jawi script, the appearance of a fetus in the womb, women with body parts exposed that must be covered per Islamic custom, and two dead bodies. The next evening, at 6:50 p.m. on July 30th, the words "Allah" and "Muhammad" appeared within or by clouds in larger Jawi script while the students were praying in a school field.[5]

Notably in the early 1990s, there were rumors of Islamic symbols miraculously appearing, particularly in the same Arabic Jawi script.

> For example, on June 12, 1990, in Algeria, the Islamic Salvation Front Party won an upset election victory. While the party leader was speaking to a crowd of supporters who were standing and shouting, "Allah Akhbar" ("God is great!") in the direction of Mecca (the Muslim Holy Land), a cloud reportedly formed the shape of the word "Allah" in Jawi letters. There was great excitement and people fainted and wept.[6]

In March in Nottingham, England, an Islamic accountant named Hussain Bhatti adamantly believed that he saw Jawi script inside of a cut eggplant. In Leicester, England, Farida Kassam believed that eggplant seeds developed into a pattern similar to "Yah-Allah" (i.e., "God is everywhere") or "Ya-Allah" (i.e., "God exists").[7]

---

apparently unexpected, was likely an objective apparition.

4. O'Connell, "Collective," 84–87.
5. Evans and Bartholomew, *Outbreak!*, 282–83.
6. Evans and Bartholomew, *Outbreak!*, 283.
7. Evans and Bartholomew, *Outbreak!*, 283.

Against this context of rumors of miracles, along with underlying conflict within the Islamic community, these Islamic students perceived a variety of different images in the skies, largely via cloud formations, over a five hour period. In fact, twenty-six images were subsequently drawn by students to describe what they saw, and these images were markedly different from one another. Such images included that of a human body; an eye that was colored red; cut pieces of a tongue that repeatedly appeared to merge into a full tongue; the wing of a bird flapping; a pig-faced female; a dog-headed man; a scorpion; a large, shiny-eyed snake; two people arguing with each other, then apparently reconciling by shaking hands; a man wearing a turban bowing towards Mecca; a map of Malaysia turned upside down, with Singapore at the top; a liquor bottle; a map of Saudi Arabia; a tombstone; etc.[8]

Remarkable though it may be that these visions occurred within a short timeframe, what was seen by the students was obviously subjective in nature. A vision of something that existed in external reality, or was projected and superimposed onto external reality by a real stimulus, would have been described similarly by the different students, with perhaps some moderate variation. Instead, we have here a diverse collection of irreconcilable perceptions.

Applying this to speculation about the risen Christ as presented in 1 Cor 15, we frankly have no idea to what degree any of O'Connell's five characteristics conformed, or not, to the visions of the percipients listed in the oral tradition. Cephas (Peter) was reportedly the first percipient. One may propose that he experienced a hallucination, or an objective bereavement apparition of Christ, and that he reported his vision to the Twelve. We may further imagine that this report created expectation and emotional excitement on the part of the disciples which caused them to have a collective hallucination of Jesus. News spread to other followers (and perhaps to some who did not initially follow Jesus?), which created more emotional excitement and expectation that eventually led to a collective hallucination involving a crowd of five hundred plus people. Later, the group that constitutes "all the apostles" experienced a similar event.

If the portmortem appearances were group hallucinations, we may reasonably speculate that some of those present saw nothing while those who did experience something saw widely diverging visions. Many of the percipients may have seen Jesus as he was prior to the crucifixion. Some

---

8. Evans and Bartholomew, *Outbreak!*, 283–84.

perhaps would have heard him utter familiar laconic statements that he commonly made in life. Others may have seen him as fully healed, appearing against a heavenly backdrop. Still others experienced him exalted at the right hand of God, as the divine "Son of Man" from Dan 7, like Stephen did.[9] Some may have had disturbing visions of Jesus bleeding and in agony on the cross while others had distressing visions of Jesus more in line with hauntings. Each vision of Christ would have been at least somewhat different while some would have been markedly different. Perhaps some sensed Jesus' presence but did not experience a vision. If we apply parallels from the cases summarized above, others may have experienced religious visions that did not contain Jesus at all, perhaps some would have seen John the Baptist and/or an angel. Others may have seen Old Testament prophets.[10]

Whatever the case, in collective hallucinations, where numerous people simultaneously experience independently produced hallucinations resulting from stress or emotional excitement and expectation, we may safely assume that the various experiences would have produced a variety of markedly different visual content while others present would not have seen anything at all. Keeping in mind that a subjective hallucination is produced by the mind of an *individual*, this conclusion is inevitable.

Whatever the postmortem appearances of Jesus were, however, they did result in the disciples' belief that Jesus had been raised *bodily* from the dead. We know that theological disputes created great controversy amongst even the pillars of the early church, most notably regarding circumcision and whether Gentile converts were to abide by the Jewish law. Paul's epistles to the various churches across the Roman Empire were in large measure written to address a litany of such controversies. As for the foundational event, however, the founding members of the church appeared to be unanimous in its understanding that Jesus had been resurrected from the dead in the final, eschatological sense.[11]

---

9. Acts 7:55.

10. This seems especially plausible depending upon what one makes of the transfiguration of Jesus, where Peter, James, and John saw Moses and Elijah. See Matt 17:1–8; Mark 9:2–8; Luke 9:28–36.

11. See Wright, *Resurrection*, 209–583, for a lengthy exposition on this matter. Also, Licona, *Resurrection*, 329–39, 400–437, 511–14. Licona notes that "without a single known exception, all of the original apostolic leaders and all of the relevant Christian literature strongly believed to have been written in the first century are of a single voice in their proclamation that Jesus had been raised bodily."

If the appearances in 1 Cor 15 were consistent with what we know of collective hallucinations, I find such apparent unanimity of interpretation extremely improbable. Indeed, I question if such diverse experiences would have led to a unified perpetuation of Jesus' movement as Messiah in the first place. At best, some would most likely conclude that they had seen Jesus' spirit.[12] Others might go a step further and conclude that Jesus had been exalted by God into heavenly glory.[13] Perhaps other percipients would have rightfully concluded that they had been hallucinating. Had some of the core disciples (the Twelve) been among those who saw nothing at all, we may have expected them to have left the movement altogether. Some others may have interpreted the appearances of Jesus as having been raised from the dead, particularly in the light of Jesus' predictions of resurrection shortly after death. In the end, if we are to imagine the followers of Jesus to have harmonized their various experiences into a common interpretation and continue Jesus' messianic movement based upon this interpretation, I doubt eschatological resurrection would have been the unanimous conclusion.

WERE JESUS' POST-RESURRECTION APPEARANCES CONSISTENT WITH APPARITIONAL PHENOMENA?

Objectively-experienced-apparitions remain by far the best potential alternative explanation to the resurrection, at least in this author's mind. Unlike collective hallucinations, the visual content of objective apparitions that are collectively perceived is usually either practically the same or at least quite similar. In what follows, I will discuss the appearances of Jesus in the light of the eight categories of apparitions, starting with what are the most unlikely categories and ending with the more likely.

WERE THE POST-RESURRECTION APPEARANCES TRANSITIONAL APPARITIONS?

I am unaware of anyone who believes that one or more of the eleven disciples was dying at the time of Jesus' appearances, which is a prerequisite

---

12. The Gospels indicate that the early church was sensitive to such an interpretation in various contexts. See Matt 14:26; Luke 24:11; Acts 12:15.

13. See below, I think this would have been the most common takeaway among the percipients.

for this kind of apparition. While some transitional apparitions are collectively perceived (including by healthy bystanders), it is universally understood by such percipients that the apparition represents the spirit of the deceased person who has come to take away the spirit of the dying. A conclusion of bodily resurrection would hardly be reached by this kind of apparition. Also, I do not know of cases of transitional apparitions appearing to large groups of percipients, certainly not a group as large as five hundred. This would also not account for the appearance to Paul.[14]

WERE THE POST-RESURRECTION APPEARANCES CRISIS APPARITIONS?

We may, I think, in short order, dispense this possibility. As the name implies, crisis apparitions occur at times of personal crisis, often about the time of the agent's death or shortly thereafter. Had the disciples experienced an apparition of Jesus while he was on the cross, or early on the Sabbath,[15] that would be more consistent with a crisis apparition. Moreover, they are frequently disturbing to the percipients, not events that would strike one as likely to ignite a religious movement. Even more problematic, crisis apparitions are not recurrent as Jesus' post-resurrection appearances were. Crisis apparitions frequently confirm to percipients that the agent has died. They do not trigger belief in bodily resurrection. Paul, who may not have even known Jesus before the crucifixion, would have been extremely unlikely to experience a crisis apparition representing Jesus.

WERE THE POST-RESURRECTION APPEARANCES RESCUE APPARITIONS?

There are cases in the literature of recurrent rescue apparitions, though usually they occur when somebody is needing delivered from a dire situation, such as a sailor caught in a storm at sea. While the Gospels depict the disciples hiding from the authorities after the crucifixion, there is nothing to indicate life-threatening danger at the time. Thus, the context

---

14. Though it is applicable in theory to Jesus' appearance to Stephen. See Acts 7:55–60.
15. Friday evening after sunset or perhaps early Saturday morning.

seems lacking for a rescue apparition. I am also unaware of any cases of rescue apparitions appearing to large groups.

WERE THE POST-RESURRECTION APPEARANCES INDUCED APPARITIONS?

Hopefully, the reader will agree that we may safely assume that the disciples were not engaged in anything resembling EMDR or other forms of psychotherapy in the aftermath of the crucifixion. If so, we may safely assume that the disciples did not experience anything like the apparitions produced by Dr. Allan Botkin in a clinical setting.

Something more akin to crystal gazing would have been more plausible in the ancient context, correlating to some degree with the experiences documented inside of Dr. Raymond Moody's homemade psychomanteum. Then there were those who attempted to contact the dead through mediums.[16] Now, if the case could be made that apparitions of Jesus were intentionally produced, and especially if they could plausibly be argued to have been induced through the deliberate use of the psychic energies of a group of people, then the psychical researcher may have struck paydirt. Recall from chapters 3 and 8 that such deliberately-produced apparitions also tend to be among the most remarkable in the literature. They are often solid, long-lasting, engage in conversations, and leave indelible changes upon the environment.

However, for several reasons this case would be very difficult to make. First, since they were pious Jews, the apostles would have been unlikely to invoke the use of necromancy or mediumship because of scriptural prohibitions.[17] Second, there is no evidence from the sources that the disciples were engaged in such practices. In fact, some evidence from Acts suggests that such practices would have been inconsistent with the spirit of early Christian preaching and practices regarding such things as divination.[18] Finally, visions of Jesus that were induced through necromancy or mediumship would not have produced belief in Jesus' resurrection, as it was understood that it was the spirit of the person that was being invoked.

---

16. See 1 Sam 28:7–19.
17. See for instance Deut 18:10–12 and Isa 8:19.
18. Acts 16:16–18; 19:17–20.

WERE THE POST-RESURRECTION APPEARANCES HAUNTING APPARITIONS?

Haunting apparitions parallel the appearances of Jesus in that they appear multiple times and are frequently collective. The Samuel Bull case is so characterized. Hauntings also, by definition, occur almost exclusively in one location. This characteristic would not eliminate hauntings based solely on the information in 1 Cor 15 since we are not told here that Jesus' appearances occurred in different locations.

Nevertheless, even without importing Gospel data into consideration here, there are significant problems. Haunting apparitions often tend to play like a three-dimensional recording. The Samuel Bull apparition, for example, always performed the same action: it walked up the stairs, entered the bedbound widow's room where it would lay its cold hand on her forehead at bedside before disappearing. The Morton Ghost likewise traversed the same pathway when it appeared. More importantly, those unfortunate enough to experience haunting apparitions often find them to be frightening and negative experiences.[19] After reading through a sufficient litany of haunting case reports in the literature, it becomes clear that these apparitions are generally unintelligent, mechanical representations of the deceased people they represent. They are mere shadows of their living counterparts.

Tyrrell, in his study on apparitions, points out two contradictory aspects of these phenomena. First, apparitions mimic human beings with varying levels of success, some even to the extent where they appear solid, at first easily mistakable for a real person; they are sometimes seen by multiple people at once; they disappear when the lighting in a room is poor, as a normal person would; and their reflections may even be visible in a mirror. Second, they tend to be very mechanical and exhibit a "somnambulistic or automatic behavior." Tyrrell suggests that such behavior reflects the widespread belief that reaches back into antiquity, that the deceased wander Hades in a semiconscious state of existence. Quoting Frederic W. H. Myers, Tyrrell puts the matter well when he says that apparitions have "no *heart* in them!"[20]

In my estimation, this difference represents the major limitation in comparing Jesus' postmortem encounters with haunting apparitions. Jesus' earliest followers would scarcely have believed that Jesus had been

19. See chapter 4.
20. Tyrrell, *Apparitions*, 40, emphasis original.

raised from the dead into a new, glorious, and immortal body, the kind of body they hoped to inherit one day, if his appearances were not markedly different from the standard ghostly encounters common to the Greco-Roman world and in more recent times. Imagine trying to convince someone (including yourself!) that the Morton Ghost or Samuel Bull apparition is really a person who was miraculously raised from the dead into a glorious new mode of existence. Now try convincing that person that our own resurrection hope is for God to one day give us an existence similar in nature to those apparitions. Somehow that does not seem to give one much to look forward to in the next world.

It is even more implausible that Paul, who was a skeptic and persecutor of the church, would have concluded that Jesus had been raised from the dead in the final, glorious, and eschatological sense if his experience had been similar in nature to ancient or modern haunts.

WERE THE POST-RESURRECTION APPEARANCES REUNION APPARITIONS?

Reunion apparitions provide us with more fertile ground for speculation. While most in this category also tend to be ephemeral in nature, these apparitions are frequently seen as younger and healthier versions of the deceased that they represent. Moreover, they often seem to come with a purpose, whether to communicate a message (verbally or, more often, nonverbally) and the percipients commonly feel a sense of closure and healing.

There are some issues that challenge this possibility. While reunion apparitions may be recurrent, they tend to center upon a single percipient rather than groups of percipients. Second, related to the last point, reunion apparitions are sometimes collectively perceived, but this is comparatively rare. Jesus appeared to groups of eleven or more three times according to 1 Cor 15. The largest group appearances I could find in the literature, at least among *spontaneously occurring, nonreligious apparitions*, were the Samuel Bull case (nine percipients), a crisis apparition seen in St. Petersburg, Russia (seven human percipients and one dog),[21] and the Captain Towns case (eight percipients), the latter of which I would categorize as a reunion apparition, but it was not recurrent.[22]

21. Bennett, *Haunted Houses*, 334–36.

22. There is an interesting report of a collective olfactory afterdeath communication where ten of eleven people present sensed a strong aroma of roses upon returning home from the cemetery shortly after the tragic death of a nine-week-old girl named Melanie.

Finally, if the disciples experienced a reunion apparition of Jesus, whether this was in a dream, or in the context of a heavenly vision, or simply an appearance in the waking state as a healthy, perhaps even as a radiant or luminous being, it remains unlikely they would have concluded he had risen from the dead. In ancient as well as modern times, seeing ghosts or apparitions of the deceased confirm to their percipients that the agent was dead, not alive again. I am not aware of an exception.[23] As we will discuss further in due course, a reunion apparition of Jesus would, I think, more likely have been interpreted as indicating his direct exaltation to heaven rather than bodily resurrection.

WERE THE POST-RESURRECTION APPEARANCES RELIGIOUS APPARITIONS?

The answer to this question seems to be, at least in a sense, an obvious "yes" given the clear religious context. Importantly, there are analogs in the literature of religious apparitions appearing to large groups of people, such as a couple of recent apparitions of Jesus to groups of fifty and two hundred people in Oakland, California, in the 1950s, along with the Marian apparitions in Knock, Ireland, (at least fifteen percipients) and in Venezuela (more than one hundred percipients). Furthermore, we know that many of the Marian apparitions are recurrent, most famously those of Fátima, Lourdes, Medjugorje, and Zeitoun. Also, the vision of Jesus seen in China by those who were not Christians and were hearing the Gospel for the first time may fairly be argued as somewhat analogous to the conversion vision of Jesus that Paul experienced.

The Marian apparitions in Zeitoun, Egypt, in 1968–69 parallel, even eclipse, Jesus' post-resurrection appearances in terms of their recurring nature and large number of percipients.[24] In a situation loosely analogous

---

This took place at Melanie and her mother's home. See Guggenheim and Guggenheim, *Hello from Heaven!*, 326–27.

23. See though below, where we will bring into consideration additional factors that make an interpretation of "resurrection" more plausible.

24. Over the course of the nearly two years that the luminous apparition appeared (from April 1968 to late 1969/early 1970), it and similar phenomena like luminous objects shaped like doves were seen by as many as thousands of people simultaneously. Zaki estimates that there were four thousand people gathered at the church when she saw the Virgin. Zaki, *Before Our Eyes*, 51–53. The author interviewed more than one hundred witnesses in 1986, roughly eighteen years after the fact. Names and summaries of more than a dozen testimonies are included. Zaki, *Before Our Eyes*, 58–65.

to the apostle Paul, a backslidden former believer had mocked the crowds that flocked to the Coptic Church hoping to see the luminous apparition. He was restored to his prior faith when, unexpectedly, the apparition made an appearance to him.[25]

Still unaddressed by parallels is the question of why the disciples concluded that Jesus was resurrected from the dead if he appeared to them as an apparition and the tomb/grave site was not vacant. If we posit that his body was left on the cross or thrown into a criminal graveyard to be devoured by carrion or wild animals as Crossan believes, there may have been no way to verify (or disprove) that the apparitions represented Jesus' reanimated body.[26] Also, if we accept as authentic Jesus' predictions of his resurrection, then perhaps later reflection would have influenced the earliest followers of Jesus to reach such an interpretation upon experiencing a series of religious visions.

WERE THE POST-RESURRECTION APPEARANCES APPARITIONS OF THE LIVING?

At first blush, the obvious answer to this question would seem to be "no." If Jesus had died by crucifixion, he could not have projected an apparition of himself while still alive days later. However, we have learned that apparitions of the living are more versatile than that. As we have considered, there is solid evidence that an agent may produce apparitions of other figures, including of people long deceased. Is it possible that one of the disciples (or more than one disciple) unintentionally produced and projected apparitions of Jesus through some poorly understood innate human ability? I think if there is a non-supernatural explanation for religious apparitions, it would go along these lines. As such, the religious apparitions that are not subjective in nature may plausibly be posited as projections of the living.

MY ALTERNATIVE THEORY TO THE RESURRECTION IN SCENARIO 1

The apostle Peter experienced either a visual hallucination or an objective apparition of Jesus, likely a reunion apparition. Either of these are

25. See Zaki, *Before Our Eyes*, 130.
26. See Crossan, *Birth*, 550–55.

theoretical possibilities since it was presumably not a collectively perceived event. Peter then reports this appearance to the rest of the Twelve, and eventually this was reported to a wider group of disciples.

The recurrent visions of Jesus revealed him to be healed (except for perhaps scars from the crucifixion?), seemed to occur to convey an intelligible purpose (whether this was through verbal or non-verbal communication), and most importantly indicated that Jesus had been vindicated by God. Given these multiple visual experiences along with consideration of Jesus' predictions of resurrection shortly before the crucifixion, the disciples concluded that Jesus' had been raised. Later, the persecutor of the church, Saul, encountered Jesus in a vision in the same way that others have throughout the Christian era, resulting in his conversion.

Finally, for the purposes of this section, we will assume that Jesus' burial by Joseph of Arimathea is not historical. We will say that Jesus' body was removed from the cross by the Romans and placed into a criminal graveyard, and perhaps by the time that the disciples came to grips with their encounters with Jesus, the disappearance of his body could not be confirmed or disconfirmed.[27]

Focusing only on the data in 1 Cor 15, I cannot affirm an alternative theory that does not involve at least some supernormal phenomena. At minimum I think objective apparitions are at play. Likely this would be of the "religious apparition" category facilitated by the minds of one or more disciples.

SCENARIO 2: APPARITIONAL HYPOTHESIS IN THE LIGHT OF 1 COR 15 AND THE EMPTY TOMB

While it is far from a point of consensus, most New Testament scholars accept that women discovered Jesus' tomb to be empty on the first Easter Sunday. Does it help or hurt the case for objective apparitions as leading to a belief in Jesus' bodily resurrection when we admit the historicity of the empty tomb into consideration?

We will not here rehash the case for crisis, rescue, transitional, induced, or religious apparitions, or of apparitions produced by the living, other than to note that an empty tomb would produce even greater strain on the explanatory power of these apparitional categories in accounting

---

27. For a recent argument that favors the probable historicity of Jesus' burial by Joseph of Arimathea and includes a response to Crossan, see Allison, *Resurrection*, 94–115.

for Jesus' post-resurrection appearances. What does a historical empty tomb do when considering haunting and reunion apparitions?

HAUNTS AND THE EMPTY TOMB

If Jesus appeared in a manner characteristic of haunting apparitions, even after discovery of an empty tomb, I think the disciples would most likely have considered this the consequence of improper burial rather than resurrection.

Apparitions in the ancient world may manifest for several reasons. As with modern times, apparitions may appear in times of crisis, haunt houses, materialize in deathbed visions,[28] tend to unfinished business, pass along important information such as the location of a will, or to exact revenge. The deceased may even manifest in physical form, as a revenant, to fight in a battle or terrorize a person or group of people. However, the most common reason in the ancient world that apparitions were thought to appear were because of improper burial.

> In the majority of cases in antiquity where the disembodied dead return to haunt the living, the motivation is the need for a proper burial. The ghost of Patroclus implies that once the proper funeral rights are performed for his body, he will not haunt the living any longer: "For I will not come again out of Hades, when you have granted me the right of funeral fire." . . .
> Elpenor complains to Odysseus that he cannot enter Hades until his body is buried.[29]

Not only was burial important, but the traditional rites must also be performed. A lack of proper burial was considered a cause for torment in the hereafter. Covering abandoned corpses with dirt was considered an act of piety.[30]

---

28. There is a story in the Talmud of Rabbi Yohanan ben Zakkai, while on his deathbed, telling those around him that he saw King Hezekiah come to greet him. Moreman, *Threshold*, ch. 2, para. 33.

29. Felton, *Haunted*, 9. Sisyphus, according to ancient myth, instructed his wife to not perform burial or the customary funerary rites so he would not be admitted to the Underworld. Given permission by the gods to return in spirit to the land of the living to request the proper rites, he proceeded to repossess his body. "Sisyphus, the ultimate trickster, made what most people feared work to his own advantage." Johnston, *Restless*, 9.

30. Felton, *Haunted*, 9–10.

> And although *lack* of burial is without question one of the main reasons ghosts haunt this world, *improper* burial or insufficient rites can also bring spirits back. After Achilles was shot by Paris, for example, his ashes were mixed in an urn with those of Patroclus. But Achilles's spirit was not at rest. When the Greeks, having taken Troy, were preparing to sail home, the ghost of Achilles appeared and restrained the troops, because they were departing without leaving any offering on his tomb. Achilles's ghost demanded the sacrifice of Priam's daughter Polyxena. When the Greeks cut her throat over Achilles's tomb, his ghost was appeased.[31]

Citing the ancient historian Suetonius, Felton relates that after Emperor Caligula's corpse was only partially burned and buried under a small amount of earth in the Lamian gardens, those who guarded these gardens were harassed by ghosts. This activity was said to have ceased when his sisters dug up, cremated, and buried Caligula's corpse.[32]

In later Jewish tradition, fear of the spirits of the deceased or demons that may cause them harm were commonly explained as the reason to prohibit leaving corpses unburied overnight.[33]

> The sooner the body was out of the way the better for the living and the dead. But the process of burial was not the least perilous—the corpse was closely accompanied by a spirit retinue during the procession to the grave, the cemetery was infested with spirits, the journey home was made hazardous by the possibility that the spirits that had not been left behind, that the ghost itself was an unseen member of the company. And when finally the funeral was over and the period of mourning commenced the danger had not yet been entirely obviated, the spirit of the deceased might still linger for a while about familiar places.[34]

The corpse was thought, in a sense, to somehow remain cognizant of its surroundings, making its proper care and burial of prime importance. The soul was believed by some to remain close to the corpse for a few days prior to departure to await the corporate resurrection of the dead.[35]

31. Felton, *Haunted*, 10, emphasis original.
32. Felton, *Haunted*, 10.
33. Trachtenberg, *Jewish Magic*, 38.
34. Trachtenberg, *Jewish Magic*, 38.
35. Moreman, *Threshold*, ch. 2, para. 27.

Repercussions from the dead were feared throughout this period, and even later, just as they were in ancient times. It became custom for the living to ask forgiveness, in front of witnesses, from the dead in order to avert any spiritual harassment. Complaints from the dead were not unheard of, with the most frequent concerning disrespect not only while living but also after death, particularly when the grave was disturbed or the dead were buried in insufficient clothing.[36]

An unoccupied tomb would likely have created concern that Jesus had been disinterred, leaving him apparently unburied. Note that, according to the Gospels, Jesus' early followers did not seem to jump to the conclusion of resurrection after initially learning that his tomb was empty.[37] The narratives at first do not betray any expectation that Jesus would appear to the disciples alive. The occurrence of shadowy haunting apparitions in the light of an unoccupied tomb and the event of his shameful death by crucifixion would be more likely to produce even more duress among his disciples. Such apparitions may have even given them the impression that Jesus was undergoing torment in the hereafter.[38]

REUNION APPARITIONS AND THE EMPTY TOMB

What of reunion apparitions? Had apparitions of Jesus presented him to the disciples in a healed, more purposeful, intelligent, and ostensibly happy postmortem state, might the appearances have been interpreted more positively? Often said, the purpose is simply to indicate something to the tune of "I'm okay" or "You should move on with your life." Importantly, some reunion apparitions that occur during bereavement can provide psychological healing and alleviation of grief to percipients.

However, there remain difficulties. In Jewish thought, resurrection in the eschatological sense was thought to be a corporate event when God would rescue his creation once and for all from the forces of evil. Not only would the righteous receive new flesh, but they would also become indestructible, inhabiting bodies fit for an earth and cosmos that had been newly created. Whatever really occurred at the time of Jesus'

---

36. Moreman, *Threshold*, ch. 2, para. 27.
37. Luke 24:22–24; John 20:11–15.
38. There is also early evidence specific to Christianity of apparitions appearing because of improper burial, though it is derived from sources several centuries after Jesus' crucifixion. See Finucane, *Ghosts*, 39–47.

postmortem encounters, the events convinced Jesus' earliest followers that he had been raised into this kind of body.

In coming to grips with how Jesus had been vindicated by God, and except for heretical sects such as the Gnostics and Docetists, the unanimous conclusion by the early church that he had been raised from the dead in this manner is significant because there was at least another option on the table. Certain heroes in Jewish history, like Enoch and Elijah, were widely thought to have ascended directly to heaven while still alive. Jewish and Christian traditions of the first century onwards believed that Enoch, Elijah, and select others were being preserved in heaven until an unspecified future date when they would return to earth, die, and *then* be raised. The Jewish apocalyptic work 4 Ezra prophesies the Messiah's reign on Earth for four hundred years, at the end of which he will die along with all others remaining. Subsequently, the Earth will rest in silence, then the general resurrection of the dead and new creation will occur.[39]

The two witnesses in Rev 11:3–12 who prophesy in the name of God are killed by the Beast, lie in the public square for three and a half days, after which they are raised from the dead, seen by witnesses, then ascend to heaven. The two witnesses here were interpreted by a litany of later Christian writers to refer to Enoch and Elijah.[40] The Coptic Apocalypse of Elijah has Enoch and Elijah descend to Earth a second time, receive their "spiritual flesh," and finally overcome the antichrist ("Shameless One"). This of course occurs within the proximity of the general resurrection.

Intriguingly, even with the precedent of Jesus having been raised in the sense of having received immortal, or spiritual, flesh, the church showed a reluctance to attribute such a privilege onto anybody else prior to the general resurrection—even Enoch and Elijah, who had already been exalted to heaven. Also, not to be missed in this tradition of the two witnesses is the following sequence of events: death -> resurrection -> seen by witnesses -> ascension to heaven. What we have here is in essence a parallel of the early Christian kerygma as it is summarized in 1 Cor 15:1–8, the early speeches in Acts, and is fleshed out in detail in the Gospels and Acts.

As was said of Jesus in the Gospels, most explicitly by the third evangelist, the postmortem appearances of the two witnesses of Rev 11 occur on Earth, *prior* to their ascension to heaven. Similarly, whatever we

---

39. 4 Ezra 7:26–32.

40. See the essays "The Martyrdom of Enoch and Elijah: Jewish or Christian?" and "Enoch and Elijah in the Coptic Apocalypse of Elijah" in Bauckham, *Jewish World*, 3–38.

make of those said to have been raised at the time of Jesus' crucifixion, the first evangelist presents the raised saints as appearing in bodily form to percipients in Jerusalem.[41] To this may be added the report that King Herod thought that Jesus was John the Baptist having been raised from the dead.[42] Resurrection was a phenomenon thought to be manifested to percipients in an *earthly* domain. I have argued elsewhere that had the initial postmortem encounters of Jesus been in the form of visions of Christ in heavenly glory that his vindication would most likely have been interpreted as a direct ascension, or exaltation, to heaven.[43]

While reunion apparitions may occur against a heavenly backdrop and others may be luminous, many seem to occur in everyday, mundane contexts at times when they are not expected. If Jesus appeared this way to the disciples, in a non-transparent form that mimicked his appearance before he underwent the horrors of the crucifixion and the brutality that preceded it, and (apparently) took up a point of space, it seems open for one to suggest that the disciples may have thought he had been raised from the dead. This may be plausible if the apparitions embodied all of apparitions' greatest hits discussed in the prior chapter, the tomb was discovered to be empty, and if, as I believe, he predicted his resurrection from the dead. Otherwise, one is left to wonder why the disciples mistook these visions to mean that Jesus had been raised, while others who experience such phenomena without exception conclude that their loved one in fact remains dead.

Given Jesus' untimely death by crucifixion, his abandonment by the disciples, and an empty tomb, I think it unlikely that an apparition of Jesus to Peter or the others would have been interpreted in a positive light. We know that some cultures tend to find afterdeath communications distressing rather than comforting.[44] The immediate historical circumstances would seem to have been more conducive to the production of disturbing, haunting apparitions, as we discussed in the previous section.

It also bears repeating that reunion apparitions occur mostly to individuals and rarely to groups of more than a few people at one time, unless they occur during séances.[45] Furthermore, Paul would not have experienced a reunion apparition of Jesus since he was not part of Jesus'

---

41. Matt 27:51–53.
42. Mark 6:14–16.
43. Kendall, "Vindication," 134–81.
44. See chapter 7.
45. See chapter 8.

movement prior to the crucifixion. Finally, if we assume the empty tomb to be historical, a second naturalistic explanation would have to be employed to account for this.[46]

MY ALTERNATIVE THEORY TO THE RESURRECTION IN SCENARIO 2

If the historicity of the empty tomb is granted, I do think we get closer to feasibly suggesting that the disciples could have interpreted the events of Easter Sunday and just beyond to be consistent with eschatological resurrection. Robust encounters with Jesus in the form of reunion/religious apparitions would, in my mind, be required, occurring to the multiple individuals listed in the creedal material at the beginning of 1 Cor 15 along with the three groups listed. While an empty tomb and visions of Jesus would have been consistent with postmortem exaltation (as opposed to eschatological resurrection), Jesus' predictions of resurrection shortly after his death persuaded the disciples to favor the latter interpretation, resulting in a mutation in Jewish' resurrection belief to allow for a single individual, the Messiah who died a righteous death to atone for the sins of many, to be raised ahead of the rest of the righteous and well before the universe is newly created. Paul's conversion was the result of an unexpected religious apparition. While any potential explanation for the empty tomb is going to be antecedently improbable (not to say impossible), if forced to choose among the numerous possibilities that have been proposed over the centuries, I would favor a sorcerer or necromancer who stole the body for purposes of magical incantations. See below for more on the empty tomb.

SCENARIO 3: APPARITIONAL HYPOTHESIS IN THE LIGHT OF 1 COR 15 AND THE GOSPELS

In chapter 20 I explained why I believe the Gospel post-resurrection accounts contain historically accurate material. More specifically, I think the evangelists probably capture the gist of what occurred on Easter and shortly afterwards. In the short space of seven weeks, these appearances embodied all the greatest hits of spontaneous apparitional encounters. As

---

46. See Allison, *Resurrection*, 10–11, for a discussion of a litany of naturalistic explanations for the empty tomb.

with scenarios one and two, I think Jesus' appearances must be considered in terms of reunion and/or religious apparitions (that were produced by living agents?) to make sense of them in terms of bodily resurrection. Additionally, the tomb was empty. A later vision to Paul ultimately resulted in his conversion to the faith.

THE RESURRECTION AS AN IDEA PATTERN—
MY ALTERNATIVE THEORY TO SCENARIO 3

Psychical research has provided, via hundreds of evidential cases, a precedent for nearly every aspect of Jesus' postmortem appearances. We have seen from various accounts in the literature that apparitions sometimes mimic the activity of living beings in extraordinary ways. The phantom hitchhiker of Montpellier, France, witnessed by four teenagers was real enough before she disappeared. On exhibit here is an idea pattern that can produce apparitions as *ostensibly* physically real as Jesus' post-resurrection appearances. Or they are non-human entities manifesting to human beings in a way that I would argue mirrors Jungian archetypes. The same may be said of materialized forms, persons, or entities produced in séances.

There is ample evidence from psychical research that challenges the notion that Jesus' consumption of food or engaging in complex conversation disproves Apparitional Hypothesis (AH). Through bilocation, Dadaji produced an apparition of himself that consumed half a biscuit and some tea and smoked part of a cigarette, leaving it still burning when he disappeared. Sathya Sai Baba performed similar feats. Bilocation apparently occurs also in the West, as Alex Tanous demonstrated by "dropping in" and drinking tea with a friend of his in Canada, while simultaneously sleeping in a New York City hotel.[47] While in New York visiting the ASPR,[48] Lloyd Auerbach had a "vivid dream" of traveling to and visiting a friend that lived forty miles away.

> A couple of days later, my friend, who has more than just the average smattering of psychic ability, asked me if I had a dream about visiting her on the night in question. When I replied, "Yes, how did you know?" (a silly question, perhaps), she said that I had been there, "physically." Apparently I had somehow been seen and touched by her (her dog reacted to me as well) at the

---

47. See chapter 3.
48. American Society for Psychical Research

time I believed I had been home dreaming. Now, assuming that I didn't sleep-drive to her house forty miles away, she either actually saw me, picked up on my dream psychically, or was just making a lucky guess.[49]

Two weeks later, Auerbach was at a bachelor party when he "suddenly had the sensation of being in two places at once." He was in his friend's kitchen and "was also standing in [his] friend Danita's living room." Danita was the same person as in the previous episode.

> We had a short conversation, partly about the bachelor party, partly about other things, and I recall her saying she knew I was having an OBE and was only "dropping in." I mentioned that I'd write down a few notes when I "got back" to Mike's and said good-bye. I found paper and pen, wrote a few notes (time, conversational details, etc.), which coincided with what Danita remembered about the situation.[50]

Surely though there are no instances, reasonably well-evidenced at least, of a supernormal appearance coinciding with a missing body, as we have with Jesus and the empty tomb? So I once believed. Yet every time I thought that I had reached the limits of what psychical research and super-psi can potentially explain regarding the resurrection, I was dealt a sobering disconfirmation. Belgian-French explorer Alexandra David-Neel relates the following regarding the Tibetan spiritual teacher, Kyongbu rimpoche.

> At that time, the new temple sheltering the huge image of the coming Buddha Maitreya was near completion and a consecration ceremony was being talked of. The Tashi Lama wished his old spiritual adviser to perform the consecration rite, but the latter declined, saying that he would have passed away before the temple could be finished.
> To this the Tashi Lama replied . . . by beseeching the hermit to delay his death till he had blessed the new building.
> Though such a request may astonish the reader, it is in accord with Tibetan ideas regarding the power which high mystics possess, of choosing the time of their death.
> The hermit promised to perform the consecration.

---

49. Auerbach, *ESP*, 46–47.
50. Auerbach, *ESP*, 47.

> Then, about one year after my visit to Shigatze, ... the Tashi Lama sent a beautiful sedan-chair and an escort to Kyongbu rimpoche to bring him to Tashilumpo's gompa.
> The men of the escort saw the lama sitting in the chair. The latter was closed and the porters started.
> Now, thousands of people had gathered at Tashilumpo for the religious festival of inauguration. To their utmost astonishment they saw the lama coming alone and on foot. Silently he crossed the temple threshold, walked straight towards the giant image of Maitreya until his body touched it, and then gradually became incorporated with it.
> Some time later the sedan-chair with the escort arrived. Attendants opened its door. ... The chair was empty.
> Many believe that the lama has never been seen again.[51]

David-Neel did not herself witness the vanishing of Kyongbu rimpoche, but she did know him from previous encounters, and more importantly, derived her information "from the account of men who affirmed that they saw the wonder."[52] She desired to go to Shigatze herself "to inquire about the lama's last days, and discover his tomb, if he was really dead," but unfortunately circumstances at the time made it impossible for her to investigate. She reports that only several years later, the political atmosphere made it unlikely that "men of rank" would say or do anything that would "increase the prestige of the Maitreya temple whose erection—according to the public rumour—had aroused unfriendly and jealous feelings at the Lhasa Court."[53] One of several opinions, however, included that the lama created a phantom that was present in the sedan-chair, then translocated to the temple of Maitreya, and disappeared after it touched the statue, while the lama himself remained in his hermitage.[54] As such, it appears to me that the apparition of Kyongbu rimpoche that appeared in Maitreya is well-attested by numerous witnesses, but the missing body component is open to speculation.

Nevertheless, a rapidly-disappearing corpse finds a home in Tibetan mysticism. In March 1874, Swami Ramalinga's body reportedly dissolved into light and finds attestation in contemporary police reports. Frank

---

51. David-Neel, *Tibet*, 280–81.
52. David-Neel, *Tibet*, 280–81.
53. David-Neel, *Tibet*, 281–82.
54. David-Neel, *Tibet*, 282.

Tiso writes that "Ramalinga's religious movement, which continues to the present day, insists on the literal disappearance of the body."[55] Moreover,

> Ramalinga is said to have appeared by bilocation to Colonel Olcott and Madame Blavatsky. Since his disappearance in 1874, he is reported to have appeared to many people in the form of a luminous hologram; there are also many reports of Ramalinga locutions. Tulasiram, a Pondicherry author and practitioner who has written voluminously on Ramalinga, reports on a woman devotee who in 2001 was awakened from sleep by a slap from Ramalinga and was put into a state of meditative absorption. Tulasiram claims to have seen a luminous apparition of Ramalinga in his private apartment in 1982.[56]

In the Tibetan Dzogchen tradition, Khenpo A Chö attained the "rainbow body," his corpse having apparently disintegrated within seven days of his death in 1998.[57] Tiso investigated the matter, having conducted several interviews of eyewitnesses. Miracles occurred around Khenpo's death besides the rainbow body itself, including the sky having become completely inundated by rainbow colors, a sweet fragrance emanating from the corpse, and a melodious song was heard by many in the vicinity whose source could not be determined.[58] Numerous disciples had visions of Khenpo, mostly in dreams, and at least one disciple Lobzang Nyendrak experienced an apparition of Khenpo while in the awake state. "At that time he had the experience of Khenpo A Chö tugging on his shirt sleeve and telling him, 'Practice well, meditate well. Be attentive.'"[59]

Finally, there are the reported bilocation episodes of Father Padre Pio.[60]

> Padre Pio, while remaining in San Giovanni Rotondo—often in full view of others—was nonetheless seen, heard, and even touched in other parts of Italy, Europe, and the world.[61]

---

55. Tiso, *Rainbow Body*, 12.
56. Tiso, *Rainbow Body*, 16.
57. Tiso, *Rainbow Body*, 34–37.
58. Tiso, *Rainbow Body*, 55–56, 59, 67, 73.
59. Tiso, *Rainbow Body*, 60.
60. Ruffin, *Padre Pio*, 365–70.
61. Ruffin, *Padre Pio*, 365.

Pio was reportedly seen in diverse locations "from Hawaii to South Africa," though the reports are of mixed quality.[62] In one report investigated by Padre Lino in 1978–1979, a nun who had been residing in a nursing facility in Montauk, Long Island claimed to have become terminally ill with stomach cancer in 1953–54 and was urged to pray to Padre Pio. One night, she was visited by a bearded priest who spoke to her in a language she did not understand, yet she somehow knew that the priest was telling her, "Don't worry. You're not going to die." He touched her on the hand and disappeared. The episode lasted about three minutes. She was declared completely healed of the cancer after her next medical evaluation. Interestingly, while she was a devotee of Padre Pio at the time, she did not know what he looked like and later identified him as the visiting priest from a photograph that she was shown of the eventual Catholic saint. Unfortunately, the authenticity of the case is compromised by the fact that Padre Lino did not record the nun's name, nor the nursing facility in which she resided at the time.[63]

Michael Grosso briefly narrates an episode that was investigated by John Schug that resonates with the Gospel report of Jesus' breaking bread with Cleopas and the unnamed disciple.[64]

> A tantalizing case is that of Cardinal Mindszenty. According to a reliable Vatican source, he once received a "visit" from Pio while imprisoned in Communist Hungary. The monk, of course, was in San Giovanni, but his double turned up with water, wine, and altar breads, served Mass and vanished. When Schug wrote to confirm this from Mindszenty, he received back a one-sentence letter: "I cannot say anything about that." If the story were false, it's not clear why the cardinal didn't say so, unless he meant to perpetuate a pious myth.[65]

Unfortunately, none of these reports are perfect from an evidential standpoint. Nevertheless, I think it more likely than not that at least one to a few of them are probably authentic.

Based on the concept of "idea pattern" from Tyrrell, could it be that the apparitional dramas were created and projected by the subliminal mind(s) of early follower(s) of Jesus beginning on the first Easter?

---

62. Ruffin, *Padre Pio*, 365.

63. Ruffin, *Padre Pio*, 365–66. For another reported healing account (of diabetes) in the context of a Padre Pio bilocation, see Grosso, *Smile*, 109.

64. Luke 24:13–32; John 21:10–14.

65. Grosso, *Smile*, 109.

According to this hypothesis, the reason that Jesus' apparitions had to be so emulative of bodily resurrection is to conform to the idea pattern of resurrection.

Perhaps then it is misguided to compare Jesus' postmortem appearances to the disciples with spontaneous apparitions of the dead, at least of the ilk that has been scrutinized by the SPR and other psychical research organizations over the past 150 years or so? The latter will conform to idea patterns of seeing haunting spirits or spirits of the deceased (or projections of living animals or humans). Therefore, such entities have proved to be more ephemeral. Jesus' postmortem appearances were conjured for a different reason, according to this theory. They do not conform to typical categories because the idea pattern produced was not for the purpose of presenting Jesus' spirit. Rather, they were supernormally produced by the early followers to conform to the idea of Jesus' *bodily* resurrection. Jesus' predictions of being raised then shortly after death planted the idea that resulted in arguably the greatest set of apparitional dramas ever created by super-psi.

PROBLEMS AND LIMITATIONS WITH THE RESURRECTION AS IDEA PATTERN

Idea patterns are shaped by culture. While the concept of eschatological resurrection was widely shared in first-century Judaism, we lack solid evidence of a belief that one person would be raised in such a way in the middle of history, so to speak. The resurrection was to be a corporate event. While one may reasonably posit that Jesus planted this idea into the subliminal minds of his earliest followers by his predictions of resurrection, things are not so straightforward.

While I believe Jesus' explicit predictions of resurrection are authentic, he also claimed that this would occur within the auspices of his role as Son of Man. Jesus also predicted his parousia as this same Son of Man, which I think hearkens to the eschatological figure in Dan 7 who receives international dominion and worldwide adoration, courtesy of the Ancient of Days.[66] As the Son of Man, Jesus will come "in his Father's

---

66. *Parousia* is the Greek word used often in the New Testament to refer to Jesus' future (second) coming.

glory with the holy angels."[67] The Son of Man will come "in clouds with great power and glory"[68] and will sit at the right hand of God.[69]

Such predictions doubtlessly contributed to the high Christology of the early church along with heavenly visions of the kind experienced by Stephen and St. John.[70] Furthermore, I tend to agree with Dale Allison that, from a pre-Easter perspective, the predictions of resurrection and the coming of the Son of Man would have been thought to occur as part of the same complex of eschatological events. Thus, the disciples would have understood Jesus' predictions of resurrection and parousia as being tied in to the general resurrection of the dead, with scriptural backing for this belief deriving from such texts as Zech 9–14 and Dan 7.[71] There is some indication that the disciples believed that they would join in Jesus' fate as they made their way to Jerusalem,[72] though I think they more likely than not would have anticipated an honorable death warring against the Romans. If this is correct, the earliest and closest followers of Jesus would have anticipated Jesus' resurrection after an *honorable* death, as well as their own, *in conjunction* with the resurrection of all the righteous, at which time Jesus would have established his kingdom as the Son of Man.

The upshot is that Jesus' predictions of resurrection would not necessarily generate an idea pattern that produced apparitions like what we find in the Gospel narratives. Any seed planted of resurrection would have been tied to the general resurrection of the dead and Jesus' coming (parousia) as Son of Man.[73] Moreover, I think there would have been other competing idea patterns.

Jesus' death by crucifixion, a *dishonorable* death, was a catastrophe.[74] Combine this with the disciples' abandonment of Jesus at the time of

67. Mark 8:38.
68. Mark 13:26.
69. Mark 14:62. This apocalyptic Son of Man is also mentioned in 1 En. 37–71 and 4 Ezra 13. In the former, he is also referred to as the "Elect One." In the latter, he is not called the "Son of Man" but the "Man" and "Mighty Man."
70. Acts 7:56; Rev 1:13–16.
71. See Allison, *Resurrection*, 198–204. Allison argues that Jesus himself probably believed this as well, at least prior to the crucifixion.
72. See Mark 14:31; John 11:16.
73. This is I think reinforced in Acts 1:6 where the disciples, after becoming convinced at the reality of Jesus' eschatological resurrection anticipated that he would imminently establish his Kingdom.
74. I think Allison downplays this factor too much. See Allison, *Resurrection*, 202n120; cf. Holding, "Shame," 185–91. First-century Jewish historian Flavius Josephus

his arrest, Peter's threefold denial, plus or minus an empty tomb, and I think a context was created that may have produced distressing apparitions of Jesus.[75] Assuming the stigma of the crucifixion would have been overcome without evidence of bodily resurrection, another potential idea pattern would have produced visions of Jesus in heavenly glory, which we know from the visions of Stephen and St. John did occur at some point in the early church. Jesus' predictions of parousia, along with his self-identification as the Son of Man from Dan 7, his application of Ps 110 to himself, and his witnessed transfiguration would have been sufficient to produce an idea pattern of exaltation to heaven, which would not have required an accompanying theology of eschatological resurrection.

Another feature worth considering is the milieu in which collective idea patterns emerge. Sightings of Sasquatch in South Dakota, Yeti in the Himalayas, phantom hitchhikers across the world, Men in Black in Point Pleasant, West Virginia, purported alien visitations/abductions, UFO sightings, etc. tend to conform with mythos that have permeated the consciousness of large communities, if not millions of people across the globe. Marian apparitions and later visions of Jesus occur(red) against a backdrop of an international community of established believers. Apparitions of the Rebbe to Meshichists occur mostly, though not exclusively, years after his death in charged religious settings steeped in visualization and absorption, along with a *prior* belief that he is currently alive and well in a parallel, spiritual reality waiting to be revealed.

Contrarily, our hypothetical resurrection idea pattern was formed shortly following Jesus' crucifixion, likely within a few days, and had a

---

referred to crucifixion as "the most wretched of deaths." Lucian said the letter T was given "evil significance" by the "evil instrument" as the medium of execution was in the form of the letter *tau*. Hengel, *Crucifixion*, 8. "From the time of Plautus, that is, from the third century BC onwards, there is evidence of the use of *crux* as a vulgar taunt among the lower classes." Hengel, *Crucifixion*, 9. Paul quotes Deut 21:23 in reference to the shame of the cross, "Christ redeemed us from the curse of the law by becoming a curse for us, for it is written: 'Cursed is everyone who is hung on a pole.'" Gal 3:13. Quoting Walter Bauer, Hengel writes of the Jewish and pagan opponents of Christianity, "The enemies of Christianity always referred to the disgracefulness of the death of Jesus with great emphasis and malicious pleasure. A god or son of god dying on the cross! That was enough to put paid to the new religion." Hengel, *Crucifixion*, 24. Hengel is thus probably correct when he said, "A crucified messiah, son of God or God must have seemed a contradiction in terms to anyone, Jew, Greek, Roman or barbarian, asked to believe such a claim, and it will certainly have been thought offensive and foolish." Hengel, *Crucifixion*, 10.

75. See above on the possibility of haunting apparitions of Jesus following the crucifixion.

profound impact on all of Jesus' earliest followers, including the eleven remaining disciples. An antecedently more probable scenario would involve the production of an apparition of Jesus to one or a few of his closest followers, at most, and perhaps a few outside of this most intimate circle. If this resulted in resurrection belief and Christianity as we know it germinated mostly peripherally to Jesus' inner circle, then the idea pattern that formed could have caused some from among (what would become) a much larger pool of believers to see visions of the resurrected Jesus, and these visions were interpreted accordingly. This is more in line with what we see with the Meshichists inside the Lubavitch movement. As such, those who happened to be among the 4 percent or so with a fantasy prone personality and/or had a low threshold for experiencing the paranormal (i.e., high transliminality) would have inevitably been those most likely to see the risen Jesus. Yet the first-century evidence indicates that Jesus' bodily resurrection was the initial, universal, and indeed foundational, belief amongst his earliest followers.

However, still more is needed. In my opinion, the least implausible non-supernatural (or non-paranormal) explanation for the empty tomb would be that a sorcerer came to steal the body of a known holy man to conduct magical incantations.[76] If we enlist super-psi to create the idea pattern of bodily resurrection, then does it follow that super-psi was responsible for the ultrarapid, supernormal decomposition of Jesus' body in the tomb?[77] As Jesus was unlikely a master of the arts of Dzogchen that is peculiar to Tibetan Buddhism, I find this possibility extremely unlikely.

Paul's vision of Jesus presents another major difficulty. As Paul did not, at the time, share in the earliest followers' social circles, and in fact was very antagonistic to the Christian movement, it seems to me very unlikely that his subliminal mind would have been subject to creating a sensory experience conforming to the idea pattern of resurrection

---

76. On this possibility see Allison, *Resurrection*, 341–44. For problems with this theory, see Holding, "Stolen," 390–93. While I find this theory to be antecedently (very highly) improbable, I think it is superior to other theories that I am aware of. If the disciples had visited the wrong tomb, it is a mistake that I think would have been corrected well before claims of resurrection were widely made. The same goes for any claim that Joseph of Arimathea moved the body or that the opposing Jewish or Roman leadership had done so, since it would presumably have been to a known location. I do not find the theory that the disciples stole the body to fabricate the resurrection tenable either since they were willing to be persecuted, and in some cases martyred, for their claims. See Matt 28:12–13.

77. See again Tiso, *Rainbow Body*, and the discussion in Allison, *Resurrection*, 272–85.

(or one of heavenly exaltation, for that matter). A different mechanism would have to account for this. There are other accounts in history of conversion visions like that of the apostle. I have read numerous remarkable examples, though I am unaware of any quite as remarkable as Paul's on the Damascus Road.[78]

FINAL THOUGHTS ON THE POST-RESURRECTION APPEARANCES OF JESUS

Collectively, AH provides a very robust data set upon which to consider Jesus' postmortem encounters with his earliest followers. I do think objective apparitions, however they are to be understood in nature, provide us a much firmer foundation than subjective visions/hallucinations do in trying to account for the evidence. The problem for one wishing to explain these phenomena under a materialistic canopy is that apparitions cannot, in my judgment, provide such an escape. At best we are still dealing here with supernormal phenomena. I am willing to go further, however. For me, the bodily resurrection of Jesus remains the most probable fit for the data. As we have seen, particularly as we admit more data into consideration, AH suffers from having to invoke numerous explanations.

By way of summary, AH would require a resurrection idea pattern to manifest in numerous dramatically compelling apparitions to individuals and groups—beginning within the space of only a few days and affecting (seemingly) all of Jesus' remaining eleven disciples (plus a wider group of followers)—the theft or psychokinetically-mediated dissolution of the crucified corpse within about thirty-six hours of burial, and the production of an apparition compelling enough to convert the apostle Paul, who was formerly a persecutor of the faith. Finally, even with authentic predictions of resurrection, the historical circumstances make the formation of a resurrection idea pattern a questionable premise at best. Despite the exploits of super-psi, I find the conspiracy of several highly unusual factors that support Jesus' bodily resurrection to remain compelling.[79]

---

78. See Allison, *Resurrection*, 89, 252–55, for numerous examples of conversion visions.

79. See Allison, *Resurrection*, 346. "The chapters in Part II have compiled parallels to much that appears in early Christian stories and traditions. Nonetheless, I know of no close phenomenological parallel to the series of likely events as a whole. Early Christianity offers us a missing body plus visions to several individuals plus collective

CONTEXT MATTERS—REFLECTIONS FROM THE THIRTEENTH DISCIPLE

There is another dimension to the historical question of the resurrection that I think is crucial to keep in mind, that being the context in which an empty tomb and postmortem appearances occurred. Consider hypothetically that there was a chemist in Oklahoma whose grave was found to be vacated a few days after his funeral and who was said to have appeared to some of his close friends and family shortly afterwards. Some of these appearances occurred to individuals. Some occurred to small and large groups. Let us also say that this chemist made no theological or even religious claims pertaining to himself. There exists no context in this hypothetical situation for why a resurrection should have occurred. While the quality of the evidence should still be evaluated and taken seriously, the pre-event probability of the chemist being raised from the dead would seem to be essentially zero. Regardless of how improbable a constellation of naturalistic alternatives may be, it would be reasonable to entertain such possibilities in our hypothetical post-event analysis.

Some would say the pre-event probability of Jesus being raised from the dead should be considered zero as well. However, I challenge the premise considering the robust theological context of Jesus' pre-Easter ministry. Unlike our hypothetical Midwest chemist, Jesus did make religious claims. Moreover, these religious claims were among the most audacious of anyone that I am aware of in history and were not without an objective foundation laid by wondrous events.

1. Jesus predicted his death and claimed that it would serve as the climax of Old Testament prophetic fulfillment. Moreover, he predicted his resurrection shortly thereafter.[80]
2. Jesus made statements that implied his pre-existence.[81]
3. Jesus claimed to be the long-awaited Messiah. Moreover, he claimed to have a unique relationship with God, indeed even claimed to be

---

apparitions plus the sense of a dead man's presence plus the conversion vision of at least one hostile outsider. Taken as a whole, this is, on any account, a remarkable, even extraordinary confluence of events and claims.... If there is a good, substantial parallel to the entire series, I have yet to run across it."

80. Allison, *Constructing*, ch. 5, "Assent to Death." Also, Licona, *Resurrection*, 284–301, and Kendall, "Passion," 51–80.

81. See Gathercole, *Pre-Existent*.

divine in some sense.[82] His earliest followers unanimously included him within the Godhead.[83]

4. Jesus performed astonishing deeds, especially healings and exorcisms, and possibly also revived the dead (in the sense of resuscitation, not eschatological resurrection).[84]

5. Although more controversial, I think the balance of the historical evidence supports that the nature miracles in the Gospels are also largely based on actual events during the ministry of Jesus. These include Jesus' walking on the surface of the Sea of Galilee, the stilling of a storm, feeding large multitudes of people with just a few loaves of bread and fish, etc.[85]

Every item in the above list is controversial to varying degrees. Unfortunately, we cannot defend any of these premises here. Since the purpose of this section is more of a personal note to readers, suffice it to say that I am convinced of the veracity of all these items, at least in the broad sense, based largely on the conclusions of rigorous historical criticism.

Against such a robust theological backdrop, I have tried a thought experiment, placing myself into the position of a thirteenth, invisible disciple on Good Friday. Given the five factors listed above regarding Jesus' words, deeds, and self-understanding, what would I have thought about Jesus' pre-event probability of rising from the dead? Of course, it helps enormously that I can do this thought experiment relatively devoid of emotion and with the benefit of hindsight that was simply unavailable to Jesus' disciples.[86]

First, Jesus' audacious claims about his work, his identity and relationship with God, and his predictions of impending death and

82. Witherington, *Christology*; Witherington, *Sage*; Wright, *Victory*.

83. Hurtado, *Lord Jesus Christ*.

84. Latourelle, *Miracles of Jesus*; Twelftree, *Miracle Worker*; Meier, *Marginal*; Harris, "Revivification."

85. Barnett, "Multitude"; Bauckham, "Coin"; Davis, "Cana." More recently, Graham Twelftree edited a volume whose various contributors approach Jesus' nature miracles from a variety of different historical and theological viewpoints, including skeptical. See Twelftree, *Nature*.

86. Given, among other things, the catastrophic implications of the crucifixion, a symbol of shame in the ancient world, and the fact that Roman control over Judea remained alive and well, it comes as no surprise that the disciples' hopes were shattered after the crucifixion. The titulus affixed to Jesus' cross that read "King of the Jews" served as Rome's declaration of victory and that was thought initially to be the end of the matter for both sides.

resurrection would not necessarily increase that pre-event probability in my mind if that is all we had. On a certain level, claims are merely claims, regardless of how bold or bizarre. However, modern studies of people with a "Christ complex" indicate that those suffering from delusions of such a magnitude are rarely functional members of society, and frequently they are committed to receive treatment in psychiatric facilities.[87] On the other hand, Jesus was, at minimum, a charismatic teacher of wisdom principles and/or ethics and was able to attract and inspire crowds wherever he went. I'm of the impression that few scholars would agree that he was a highly dysfunctional member of first-century Judeo-Roman society.

Then there are the healings. When I further reflect upon the cleansed lepers, the healing of those that had been stricken for decades with blindness or paralysis, those raised from the dead such as Lazarus, and the repeated demonstrations of mastery over natural processes (such as storms), against the backdrop of Jesus' own predictions of death and resurrection, I may plausibly reach the belief that some interesting things might occur within the few days following the crucifixion. That is, interesting things that would indicate Jesus had been vindicated. After all, I've already seen numerous other things that I cannot plausibly explain as mundane events in nature, and Jesus did predict said vindication.

Given this, how can I be so certain that one more miracle, albeit the best and most important of all, would not occur? However, if I did expect Jesus to soon rise in the eschatological sense, I would probably have expected it in conjunction with the general resurrection of the dead, not an isolated raising.

It is against the backdrop of such a theological context that women followers of Jesus found his tomb empty two mornings later. Shortly thereafter, his closest disciples, particularly the eleven, individually and in groups, claimed to see Jesus alive. Against the expectations of the time, they interpreted these numerous appearances to mean that he had been raised in the eschatological sense ahead of all the righteous, not only revived from death but also having received immortal flesh.

---

87. See Dyga and Stupak, "Religious Delusions."

23

Comparing the Postmortem Appearances of the Lubavitcher Rebbe and Jesus Christ

THOUSANDS OF LUBAVITCHER HASIDIM, including many Meshichists, make pilgrimages to and perform elaborate rituals at the Rebbe's gravesite every year, the implication being the belief of most that the Rebbe is still buried there. Lubavitchers are divided on the question of the Rebbe's messiahship and only a minority believe him to have been raised from the dead. We have seen that the leaders of Agudas Chasidei Chabad and most emissaries were and are more likely to disavow rigid declarations that the Rebbe is Messiah, and virtually none endorse that he has been raised from the dead. At best, some hope that God will reveal the Rebbe to be Israel's Messiah after all, and this may culminate in his *future* resurrection from the dead. A small minority claim the Rebbe is alive but concealed or invisible and will be revealed by God at the appointed time. This belief is not based on postmortem appearances of the Rebbe to followers in the immediate aftermath of his death. Rather, the postmortem encounters that occur later are largely outpourings of a prior belief, based on the principal of *histalkus*, that is the Rebbe's concealment.

Hypothetically speaking, the rise of Christianity would have served a more fitting parallel to the Lubavitch movement if it had unfolded something like this. A peripheral member of Jesus' movement leading up to the crucifixion, or perhaps one of the eleven remaining disciples, came to the conviction that he was still alive and somehow still the Messiah of Israel. God had indeed vindicated Jesus, but this was concealed from the world, including his followers. This world where Jesus is alive can only be seen with spiritual eyes rather than with the eyes of flesh. One day, perhaps when all the Jewish nation accepts him as Messiah, will we receive the ability to perceive this reality in which Jesus had been raised.

In the world that we all know and live, Jesus' body is still interred in Joseph of Arimathea's tomb, though later some that express this same conviction about Jesus' concealment speculate that perhaps his body would either not be found there if one were to look, or perhaps the body would exhibit miraculous preservation from corruption. Based on this *established* conviction that Jesus has been raised in some parallel reality and would inevitably show himself to be Messiah, some see apparitions of Jesus both in mundane contexts, and more often in charged religious environments where his life and memory and this messianic conviction are routinely celebrated.

Meanwhile, this messianic faction finds fierce resistance from the movement's central leadership, particularly the vast majority (or all) of the remaining eleven disciples, James, and the vast majority of those who were within Jesus' inner circle prior to his death. The seventy disciples Jesus would later commission come to mind here.[1] This central leadership still holds out hope that Jesus will be raised in the future, and perhaps may even be declared Messiah, but this is not a foregone conclusion. After all, there is a potential Messiah in every generation. Whether or not that will prove to be Jesus is God's discretion.

Much like the Chabadniks, in the aftermath of the crucifixion, the messianic hopes of Jesus' closest followers were dashed. Unlike the Chabadniks, the renewed vigor and passion with which Jesus' disciples subsequently preached Jesus' messiahship, often in the face of suffering and persecution, were the result of experiences that they deemed to be irrefutable evidence that God had raised Jesus from the dead. Although controversial, good evidence exists that Jesus' tomb was found empty on Easter Sunday. The reported post-resurrection appearances to Jesus' earliest disciples, and wider groups of followers on at least one or two occasions, were essential and formative to the belief that Jesus had been raised and is Messiah indeed.

---

1. Luke 10:1–23.

Concluding Reflections

IN THIS VOLUME, WE have argued that the Apparitional Hypothesis (AH) serves as the best potential alternative to Jesus' resurrection other than the Resurrection Hypothesis. Much of what we see in the Gospel narratives and the appearance accounts of the Lubavitcher Rebbe finds parallel among well-evidenced cases of apparitions. While apparitional and other psi phenomena plausibly account for the postmortem appearances of the Rebbe, they do so only with great difficulty when applied to Jesus' postmortem appearances.

This research has resulted in epiphanies that have demanded modification of my worldview in significant ways. Ostensible encounters with the dead occur in nature, but in many cases, I think these are best explained as products of telepathic impulses rather than visitations from conscious spirits or demonic manifestations. In fact, such encounters are arguably explainable as subliminal projections of living persons rather than from the dead. I would even include in this potentially explainable vein the remarkable cases of religious apparitions that are witnessed by dozens, hundreds, or even thousands of people, particularly those of Jesus and the Blessed Virgin Mary.

The implications of psi in nature, the mechanisms of which would be responsible for producing such apparitions of the living among other things, add other dimensions to reality that demand consideration. Some of these considerations would, I think, challenge theistic interpretations of certain remarkable events.

1. Are visions of religious figures of divine origin or merely apparitions produced unconsciously from the subliminal minds of living agents?

2. Is demonic possession merely a case of dissociative identity disorder (DID) or the manifestation of a secondary center of consciousness, that, because of its proximity to the subliminal mind, is capable of exhibiting psi abilities that may be mistaken as supernatural expressions of power?[1]

3. Are healing miracles mere expressions of psychokinetic ability on the part of the healed or the healer? Perhaps in rare circumstances the placebo effect is capable of being harnessed and used in dramatically exceptional ways.[2] As a medical doctor who knows of and has witnessed firsthand the power of the placebo effect, and its limitations, there was a time I would have found this idea laughable. As I write this more than five years later, I am not laughing.

4. Similarly, perhaps miracles that affect the environment are also dramatic instances of super-psi.[3]

Psychical research has demonstrated that conscious, sentient organisms, preeminently human beings, have latent abilities (psi) that are at present very poorly understood but can theoretically account for much of the anomalous phenomena we have surveyed in this book. Even evidence that ostensibly points to survival of bodily death could debatably be accounted for by super-psi. Be that as it may, many from among the ranks of the founding members of the Society for Psychical Research and their modern counterparts tend to lean towards the interpretation that the relevant data favors the survival hypothesis over and against

---

1. Once more widely labeled multiple personality disorder (MPD).

2. I believe this line of reasoning can only take us so far, as revivifications of the dead can scarcely be the result of psychosomatic causes. On the historicity of Gospel claims that Jesus raised the dead, see Harris, "Revivification"; Latourelle, *Miracles*, 121–27, 185–94, 229–37; Meier, *Marginal*, 773–837; Twelftree, *Miracle Worker*, 304–10. For further discussion, including well-evidenced revivifications in modern times, including in Africa, Asia, the Philippines, Latin America, and the West, see Keener, *Miracles*, 536–79; also Keener, *Miracles Today*, 137–74. For a briefer summary of modern raisings, see Keener, *Acts*, 2:1711–14.

3. On miracles that affect the environment, such as controlling the weather, multiplying food, etc., see Keener, *Miracles*, 579–99; Keener, *Miracles Today*, 175–90. Famous Indian holy man Sathya Sai Baba is said to have miraculously produced a variety of delicious Indian dishes inside of empty vessels on the banks of the Chitravati River. Haraldsson, *Modern Miracles*, 99–100.

that of super-psi. Worth noting is that this very formidable collaboration of scholars, historians, philosophers, and scientists does not tend to subscribe to traditional religions. Yet, to my mind, they persuasively demonstrate that scientific materialism cannot explain the phenomenon of consciousness or certain facets of nature.[4]

I believe that the historical Jesus claimed to be not only the Jewish Messiah, but even divinity incarnate, and that his predicted, atoning death would be required for salvation. Crucially, I believe these claims were given a divine stamp of authority when he was raised from the dead into a transformed, immortal, and glorified body. In whatever ways my own worldview is to be modified by the data and implications of psi, I am compelled to keep Jesus' atoning death and resurrection at the center.

Nevertheless, I am very much inclined to think that the Esalen thinktank and those likeminded are onto something very important.[5] Could it be, along the lines of forces like gravity and electromagnetism, that there are "psi fields" or "morphogenetic fields," to borrow terminology from English biologist Rupert Sheldrake, which connect all conscious beings with each other and with the virtually infinite sea of matter in the universe? If such fields exist and could be discovered and understood, it will shine a light on many topics discussed in this book. Importantly, as with discoveries like Einstein's general and special relativity, quantum mechanics, and electromagnetism, understanding and harnessing whatever makes psi phenomena possible could result in technological innovations that would revolutionize such things as medicine, communications, information-gathering capacities, and religion.

Our Judeo-Christian traditions assert that God acted in human history to affect such ends as the liberation of the Israelites from Pharaoh and the resurrection of Jesus Christ. Furthermore, as believers in a rational Creator who brought forth an orderly universe that can be studied, it

---

4. For seminal works, see Gurney et al., *Phantasms I* and *Phantasms II*; Sidgwick et al., "Census"; Myers, *Human Personality*, vols. 1 and 2. For modern treatments, see Kelly et al., *Irreducible*; Kelly et al., *Beyond Physicalism*; Kelly and Marshall, *Consciousness Unbound*; Murphy, *Future*; Grosso, *Next World*; Targ, *Limitless*; Targ and Puthoff, *Mind-Reach*. For deep dives into psi, see Braude, *Limits*; Braude, *Immortal*; On NDEs from the vantage point of a medical doctor, see Greyson, *After*; Long and Perry, *Evidence of the Afterlife*; Long and Perry, *God and the Afterlife*; Rivas et al., *Self Does Not Die*; van Lommel, *Consciousness*. See Grosso, *Smile*, for a great volume on miracles. For further critiques of materialism/physicalism and support for the belief that consciousness can exist apart from a functioning brain/body, see Beauregard and O'Leary, *Spiritual*; Doidge, *Brain*; Schwartz and Begley, *Mind*.

5. Kripal, *Esalen*.

behooves us twenty-first century Christians to open-mindedly consider where the evidence leads us to better understand the phenomena inherent in nature, regardless of whether or not we are expelled from our current comfort zone. If we close our minds to such things, not only do we risk stifling progress that could ultimately result in the betterment of humanity, but we would be guilty of the very sort of closed-mindedness of which we accuse our physicalist counterparts.

Appendix A

Statistics on Apparitional Phenomena

SOME CHARACTERISTICS OF APPARITIONS are more common than others. Collectively experienced apparitions, for instance, tend to be exceptional compared with those that are seen by a single percipient. Apparitions that produce tactile sensations, such as ostensibly touching a percipient, are also among the minority. Here I will discuss the incidence of some of these characteristics of apparitions through the lens of statistics yielded by collections that have been referenced in this volume.

CHARACTERISTICS OF BEREAVEMENT ENCOUNTERS

W. Dewi Rees in 1971 performed a study of aggrieved widows and widowers in Wales, United Kingdom. To the surprise of many, he found that roughly 50 percent reported encounters with their deceased spouse. Of those surveyed, a sense of presence was the most common phenomenon reported (39 percent). Visual encounters (apparitions) were experienced in 14 percent. Auditory encounters, which usually meant hearing the voice of the deceased spouse, occurred in 13 percent. Fewer than 3 percent reported tactile (touch) experiences. Frequently, more than one sensory modality was involved in bereavement encounters. In exceptional cases, for example, a widow may have seen an apparition of her spouse, heard the apparition speak, and even felt the touch of the apparition.[1]

---

1. Rees, *Eternity*, Ch. 10, "The Llanidloes Study of Widowhood," para 7.

Rees's survey sparked a spate of similar studies in the ensuing decades that essentially confirmed the commonality of these ostensible afterlife encounters. However, I have found that the literature varies widely as to which sensory modality predominates. Glick et al. report that even thirteen months after bereavement, 47 percent of widows in their sample agreed that "I have the feeling that my husband watches over me."[2]

> Some widows occasionally experienced near hallucinations. One reported hearing her husband come to the door after work and put his key in the lock. Four others reported catching sight of their husband out of the corners of their eyes. In one case he was sitting in the living room reading his paper, in another he was standing by the door. These widows, it should be emphasized, knew better, no matter what they heard or saw. Unlike the hallucinating psychotic, they had full insight into the illusory character of their perceptions.[3]

Interestingly, in this study, the sense of presence of the deceased did not diminish with time after its initial onset (usually a few weeks after death). Numerous widows even deliberately and successfully *invoked* the sense of presence, especially when they felt depressed or especially lonely.[4]

Arcangel's "Afterlife Encounters Survey" revealed that 69 percent of those that affirmed an afterlife encounter experienced the encounter visually (an apparition). Haraldsson's study was similar, with 67 percent reporting a visual encounter of the deceased. Kalish and Reynolds interviewed at least one hundred members each of four demographics: African Americans, Anglo-Americans, Mexican Americans, and Japanese Americans in Los Angeles County regarding a litany of matters pertaining to death, including grief. Extrapolating from the data listed in the appendix, about 44 percent answered "yes" to the question, "Have you ever experienced or felt the presence of anyone after he had died?"[5] Of those, well over half responded in the next survey question that this occurred

---

2. Glick et al., *Bereavement*, 146n2.
3. Glick et al., *Bereavement*, 147.
4. Glick et al., *Bereavement*, 147.
5. Kalish and Reynolds, *Death*, Appendix, 215. One hundred and ninety-three of 434 answered in the affirmative.

in a dream.[6] The next closest category was those that experienced a visit while in the awake state.[7]

The differences may relate to geographical, situational, and cultural factors. Whereas Rees specifically surveyed widows and widowers in Wales, Arcangel's survey was international and drew participants from a general pool of respondents (not primarily widows and widowers). Haraldsson likewise drew from a general pool in Iceland.

There have been other studies that confirm the predominance of visual encounters while others found, similar with Rees, the sense of presence was the most common.[8] The only firm conclusion I can draw from the collective data set is that the two most common forms of afterlife encounter experiences (or ADCs) are the sense of presence and apparitions. Depending upon the specific case, both modalities may be present plus or minus auditory occurrences (especially hearing the deceased speak), tactile phenomena, and olfactory experiences. Also worthy of note is that tactile experiences were more common than I would have thought at the outset of this research, being present in about 13 percent of the cases reported by Arcangel and Haraldsson.

WHO APPEARS, OR MANIFESTS, TO PERCIPIENTS?

Of the 596 affirmative respondents in Dianne Arcangel's "Afterlife Encounters Survey," there were 950 reported entities that manifested. A parent or "other family member" were the most common encounters, at 21 percent each. Unrelated people were encountered 13 percent of the time while unknown figures appeared 11 percent of the time.[9] Children were perceived 11 percent of the time while pets were perceived 10 percent of

---

6. Kalish and Reynolds, *Death*, Appendix, Q 127. Specifically, 65 percent of African Americans, 63 percent of Japanese Americans, 74 percent of Mexican Americans, and 45 percent of Anglo-Americans experienced the deceased in a dream.

7. The text does not specify what kind of visit, presumably this category would include but would not be exclusive to visual phenomena (apparitions). Twenty-nine percent of African Americans, 6 percent of Japanese Americans, 21 percent of Mexican Americans, and 42 percent of Anglo-Americans claimed to receive visits from the deceased.

8. Arcangel, *Afterlife*, 283–85 and Aleman and Larøi, *Hallucinations*, "Hallucinations in Nonclinical Groups," paras. 18–20.

9. Many in this category were not known to the percipient at the time of the experience but were discovered later from photographs to be relatives from the distant past.

the time.[10] Interestingly only 6 percent of the time was a deceased spouse encountered. Spiritual figures manifested 5 percent of the time while contemporary or historically famous personages comprised 2 percent of such encounters.[11]

In Haraldsson's Icelandic survey, 51 percent of those perceived were family members, slightly more than half of which were described as either "very close" or "quite close" to the percipient (33 percent and 19 percent, respectively). Friends, colleagues, and acquaintances comprised another 23 percent of those perceived, and 24 percent were strangers that were "almost unknown or completely unknown by the informants until after the experience."

Of the 214 family members that were perceived, as with Arcangel's survey, parents predominated. Fathers were perceived in forty-three cases (20 percent), mothers in twenty-two cases (10 percent), and children in sixteen cases (7.5 percent). Spouses did appear more often in this study, more than 12 percent of the total: husbands in eighteen cases (8.4 percent) and wives in nine cases (4.2 percent). Haraldsson adds that "those who have lost their life partners probably have more contact with the dead than any other group."[12]

Both Arcangel's and Haraldsson's studies inquired specifically of apparitions of the dead. However, outside of deathbed visions, apparitions of the living are more common than apparitions of the dead in most studies that do not discriminate.[13] In the "Census of Hallucinations", 31.6 percent of visual encounters were apparitions of the living, more than double that of apparitions of the dead (14.6 percent). Another 28.3 percent were apparitions of unrecognized figures.[14] West's study in 1947 revealed similar statistics: 40 percent were apparitions of the living; a mere 9 percent were apparitions of the dead; 27 percent were apparitions of unrecognized figures.[15] However, an international collection based on questionnaires per-

---

10. In the case of pets, more than half of such encounters were accompanied by deceased family members.

11. Arcangel, *Afterlife*, 291.

12. Haraldsson, *Departed*, 59–60.

13. On deathbed visions (i.e., transitional apparitions), see Osis and Haraldsson, *Hour of Death*.

14. These percentages are based on my calculations from the data in Sidgwick et al., "Census," 43. Note the numbers do not add up to 100 percent because other apparitions that did not appear as "realistic human phantasms" were classified differently.

15. West, "Mass-Observation," 190. Again, the numbers do not add up to 100 percent because other apparitions that did not appear as "realistic human phantasms" were

formed in 1968 and 1974 revealed about twice as many apparitions of the dead compared with those of the living among *recognized* apparitions.[16] However, this collection had a comparatively disproportionate number of apparitions of unrecognized figures (72 percent).[17] Extrapolating from Green and McCreery's data, this would leave about 18–19 percent of the collection comprising apparitions of the dead with another 9 percent representing apparitions of the living.

COLLECTIVE APPEARANCES

We have noted that most apparitions, and other nonvisual encounters, occur to individuals. However, we have also seen that collective experiences are far from unheard of. In the "Report on the Census of Hallucinations," ninety-five of the 1,087 visual cases were collectively perceived, about 9 percent. However, in only 283 of the 1,087 cases there were more than one person present at the time of the appearance. This data suggests that if an apparition appears to a group of two or more people, it will be seen collectively about one-third of the time.

In Erlendur Haraldsson's survey of 349 accounts, in half (174) the perceiver claimed that another person was present or at least close by at the time of the appearance. However, only around half of these (eighty-nine) were reportedly in position to make a similar observation. Of these eighty-nine occurrences, in forty-one of them another percipient reportedly had the same experience as the informant (46 percent). Haraldsson was able to confirm twenty-nine of these forty-one accounts by the co-witness.[18]

RECURRENT ENCOUNTERS

According to the "Census," 66 percent of the percipients had only one encounter in their lives up to the point of interview.[19] Of the 34 percent who

---

classified differently.

16. Green and McCreery, *Apparitions*, 178 and 188.

17. Green and McCreery, *Apparitions*, 178.

18. Haraldsson, *Departed*, 201. Of the other twelve cases, Haraldsson states that seven of the co-witnesses had passed away, another two could not be contacted, and in three the witnesses either could not remember the occurrence or declined to give their opinion.

19. There were similar findings in the follow-up study in 1947 where 38.7 percent

experienced more than one encounter, roughly two-thirds (23 percent of the total) of these contained visual elements (with or without auditory and/or tactile components). Only 12.4 percent of those that answered "yes" to having seen an apparition claimed to see one three or more times.[20] Similarly, Erlendur Haraldsson found that of those perceiving a deceased person, a similar 66 percent perceived this person only once while 17 percent experienced two such events, and 15 percent experienced three or more such perceptions of the deceased person.[21] In Arcangel's study, 78 percent of respondents that answered "yes" to having had an apparitional encounter reported that they experienced at least two such encounters of *different* persons or entities during their lives. It isn't clear to me from the survey results, however, how many of her respondents had multiple encounters of the *same* person or entity. Also, the "Census" and Haraldsson's study counted only direct sensory phenomena, be they visual, auditory, tactile, olfactory, or a combination of more than one in the waking state. Arcangel's study included ADCs that occurred in dreams and the sense of presence in the awake state, which as we have seen the latter is the most common kind of occurrence according to some studies.

TIMING OF ENCOUNTERS IN RELATION TO DEATH

Apparitions occur more frequently closer to the time of death and tend to taper off with time. We mentioned in chapter two that a disproportionate number of apparitions occur very near the time of death. In Haraldsson's Icelandic study, about 7 percent occurred at the time of death and 14 percent occurred within twenty-four hours of death. Typically, this 14 percent would entail crisis apparitions which commonly inform percipients of the agent's death. Twenty-two percent of apparitions occur within one week of death, nearly one-third occur within one month, and about half occur within one year.[22] Sometimes apparitions may manifest for the first time between one and five years after death, about 21 percent in

---

of respondents that confirmed having experienced an encounter also claimed to experience more than one. See West, "Mass-Observation," 193.

20. These are my calculations based on the data from Sidgwick et al., "Census," 39, 42.

21. Sidgwick et al., "Census," 120.

22. Haraldsson, *Departed*, 53.

Haraldsson's study. Another 9 percent appear between five and ten years, and the remaining 18 percent after ten years.[23]

Per W. D. Rees' Welsh study, bereavement encounters tend to start weeks to months after death. However, in extrapolating from Haraldsson's data, along with some of the cases I've run across in the literature, it's likely that a minority of such encounters (perhaps, as an educated guess, around 8–10 percent) occur between twenty-four hours and one week of death.

Hauntings do not usually have their onset before at least several months following death, and in many cases likely years later. This much may be reasonably postulated because they tend to be of unrecognized figures for the most part. In most cases, haunting apparitions likely represent a person who once occupied a particular house, or frequented some other locale, and those that knew them in life have moved on to somewhere else. There are exceptions. The appearances of the Samuel Bull apparition to his family began about six months following his death.

Rescue apparitions tend to be of unrecognized people as well, or represent the mysterious "Third Man." When representing a person that once lived, rescue apparitions tend to be of people long passed. Transition apparitions may represent anyone that has passed on, usually a lost loved one from the percipient's family that passed on any time between days and decades earlier. As we discussed in chapter 6, numerous cases in the literature narrate apparitions of the deceased that represent people in which the percipient was not yet aware of their death. Apparitions that represent those still living, of course, do not apply to this situation. Finally, religious apparitions tend to occur anywhere between years and centuries later. Religious apparitions of the Rebbe have been occurring for at least the past couple of decades. In the case of Jesus Christ and the Blessed Virgin Mary, they have occurred for nearly two thousand years and counting.

23. Haraldsson, *Departed*, 53–54.

Appendix B

Apparitions and Quantum Entanglement

PHYSICALISM DOMINATES WESTERN SCIENCE and philosophy. Although there are notable exceptions, the current consensus takes for granted that consciousness is somehow produced by the complex neurocircuitry that makes up the brain. In other words, what makes you wake up as yourself every morning (and not somebody else) depends upon the makeup of your brain's particular neural network. Given sufficient advancement in technology, if we were to construct a neural network identical to yours, that *is* you. Consciousness cannot exist, says the scientific materialist, outside of a functioning brain.

This concept sits well within the realm of classical physics, which posits that if we know enough information about an object's position and motion, along with extrinsic factors such as the force of gravity, the magnitude of friction present along its path, or wind resistance in the case of projectiles, etc. then we can predict where that object will be ten seconds, ten minutes, or one thousand years into the future. Apply this logic to the microscopic world, down to the very subatomic particles that comprise our existence, and you have both a mechanical and predictable universe. That is, given enough information, the lifetime of events of both animals and humans could be mapped out and predicted in advance. Not only that, the past histories of all objects and living creatures could be reconstructed. This of course raises the question of whether we have free will or the apparent freedom we have to make choices is merely an illusion. There is no room for free will if consciousness cannot exist independently of the brain but merely *results* from a functioning brain.

More emphatically, there is certainly no room for objectively produced apparitions, telepathy, psychokinesis, or any kind of psi phenomena in a materialistic universe.

Enter quantum mechanics in the early twentieth century. The discoveries of quantum mechanics literally threw a wrench of uncertainty into the deterministic universe of classical mechanics, even to the point where the nature of reality has become controversial. It was discovered that matter, or at least subatomic particles like photons and electrons, exhibit wave-particle duality. When a single photon[1] is fired from a laser and forced to "choose" one of two paths on its way to a photographic plate, it will act as a particle when measured. However, in a similar experimental set up, if the photon is not forced to choose one path or another, it will traverse *both* paths. That is, the photon will exist as a wave, not a particle, and it will manifest on the photographic plate as an interference pattern with alternating bands of darkness and light. Whether or not one observes, by measurement, the path the photon takes literally decides whether it will act as a particle or a wave.

Even more mysteriously, the photon will always seem to make an appropriate choice even in experimental setups where the experimenter makes the decision to observe, or not, at a point in time *after* the photon goes through a beam splitter. The upshot of these experiments is that not only does consciousness seem to produce reality, at least on a microscopic scale, but in theory one may extrapolate from the data that even past events are determined from decisions made by conscious individuals in the *future*.

Prior to the advent of quantum entanglement, information was considered to be unable to travel faster than the speed of light. Suppose the sun simply ceases to exist in an instant. Obviously, this would be catastrophic for our solar system, including the Earth and all of us living upon it. No longer held in orbit by the sun's gravity, the Earth would be thrown into deep space and that would quickly, violently be the end of life on this planet. However, this catastrophic process would not occur at the exact moment of the sun's disappearance. Rather, it would begin about eight minutes later, or the time required for the last glimmer of light and gravitational influence that emanated from the sun to reach us. The gravitational disruption of the sun's disappearance likewise can only travel at the speed of light. The speed of light is essentially the physical

---

1. A photon is a unit of light.

speed limit of our universe. According to the conception of classical physics, it is impossible for anything, including any form of information, to be conveyed faster than one hundred eighty six thousand miles per second. However, the experimental proofs of quantum entanglement revealed that in some situations this speed limit is irrelevant.

A famous thought experiment called the EPR paradox, authored by Albert Einstein, Boris Podolsky, and Nathan Rosen, suggested that, using twin state photons (paired, complementary particles), the implications of quantum mechanics proved that this physical speed limit could be violated. The EPR paradox implied that using a measuring device to determine one twin particle's position or velocity gives the experimenter similar information instantly about the other particle, whose properties are complementary. Einstein eschewed the idea of entanglement, reportedly referring to it as "spooky actions at a distance." Einstein used this to argue that quantum mechanics could not possibly be a complete theory and these effects must be accounted for by some unknown "hidden variables."

However, with the advent of newer technologies, the predictions of EPR would eventually be proven correct. The physical speed limit of the universe is violable through the implications of quantum entanglement. As it turns out, information can travel faster than the speed of light.

It is understandable that some readers hearing of these fascinating physical realities for the first time will find them counterintuitive, or perhaps even insane. That was my reaction when I first learned of wave particle duality and quantum entanglement and the implications thereof. It also was the initial reaction it seems of most (all?) the scientists that brought it to us. Unlike with classical mechanics, quantum entanglement purports a universe where everything is connected, not only in space but also in time.[2]

Quantum physicists generally eschew interpretations of quantum mechanics that make room for mystical interpretations of reality. Be that as it may, while quantum theory does not necessitate a reality that permits objective apparitions and other psi phenomena, it clearly is more conducive to such events transpiring than classical mechanics. The insight of quantum mechanics serves as a plausible framework in which

---

2. Rosenblum and Kuttner, *Quantum Enigma*, and Greene, *Fabric of the Cosmos*, provide excellent introductions to quantum mechanics. Schwartz and Begley, *Mind*, Ch. 8, "The Quantum Brain" is helpful. For a more technical read, see Stapp, "Quantum-Mechanical."

to place the substantial empirical evidence that has been amassed for the reality of psi phenomena. Telepathy and psychokinesis, if valid, requires some theory that would allow connectedness at a distance. Theoretically, quantum entanglement may ground such a connectedness within scientific theory.

There is also some experimental evidence that supports this contention. Pim van Lommel describes an experiment where people were paired and placed in separate Faraday cages.[3] According to van Lommel, if the pair were strongly bonded, such as a mother and child or two people that had practiced joint meditation for years, their EEGs would register simultaneous discharges when one of the two received sensory stimuli via light flashes. Specifically, visual evoked potentials would register on the EEG of both the stimulated person *and* the other person who was isolated in a different Faraday cage.[4]

When groups of cells that line the intestine (epithelial cells) are deliberately separated to seemingly preclude communication by electrical or chemical means, and one group of cells is damaged by a toxic agent, the group of cells that is *not* exposed to the toxic agent also exhibit similar changes as the group that was exposed.[5] Moreover, immune cells (white blood cells) demonstrate a similar connectedness when separated from the individual that produced them. In an experimental study in which immune cells were separated by twelve to twenty kilometers from a subject, and placed in a Faraday cage, these separated cells reacted when the subject was shown horrifying or sexually arousing images.[6] Experimental evidence for psi is not insubstantial.[7]

Rupert Sheldrake's theory of "Formative Causation" makes some sense in a universe of quantum connectedness. His controversial theory involves the presence of morphic fields of various kinds that are operative among members especially of the same species. While not yet having gained widespread acceptance in the scientific community, Sheldrake amasses a wealth of data from various disciplines to make a formidable case. This includes numerous examples from nature including the behavior of insect colonies, schools of fish, and flocks of birds.

---

3. Faraday cages are areas shielded from electromagnetic radiation.
4. van Lommel, *Consciousness*, 269.
5. van Lommel, *Consciousness*. 294.
6. van Lommel, *Consciousness*. 298–99.
7. See especially Radin, *Conscious Universe*; Radin, *Supernormal*.

Citing but one example here, Sheldrake discusses the banking movements of flocks of dunlins. When the flock changes directions, the wave of propagation effecting this change moves from dunlin to dunlin at an average speed of fifteen milliseconds, or fifteen thousandths of a second. However, the average reaction of dunlins in the lab to a sudden flash of flight is thirty-eight milliseconds. The potential implication is that something more than simple visual stimuli is responsible for how quickly dunlins change directions while in flock. One potential explanation for this is the presence of a field that connects the various members of the flock.[8] Until such fields are discovered, the theories of morphic resonance will remain within the realm of educated conjecture. Be that as it may, I find the cumulative case made by Sheldrake to be impressive.[9]

Despite some promising experimental results, the degree to which quantum theory, especially quantum entanglement, accommodates psi phenomena is controversial. Generally, such accommodation is made to the chagrin of quantum scientists and theoretical physicists. Regardless of where future discoveries may lead, and whether they confirm or refute what is being suggested here, the grounding of psi phenomena, including apparitions, near-death experiences, and mystical experiences within a scientific framework will continue to be met by resistance, and even hostility. We should expect nothing less, after all, "The first one through the wall always gets bloody."

---

8. Sheldrake, *Presence of the Past*, 284–87.
9. Sheldrake, *Presence of the Past*; Sheldrake, *Morphic Resonance*.

Bibliography

Aleman, André, and Frank Larøi. *Hallucinations: The Science of Idiosyncratic Perception.* Washington, DC: American Psychological Association, 2008. Kindle.
Alexander, Stewart. *An Extraordinary Journey: The Memoirs of a Physical Medium.* 2nd ed. Guildford, UK: White Crow, 2020. Kindle.
Allison, Dale C., Jr. *Constructing Jesus: Memory, Imagination, and History.* Grand Rapids: Baker, 2010. Kindle.
———. *Encountering Mystery: Religious Experience in a Secular Age.* Grand Rapids: Eerdmans, 2022.
———. *Resurrecting Jesus: The Earliest Christian Tradition and Its Interpreters.* New York: T&T Clark, 2005.
———. *The Resurrection of Jesus: Apologetics, Polemics, History.* New York: T&T Clark, 2021.
"An Apparition." *Journal of the Society for Psychical Research* 7 (1895) 25–28.
Arcangel, Dianne. *Afterlife Encounters: Ordinary People, Extraordinary Experiences.* Charlottesville, VA: Hampton Roads, 2005.
Auerbach, Loyd. *ESP, Hauntings, and Poltergeists: A Parapsychologist's Handbook.* 30th Anniversary ed. 1986. Self-published, 2016. Kindle.
Barnett, P. W. "The Feeding of the Multitude in Mark 6/John 6." In *The Miracles of Jesus*, edited by David Wenham and Craig Blomberg, 273–93. Gospel Perspectives 6. Eugene, OR: Wipf & Stock, 2003.
Barrett, Sir William. *Death-Bed Visions: How the Dead Talk to the Dying.* London: Methuen, 1926.
Barrow, John D. *The Book of Universes: Exploring the Limits of the Cosmos.* New York: Norton, 2011.
Bauckham, Richard. "The Coin in the Fish's Mouth." In *The Miracles of Jesus*, edited by David Wenham and Craig Blomberg, 219–52. Gospel Perspectives 6. Eugene, OR: Wipf & Stock, 2003.
———. *Gospel Women: Studies of the Named Women in the Gospels.* Grand Rapids: Eerdmans, 2002.
———. *Jesus and the Eyewitnesses: The Gospels as Eyewitness Testimony.* 2nd ed. Grand Rapids: Eerdmans, 2017. Logos.
———. *The Jewish World Around the New Testament.* Grand Rapids: Baker, 2010.
Beauregard, Mario, and Denyse O'Leary. *The Spiritual Brain: A Neuroscientist's Case for the Existence of the Soul.* San Francisco: HarperOne, 2007.

Benedetti, Fabrizio, et al. "Conscious Expectation and Unconscious Conditioning in Analgesic, Motor, and Hormonal Placebo/Nocebo Responses." *Journal of Neuroscience* 23 (2003) 4315–23.

Benedetti, Fabrizio, et al. "How Placebos Change the Patient's Brain." *Neuropsychopharmacology* 36 (2011) 339–54.

Bennett, Sir Ernest. *Apparitions and Haunted Houses: A Survey of the Evidence.* London: Faber and Faber, 1939.

Bilu, Yoram. "'We Want to See Our King': Apparitions in Messianic Habad." *ETHOS* 41 (2013) 98–126.

———. *With Us More Than Ever: Making the Absent Rebbe Present in Messianic Chabad.* Translated by Haim Watzman. Stanford, CA: Stanford University Press, 2020. Kindle.

Botkin, Allan L., and Craig Hogan. *Induced After Death Communication: A Miraculous Therapy for Grief and Loss.* 2nd ed. Charlottesville, VA: Hampton Roads, 2014. Kindle.

Braude, Stephen E. *Dangerous Pursuits: Mediumship, Mind, and Music.* San Antonio: Anomalist, 2020.

———. *First Person Plural: Multiple Personality and the Philosophy of Mind*, rev. ed. Lanham, MD: Rowman & Littlefield, 1995.

———. *Immortal Remains: The Evidence for Life After Death.* Lanham, MD: Rowman & Littlefield, 2003.

———. *The Limits of Influence: Psychokinesis and the Philosophy of Science.* Rev. ed. Lanham, MD: University Press of America, 1997.

Brown, Alan. *Haunted Kentucky: Ghosts and Strange Phenomena of the Bluegrass State.* Mechanicsburg, PA: Stackpole, 2009. Kindle.

Brown, Raymond E. *The Gospel According to John (I–XII): Introduction, Translation, and Notes.* Anchor Yale Bible 29. Garden City, NY: Doubleday, 1966. Logos.

Casdorph, H. Richard. *The Miracles.* Plainfield, NJ: Logos International, 1976.

"Case of Haunting at Ramsbury, Wilts." *Journal of the Society for Psychical Research* 27 (1931–32) 297–304.

Cavendish, Richard. *Man, Myth and Magic: An Illustrated Encyclopedia of the Supernatural.* Vol. 8. New York: Marshall Cavendish Corporation, 1970.

Charman, Robert A. *Telepathy, Clairvoyance, and Precognition: A Re-Evaluation of Some Fascinating Case Studies.* Published by the author, 2022.

"G.—476—Collective." *Journal of the Society for Psychical Research* 2 (1885–86) 274–76.

"Collective Apparition." *Journal of the Society for Psychical Research* 6 (1893–94) 146–50.

Colloca, Luana, and Arthur J. Barsky. "Placebo and Nocebo Effects." *New England Journal of Medicine* 382 (2020) 554–61.

Conner, Robert. *Apparitions of Jesus: The Resurrection as Ghost Story.* Valley, WA: Tellectual Press, 2018. Kindle.

Crabtree, Adam. "Automatism and Secondary Centers of Consciousness." In *Irreducible Mind: Toward a Psychology for the 21st Century*, edited by Edward F. Kelly et al., 301–65. Lanham, MD: Rowman & Littlefield, 2007.

Crossan, John Dominic. *The Birth of Christianity: Discovering What Happened in the Years Immediately After the Execution of Jesus.* New York: HarperCollins, 1998. Kindle.

Cutchin, Joshua. *Fourth Wall Phantoms: Reflections on the Paranormal, Narrative, and Fictions Becoming Fact.* Marrietta, GA: Horse & Barrel, 2025. Kindle.

David-Neel, Alexandra. *Magic and Mystery in Tibet*. New York: Dover, 1971. Kindle.
Davies, W. D., and Dale C. Allison. *A Critical and Exegetical Commentary on the Gospel According to Saint Matthew (I–VII)*. Vol. 1. 2nd ed. London: T&T Clark, 2000. Logos.
Davis, Stephen T. "The Miracle at Cana: A Philosopher's Perspective." In *The Miracles of Jesus*, edited by David Wenham and Craig Blomberg, 419–442. Gospel Perspectives 6. Eugene, OR: Wipf & Stock, 2003.
Dein, Simon. *What Really Happens When Prophecy Fails?* London: Continuum, 2011. E-book.
Derr, John S., and Michael A. Persinger. "Geophysical Variables and Behavior: LIV. Zeitoun (Egypt) Apparitions of the Virgin Mary as Tectonic Strain-Induced Luminosities." *Perceptual and Motor Skills* 68 (1989) 123–28.
Dingwall, Eric J. "An Amazing Case: The Mediumship of Carlos Mirabelli." *Psychic Research* 24 (1930) 296–302.
Dispenza, Joe. *You Are the Placebo: Making Your Mind Matter*. Carlsbad, CA: Hay House, 2014.
Doidge, Norman. *The Brain That Changes Itself: Stories of Personal Triumph from the Frontiers of Brain Science*. New York: Viking, 2007.
Driesch, Hans. "The Mediumship of Carlos Mirabelli." *Psychic Research* 24 (1930) 302–6.
Duffin, Jacalyn. *Medical Miracles: Doctors, Saints, and Healing in the Modern World*. New York: Oxford University Press, 2009.
Dunn, James D. G. *Beginning from Jerusalem*. Christianity in the Making 2. Grand Rapids: Eerdmans, 2009.
Dyga, Krzysztof, and Radoslaw Stupak. "Ways of Understanding of Religious Delusions Associated with a Change of Identity on the Example of Identification with Jesus Christ." *Psychiatria Polska* 52 (2018) 69–80.
Evans, Hilary. "The Ghost Experience in a Wider Context." In *Hauntings and Poltergeists: Multidisciplinary Perspectives*, edited by James Houran and Rense Lange, 41–61. Jefferson, NC: McFarland, 2001.
———. *Visions, Apparitions, Alien Visitors: A Comparative Study of the Entity Enigma*. Wellingborough, Northamptonshire: Aquarian Press, 1984.
Evans, Hilary, and Robert E. Bartholomew. *Outbreak! The Encyclopedia of Extraordinary Social Behavior*. San Antonio: Anomalist, 2009.
Feaver, Karen M. "Chinese Lessons: What Chinese Christians Taught a US Congressional Delegation." *Christianity Today* 38 (1994) 33–35.
Felton, D. *Haunted Greece and Rome: Ghost Stories from Classical Antiquity*. Austin: University of Texas Press, 1999. Kindle.
Fernandes, Fernando, et al. *Fátima Revisited: The Apparition Phenomenon in Ufology, Psychology, and Science*. Translated and edited by Andrew D. Basiago and Eva M. Thompson. Charlottesville, VA: Anomalist, 2008.
Fernandes, Joaquim, and Fina D'Armada. *Celestial Secrets: The Hidden History of the Fátima Incident*. Translated by Alexandra Bruce. Edited by Andrew D. Basiago. Charlottesville, VA: Anomalist, 2006.
———. *Heavenly Lights: The Apparitions of Fátima and the UFO Phenomenon*. Translated and edited by Andrew D. Basiago and Eva M. Thompson. Charlottesville, VA: Anomalist, 2005.

Ferrer, Jorge N. *Participation and the Mystery: Transpersonal Essays in Psychology, Education, and Religion.* New York: State University of New York, 2017. Kindle.

Finucane, R. C. *Ghosts: Appearances of the Dead and Cultural Transformation.* Amherst, NY: Prometheus, 1996.

Fishkoff, Sue. *The Rebbe's Army: Inside the World of Chabad—Lubavitch.* New York: Schocken Books, 2003. Kindle.

Fitzmyer, Joseph A. *The Gospel According to Luke (1–9): Introduction, Translation, and Notes.* Anchor Yale Bible 28. Garden City, NY: Doubleday, 1970. Logos.

France, R. T. *The Gospel of Mark: A Commentary on the Greek Text.* Grand Rapids: Eerdmans, 2002. Logos.

Garriss, James J. "What Are Sun Dogs? And How Did They Get Their Name?" *The Old Farmers Almanac.* Accessed on 6/20/2025. https://www.almanac.com/what-are-sundogs-rainbows-beside-sun

Gathercole, Simon J. *The Pre-Existent Son: Recovering the Christologies of Matthew, Mark, and Luke.* Grand Rapids: Eerdmans, 2006.

Gauld, Alan. *The Founders of Psychical Research.* London: Routledge & Kegan Paul, 1968.

———. *A History of Hypnotism.* Cambridge; New York: Cambridge University Press, 1992.

———. *Mediumship and Survival: A Century of Investigations.* Exeter, England: David & Charles, 2012. Kindle.

Geiger, John. *The Third Man Factor: Surviving the Impossible.* New York: Weinstein, 2009. Kindle.

Glick, Ira O., et al. *The First Year of Bereavement.* New York: Wiley & Sons, 1974.

Goss, Michael. *The Evidence for Phantom Hitch-Hikers.* San Francisco, CA: Weiser, 1984. Kindle.

Green, Celia, and Charles McCreery. *Apparitions.* London: Hamish Hamilton, 1975.

Greene, Brian. *The Fabric of the Cosmos: Space, Time, and the Texture of Reality.* New York: Vintage, 2004.

———. *The Hidden Reality: Parallel Universes and the Deep Laws of the Cosmos.* New York: Knopf, 2011.

Greyson, Bruce. *After: A Doctor Explores What Near-Death Experiences Reveal About Life and Beyond.* New York: St. Martin's Essentials, 2021. Kindle.

Grosso, Michael. *Experiencing the Next World Now.* New York: Paraview, 2004. Kindle.

———. *Smile of the Universe: Miracles in an Age of Disbelief.* Charlottesville, VA: Anomalist, 2020. Kindle.

Guggenheim, Bill, and Judy Guggenheim. *Hello from Heaven! A New Field of Research—After-Death Communication—Confirms That Life and Love Are Eternal.* 3rd ed. New York: Bantam, 1995. Kindle.

Gurney, Edmund, et al. *Phantasms of the Living.* Vol. 1. 1886. Reprint, Redditch, UK: Read Books Ltd, 2018.

———. *Phantasms of the Living.* Vol. 2. 1886. Reprint, Redditch, UK: Read Books Ltd, 2018.

Gurney, Edmund and Frederic W. H. Myers. "On Apparitions Occurring Soon After Death." *Proceedings of the Society for Psychical Research.* 5 (1888–89) 403–85.

Habermas, Gary. *On the Resurrection 1: Evidences.* Brentwood, TN: B&H Academic, 2024. Kindle.

———. *The Risen Jesus and Future Hope.* Lanham, MD: Rowman & Littlefield, 2003.

Haffert, John. *Meet the Witnesses of the Miracle of the Sun.* 2nd ed. Spring Grove, PA: The American Society for the Defense of Tradition, Family and Property, 2006.

Haraldsson, Erlendur. *The Departed Among the Living: An Investigative Study of Afterlife Encounters.* Guildford, UK: White Crow, 2012. Kindle.

———. *Modern Miracles: The Story of Sathya Sai Baba: A Modern Day Prophet.* Guildford, UK: White Crow, 2013. Kindle.

———. "Possible Evidence of Survival." In *Surviving Death: A Journalist Investigates Evidence for an Afterlife.* Edited by Leslie Kean, 293–304. New York: Three Rivers, 2017. Kindle.

Haraldsson, Erlendur, and Loftur R. Gissurarson. *Indridi Indridason: The Icelandic Physical Medium.* Guildford, UK: White Crow, 2015. Kindle.

Harpur, Patrick. *Daimonic Reality: A Field Guide to the Otherworld.* Bedford, IN: Pine Winds, 2003.

Harris, Murray J. "'The Dead Are Restored to Life': Miracles of Revivification in the Gospels." In *The Miracles of Jesus,* edited by David Wenham and Craig Blomberg, 295–326. Gospel Perspectives 6. Eugene, OR: Wipf & Stock, 2003.

Harris, Ruth. *Lourdes: Body and Spirit in the Secular Age.* New York: Penguin, 1999.

Hengel, Martin. *Crucifixion in the Ancient World and the Folly of the Message of the Cross.* Translated by John Bowden. Philadelphia: Fortress, 1977.

———. *The Four Gospels and the One Gospel of Jesus Christ: An Investigation of the Collection and Origin of the Canonical Gospels.* Translated by John Bowden. Harrisburg, PA: Trinity Press International, 2000.

Holding, James Patrick. "The Shame of Crucifixion." In *Defending the Resurrection: Did Jesus Rise from the Dead?* edited by James Patrick Holding. Maitland, FL: Xulon Press, 2010.

———. "The Stolen Body Theory." In *Defending the Resurrection: Did Jesus Rise from the Dead?* edited by James Patrick Holding. Maitland, FL: Xulon Press, 2010.

———. *Trusting the New Testament: Is the Bible Reliable?* edited by James Patrick Holding. Maitland, FL: Xulon Press, 2009.

Houran, James, and Rense Lange. *Hauntings and Poltergeists: Multidisciplinary Perspectives.* Jefferson, NC: McFarland, 2001.

Hróbjartsson, Asbjørn, and Peter C. Gøtzsche. "Is the Placebo Powerless?—An Analysis of Clinical Trials Comparing Placebo with No Treatment." *New England Journal of Medicine* 344 (2001) 1594–1602.

Hufford, David J. *The Terror That Comes in the Night: An Experience-Centered Study of Supernatural Assault Traditions.* Philadelphia: University of Pennsylvania Press, 1982. Kindle.

Hurtado, Larry W. *Lord Jesus Christ: Devotion to Jesus in Earliest Christianity.* Grand Rapids: Eerdmans, 2003.

Hynes, Eugene. *Knock: The Virgin's Apparition in Nineteenth-Century Ireland.* Cork: Cork University Press, 2008.

Induced After-Death Communication. "IADC Therapy and The Center for Grief and Traumatic Loss." https://www.induced-adc.com.

James, William. "What Psychical Research Has Accomplished." In *The Will to Believe and Other Essays in Popular Philosophy,* 299–327. New York: Longmans, Green, 1897.

Jawer, Michael A., et al. "Environmental 'Gestalt Influences' Pertinent to Studies of Haunted Houses." *Journal of the Society for Psychical Research* 84 (2020) 65–92.

Johnston, Sarah Iles. *Restless Dead: Encounters Between the Living and the Dead in Ancient Greece*. Oakland: University of California Press, 1999.

Jung, Carl Gustav. *The Archetypes and the Collective Unconscious*. The Collected Works of C. G. Jung, vol. 9, edited by Gerhard Adler et al., translated by R. F. C. Hull, Princeton: Princeton University Press, 1981. Kindle.

Kaku, Michio. *Parallel Worlds: A Journey Through Creation, Higher Dimensions, and the Future of the Cosmos*. New York: Anchor, 2005.

Kalish, Richard A., and David K. Reynolds. *Death and Ethnicity: A Psychocultural Study*. Farmingdale, NY: Baywood, 1981.

Kaptchuk, Ted J., and Franklin G. Miller. "Placebo Effects in Medicine." *New England Journal of Medicine* 373 (2015) 8–9.

Kean, Leslie. *Surviving Death: A Journalist Investigates Evidence for an Afterlife*. New York: Three Rivers, 2017. Kindle.

Keel, John A. *Operation Trojan Horse: The Classic Breakthrough Study of UFOs*. 3rd ed. Charlottesville, VA: Anomalist, 2013.

Keener, Craig S. *Acts: An Exegetical Commentary; 3:1–14:28*. Vol. 2. Grand Rapids: Baker, 2014.

———. *Acts: An Exegetical Commentary; 15:1–23:35*. Vol. 3. Grand Rapids: Baker, 2014.

———. *Christobiography: Memory, History, and the Reliability of the Gospels*. Grand Rapids: Eerdmans, 2019. Kindle.

———. *A Commentary on the Gospel of Matthew*. Grand Rapids: Eerdmans, 1999. Kindle.

———. *Miracles: The Credibility of the New Testament Accounts*. Vol. 1. Grand Rapids: Baker, 2011.

———. *Miracles Today: The Supernatural Work of God in the Modern World*. Grand Rapids: Baker, 2021.

Kelly, Edward F., et al., eds. *Beyond Physicalism: Toward Reconciliation of Science and Spirituality*. Lanham, MD: Rowman & Littlefield, 2015.

Kelly, Edward F., et al., eds. *Irreducible Mind: Toward a Psychology for the 21st Century*. Lanham, MD: Rowman & Littlefield, 2007.

Kelly, Edward F., and Michael Grosso. "Mystical Experience." In *Irreducible Mind: Toward a Psychology for the 21st Century*, edited by Edward F. Kelly et al., 495–575. Lanham, MD: Rowman & Littlefield, 2007.

Kelly, Edward F., and Paul Marshall, eds. *Consciousness Unbound: Liberating Mind from the Tyranny of Materialism*. Lanham, MD: Rowman & Littlefield, 2021.

Kelly, Edward F., and Ian Whicher. "Patañjali's Yoga *Sūtras* and the *Siddhis*." In *Beyond Physicalism: Toward Reconciliation of Science and Spirituality*, edited by Edward F. Kelly et al., 315–48. Lanham, MD: Rowman & Littlefield, 2015.

Kelly, Emily Williams. "Psychophysiological Influence." In *Irreducible Mind: Toward a Psychology for the 21st Century*, edited by Edward F. Kelly et al., 117–239. Lanham, MD: Rowman & Littlefield, 2007.

Kendall, Jonathan. "Pondering the Passion Prognostications." In *Defending the Resurrection: Did Jesus Rise from the Dead?* Edited by James Patrick Holding, 51–80. Maitland, FL: Xulon, 2010.

———. "The Vindication of the Messiah: Why Resurrection?" In *Defending the Resurrection: Did Jesus Rise from the Dead?*, edited by James Patrick Holding, 134–81. Maitland, FL: Xulon, 2010.

Kripal, Jeffrey J. *Esalen: America and The Religion of No Religion*. Chicago: University of Chicago Press, 2007.

"L. 1139 Dream." *Journal of the Society for Psychical Research* 11 (1903–4) 278–90.

Ladd, George Eldon. *I Believe in the Resurrection of Jesus*. Grand Rapids: Eerdmans, 1984.

Latourelle, René. *The Miracles of Jesus and the Theology of Miracles*. Translated by Matthew J. O'Connell. Mahwah, NJ: Paulist, 1988.

Licona, Michael R. "Are the Gospels 'Historically Reliable'? A Focused Comparison of Suetonius's Life of Augustus and the Gospel of Mark." *Religions* 10 (2019). https://www.mdpi.com/2077-1444/10/3/148.

———. *Jesus, Contradicted: Why the Gospels Tell the Same Story Differently*. Grand Rapids: Zondervan, 2024.

———. "Jesus's Resurrection, Realism, and the Role of the Criteria of Authenticity." In *Jesus, Skepticism and the Problem of History: Criteria and Context in the Study of Christian Origins*, edited by Darrel L. Bock and J. Ed Komoszewski, 285–302. Grand Rapids: Zondervan, 2019.

———. *The Resurrection of Jesus: A New Historiographical Approach*. Downers Grove, IL: InterVarsity Press Academic, 2010.

Long, Jeffrey, and Paul Perry. *Evidence of the Afterlife: The Science of Near-Death Experiences*. New York: HarperCollins, 2010.

———. *God and the Afterlife: The Groundbreaking New Evidence for God and Near-Death Experience*. San Francisco: HarperOne, 2016.

Luke, David, and Rory Spowers, eds. *DMT Entity Encounters: Dialogues on the Spirit Molecule*. Rochester, VT: Park Street. 2021.

Lüdemann, Gerd. "First Rebuttal." In *Jesus' Resurrection: Fact or Figment?* Edited by Paul Copan and Ronald K. Tacelli, 52–55. Downers Grove, IL: InterVarsity. 2000.

MacKenzie, Andrew. *Hauntings and Apparitions*. London: Heinemann, 1982.

MacPhilpin, John. *The Apparitions and Miracles at Knock: The Official Depositions of the Eye-Witnesses*. 1880. Reprint, Potosi, WI: St. Athanasius Press. 2021.

Marcus, Joel. *Mark 1–8: A New Translation with Introduction and Commentary*. Anchor Yale Bible Commentaries, vol. 27. New Haven: Yale University Press, 2002. Logos.

Massullo, Brandon. *The Ghost Studies: New Perspectives on the Origins of Paranormal Experiences*. Wayne, NJ: Career Press, 2017. Kindle.

McClenon, James. "The Sociological Investigation of Haunting Cases." In *Hauntings and Poltergeists: Multidisciplinary Perspectives*, edited by James Houran and Rense Lange, 62–81. Jefferson, NC: McFarland, 2001.

Meier, John P. *A Marginal Jew: Rethinking the Historical Jesus, Volume 2—Mentor, Message and Miracles*. New York: Doubleday, 1994. Logos.

Metzger, Bruce M. *A Textual Commentary of the Greek New Testament*. 4th rev. ed. Stuttgart: Deutsche Bibelgesellschaft, 2000.

Moody, Raymond, and Paul Perry. *Glimpses of Eternity: Sharing a Loved One's Passage from This Life to the Next*. Nashville: Ideals Publications, 2010. Kindle.

———. *Paranormal: My Life in Pursuit of the Afterlife*. New York: HarperCollins, 2012. Kindle.

———. *Reunions: Visionary Encounters with Departed Loved Ones*. New York: Ivy Books, 1993. Kindle.

Moreman, Christopher A. *Beyond the Threshold: Afterlife Beliefs and Experiences in World Religions*. 2nd ed. Lanham, MD: Rowman & Littlefield, 2018. Kindle.

Morton, R. C. "A Record of a Haunted House." *Proceedings of the Society for Psychical Research* 8 (1892) 331–32.

Murphy, Michael. *The Future of the Body: Explorations into the Further Evolution of Human Nature.* Los Angeles: Jeremy P. Tarcher, 1992.

Myers, Frederic W. H. *Human Personality and Its Survival of Bodily Death.* Vol. 1–2. 1903.London: Forgotten Books, 2012.

———. "On Recognized Apparitions Occurring More Than a Year After Death." *Proceedings of the Society for Psychical Research* 6 (1889–90) 13–65.

National Weather Service. "What Causes Halos, Sundogs and Sun Pillars?" https://www.weather.gov/arx/why_halos_sundogs_pillars.

Nickell, Joe. *Looking for a Miracle: Weeping Icons, Relics, Stigmata, Visions and Healing Cures.* Amherst, NY: Prometheus, 1998. Kindle.

———. "Miracle Tableau: Knock, Ireland, 1879." *Skeptical Inquirer* 41 (2017). https://skepticalinquirer.org/2017/03/miracle-tableau-knock-ireland-1879/. Accessed on 6/1/2025.

———. "Phantoms, Frauds, or Fantasies?" In *Hauntings and Poltergeists: Multidisciplinary Perspectives*, edited by James Houran and Rense Lange, 214–23. Jefferson, NC: McFarland, 2001.

———. *The Science of Ghosts: Searching for Spirits of the Dead.* Amherst, NY: Prometheus, 2012.

———. *The Science of Miracles: Investigating the Incredible.* Amherst, NY: Prometheus, 2013.

Noyes, Russell, Jr., et al. "Aftereffects of Pleasurable Western Adult Near-Death Experiences." In *The Handbook of Near-Death Experiences: Thirty Years of Investigation*, edited by Janice Miner Holden et al. New York: Praeger, 2009. Kindle.

O'Connell, Jake. *Jesus' Resurrection and Apparitions: A Bayesian Analysis.* Eugene, OR: Resource, 2016.

———. "Jesus' Resurrection and Collective Hallucinations." *Tyndale Bulletin* 60 (2009) 69–105.

Odell, Catherine M. *Those Who Saw Her: Apparitions of Mary*, rev. 4th ed. Huntington, IN: Our Sunday Visitor, 2023.

Osis, Karlis, and Erlendur Haraldsson. *At the Hour of Death*, rev. ed. Guildford, UK: White Crow, 2012.

———. "OOBEs in Indian Swamis: Sathya Sai Baba and Dadaji." In *Research in Parapsychology 1975: Abstracts and Papers from the Eighteenth Annual Convention of the Parapsychological Association*, edited by J. D. Morris et al., 147–50. Metuchen, NJ: Scarecrow, 1976.

Perry, Michael C. *The Easter Enigma: An Essay on the Resurrection with Special Reference to the Data of Psychical Research.* London: Faber and Faber, 1959.

Persinger, Michael A., and Stanley A. Koren. "Predicting the Characteristics of Haunt Phenomena from Geomagnetic Factors and Brain Sensitivity: Evidence from Field and Experimental Studies." In *Hauntings and Poltergeists: Multidisciplinary Perspectives*, edited by James Houran and Rense Lange, 179–94. Jefferson, NC: McFarland, 2001.

Persinger, Michael A. "The Neuropsychiatry of Paranormal Experiences." *Journal of Neuropsychiatry and Clinical Neurosciences* 13 (2001) 515–24.

Playfair, Guy Lyon. *If This Be Magic: The Forgotten Power of Hypnotism.* Guildford, UK: White Crow, 2011. Kindle.

Radin, Dean. *The Conscious Universe: The Universal Truth of Psychic Phenomena.* New York: HarperOne, 2009.

———. *Supernormal: Science, Yoga, and the Evidence for Extraordinary Psychic Abilities.* New York: Harmony, 2013.

Ramesh, Chidambaram. *Embodied Imaginations: Fictional Characters Making Experiential Crossings into Real Life: An Unusual Phenomenon.* New Delhi: New Age, 2023.

Rees, Dewi. *Pointers to Eternity.* Talybont, Ceredigion: Y Lolfa, 2010. Kindle.

Richet, Charles. *Thirty Years of Psychical Research.* Translated by Stanley DeBrath. Whitefish, MT: Kessinger, 2010.

Rhine, Louisa. "Hallucinatory Experiences and Psychosomatic Psi." *Journal of Parapsychology* 31 (1967) 111–34.

Rivas, Titus, et al. *The Self Does Not Die: Verified Paranormal Phenomena from Near-Death Experiences.* 2nd ed. Durham, NC: IANDS, 2023.

Roll, William G., and Michael A. Persinger. "Investigations of Poltergeists and Haunts: A Review and Interpretation." In *Hauntings and Poltergeists: Multidisciplinary Perspectives,* edited by James Houran and Rense Lange, 123–63. Jefferson, NC: McFarland, 2001.

Roll, William G. *The Poltergeist.* New York: Paraview, 2004.

———. "Survival Research: Problems and Possibilities." In *Psychic Exploration: A Challenge for Science,* edited by John White, 397–424. 2nd ed. New York: Cosimo, 2011.

Rosenblum, Bruce, and Fred Kuttner. *Quantum Enigma: Physics Encounters Consciousness.* 2nd ed. New York: Oxford University Press, 2011.

Rossettini, Giacomo, et al. "Context Matters: The Psychoneurobiological Determinants of Placebo, Nocebo and Context-Related Effects in Physiotherapy." *Archives of Physiotherapy* 10 (2020) 1–12.

Ruffin, C. Bernard. *Padre Pio: The True Story.* 3rd ed. Huntington, IN: Our Sunday Visitor, 2018. Kindle.

Sabucedo, Pablo, et al. "Perceiving Those Who Are Gone: Cultural Research on Post-Bereavement Perception or Hallucination of the Deceased." *Transcultural Psychiatry* 60 (2023) 879–90.

Schatzman, Morton. *The Story of Ruth.* New York: Zebra, 1980.

Schwartz, Jeffrey M., and Sharon Begley. *The Mind and the Brain: Neuroplasticity and the Power of Mental Force.* New York: HarperCollins, 2009.

Shaw, Gregory. "Platonic Siddhas: Supernatural Philosophers of Neoplatonism." In *Beyond Physicalism: Toward Reconciliation of Science and Spirituality,* edited by Edward F. Kelly et al., 275–313. Lanham, MD: Rowman & Littlefield, 2015.

Sheldrake, Rupert. *Dogs That Know When Their Owners Are Coming Home: And Other Unexplained Powers of Animals.* 2nd ed. New York: Three Rivers, 2011.

———. *Morphic Resonance: The Nature of Formative Causation.* 5th ed. Rochester, VT: Park Street, 2009.

———. *The Presence of the Past: The Memory of Nature.* 4th ed. Rochester, VT: Park Street, 2012.

Sidgwick, Eleanor. "On the Evidence for Clairvoyance." *Proceedings of the Society for Psychical Research* 7 (1891–1892) 30–99.

Sidgwick, Henry, et al. "Report on the Census of Hallucinations." *Proceedings of the Society for Psychical Research* 10 (1894) 25–422.

Sparrow, G. Scott. *I Am with You Always: True Stories of Encounters with Jesus*. New York: Bantam, 1995.

———. *Sacred Encounters with Jesus*. Notre Dame, IN: Thomas More, 2003.

Stapp, Henry P. "A Quantum-Mechanical Theory of the Mind/Brain Connection." In *Beyond Physicalism: Toward Reconciliation of Science and Spirituality*, edited by Edward F. Kelly et al., 157–93. Lanham, MD: Rowman & Littlefield, 2015.

Stevenson, Ian. "Cryptomnesia and Parapsychology." *Journal of the Society for Psychical Research* 52 (1983) 1–30.

Strieber, Whitley, and Jeffrey J. Kripal. *The Super Natural: Why the Unexplained Is Real*. New York: Walker & Collier, 2016. Kindle.

Tanous, Alex, et al. *Psi in Psychotherapy: Conventional and Nonconventional Healing of Mental Illness*. Guildford, UK: White Crow, 2019.

Targ, Russell. *Limitless Mind: A Guide to Remote Viewing and Transformation of Consciousness*. Novato, CA: New World Library, 2004.

Targ, Russell, and Harold E. Puthoff. *Mind-Reach: Scientists Look at Psychic Abilities*. Charlottesville, VA: Hampton Roads, 1977.

Telushkin, Joseph. *Rebbe: The Life and Teachings of Menachem M. Schneerson, the Most Influential Rabbi in Modern History*. New York: Harper Wave, 2016. Kindle.

Thompson, Keith. *Angels and Aliens: UFOs and the Mythic Imagination*. New York: Ballantine, 1991.

Thurston, Herbert. *Ghosts and Poltergeists*. Edited by J. H. Crehan. Chicago: Henry Regnery, 1954.

———. *The Physical Phenomena of Mysticism*. Guildford, UK: White Crow, 1952.

Tiso, Francis V. *Rainbow Body and Resurrection: Spiritual Attainment, the Dissolution of the Material Body, and the Case of Khenpo A Chö*. Berkeley, CA: North Atlantic, 2016. Kindle.

Trachtenberg, Joshua. *Jewish Magic and Superstition: A Study in Folk Religion*. Eastford, CT: Martino Fine, 2012. Kindle.

Twelftree, Graham H. *Jesus the Miracle Worker: A Historical and Theological Study*. Downers Grove, IL: InterVarsity, 1999.

———. *The Nature Miracles of Jesus: Problems, Perspectives, and Prospects*. Eugene, OR: Cascade, 2017.

Tyrrell, G. N. M., and H. H. Price. *Apparitions*. Whitefish, MT: Kessinger, 2010.

Vallée, Jacques. *Dimensions: A Casebook of Alien Contact*. 2nd ed. San Antonio: Anomalist, 2008. Kindle.

———. *The Invisible College: What a Group of Scientists Has Discovered About UFO Influence on the Human Race*. Charlottesville, VA: Anomalist, 1975. Kindle.

———. *Passport to Magonia: From Folklore to Flying Saucers*. Adelaide, SA: Daily Grail, 2014. Kindle.

van Lommel, Pim. *Consciousness Beyond Life: The Science of the Near-Death Experience*. New York: HarperCollins, 2010. Kindle.

Wedderburn, A. J. M. *Beyond Resurrection*. Peabody, MA: Hendrickson, 1999.

West, D. J. "A Mass-Observation Questionnaire on Hallucinations." *Journal of the Society for Psychical Research* 34 (1948) 187–96.

Wiebe, Phillip. *Visions and Appearances of Jesus*. Abilene, TX: Leafwood, 2014. Kindle.

Wilson, Sheryl C., and Theodore X. Barber. "The Fantasy-Prone Personality: Implications for Understanding Imagery, Hypnosis, and Parapsychological

Phenomena." In *Imagery: Current Theory, Research, and Application*, edited by Anees A. Sheikh, 340–87. New York: Wiley & Sons, 1986.

Witherington, Ben, III. *The Christology of Jesus*. Philadelphia: Fortress, 1990.

———. *Jesus the Sage: The Pilgrimage of Wisdom*. Philadelphia: Fortress, 1994.

Wright, N. T. *Jesus and the Victory of God*. Philadelphia: Fortress, 1996.

———. *The Resurrection of the Son of God*. Philadelphia: Fortress, 2003.

Yogananda, Paramahansa. *Autobiography of a Yogi*. Los Angeles: Self-Realization Fellowship, 2019. Kindle.

Zaki, Pearl. *Before Our Eyes: The Virgin Mary Zeitun Egypt 1968 and 1969*. Goleta, CA: Queenship, 2002.

Zimdars-Swartz, Sandra L. *Encountering Mary: Visions of Mary from La Salette to Medjugorje*. New York: Avon, 1991.

www.ingramcontent.com/pod-product-compliance
Lightning Source LLC
Chambersburg PA
CBHW051632230426
43669CB00013B/2272